second edition

SYMBOLIC INTERACTIONISM
an introduction,
an interpretation,
an integration

Joel M. Charon

Moorhead State University

PRENTICE-HALL, INC., Englewood Cliffs, N.J. 07632

Library of Congress Cataloging in Publication Data

CHARON, JOEL M. (date)
    Symbolic interactionism.

    Bibliography: p.
    Includes index.
    1. Symbolic interactionism.   I. Title.
HM251.C46 1985   302   84-15068
ISBN   0-13-879966-0

Editorial/production supervision and
    interior design: Helen Maertens and Eva Jaunzems
Cover design: Ben Santora
Manufacturing buyer: John B. Hall

Printed in the United States of America

10   9   8   7   6   5   4   3   2   1

ISBN   0-13-879966-0   01

Prentice-Hall International, Inc., *London*
Prentice-Hall of Australia Pty. Limited, *Sydney*
Editora Prentice-Hall do Brasil, Ltda., *Rio de Janeiro*
Prentice-Hall Canada Inc., *Toronto*
Prentice-Hall of India Private Limited, *New Delhi*
Prentice-Hall of Japan, Inc., *Tokyo*
Prentice-Hall of Southeast Asia Pte. Ltd., *Singapore*
Whitehall Books Limited, *Wellington, New Zealand*

CONTENTS

7

The Human Mind   88

8

Taking the Role of the Other   99

9

Action and Social Action   113

PREFACE

This book is an attempt to fulfill a promise I made to myself in graduate school: to write a clear, organized, and interesting introduction to symbolic interactionism. It is meant to integrate that perspective, to be as accurate as possible, and to help the reader apply the ideas to real life.

The second edition is meant to bring in some ideas and studies left out of the first. The book's basic organization is the same. In my judgment, symbolic interactionism as a perspective is even more important today than it was when this book first came out. As sociology has become more diverse in both its research and ideas, more and more sociologists have turned to many of the core ideas in symbolic interactionism.

Many people have contributed to my understanding of symbolic interactionism and to the writing of this book. Special thanks go to Herbert Blumer and David Olday who guided me through the first edition. However, it is my wife Susan who has helped me the most throughout my whole academic life. Her continued support makes my work meaningful.

1
THE NATURE OF "PERSPECTIVE"

Teachers and authors throughout my educational career have warned me that truth is very difficult to find indeed. The more I understood, of course, the more I realized they were right. A new dimension to the problem of truth opened up, however, as I was introduced to the concept of *perspective*. Once taken literally, the concept of perspective must lead one to the conclusion that for human beings, truth about physical reality is impossible in any absolute sense.

Many years ago, I read the following story by A. Averchenko. It underlined the difficulty the human has in knowing what is really happening "out there." I interpreted it as an illustration of bias in perception. I explained to others that here was a good example of how people take a single situation and twist it to meet their needs. Underlying my interpretation of the story was the belief that people tend to be close-minded, narrow, and less than truthful.

POINT OF VIEW
A. Averchenko

"Men are comic," she said, smiling dreamily. Not knowing whether this indicated praise or blame, I answered noncommitally: "Quite true."

"Really, my husband's a regular Othello. Sometimes I'm sorry I married him." I looked helplessly at her. "Until you explain—" I began.

"Oh, I forgot that you haven't heard. About three weeks ago, I was walking home with my husband through the square. I had a large black hat on, which suits me awfully well, and my cheeks were quite pink from walking. As we passed under a street light, a pale, dark-haired fellow standing near by glanced at me and suddenly took my husband by his sleeve."

" 'Would you oblige me with a light,' he says. Alexander pulled his arm away, stooped down, and quicker than lightning, banged him on the head with a brick. He fell like a log. Awful!"

"Why, what on earth made your husband get jealous all of a sudden?" She shrugged her shoulders. "I told you men are very comic."

"Bidding her farewell, I went out, and at the corner came across her husband.

"Hello, old chap," I said. "They tell me you've been breaking people's heads."

He burst out laughing. "So, you've been talking to my wife. It was jolly lucky that brick came so pat into my hand. Otherwise, just think: I had about fifteen hundred rubles in my pocket, and my wife was wearing her diamond earrings."

"Do you think he wanted to rob you?"

"A man accosts you in a deserted spot, asks for a light and gets hold of your arm. What more do you want?"

Perplexed, I left him and walked on.

"There's no catching you today," I heard a voice say from behind.

I looked around and saw a friend I hadn't set eyes upon for three weeks.

"Lord!" I exclaimed. "What on earth has happened to you?"

He smiled faintly and asked in turn: "Do you know whether any lunatics have been at large lately? I was attacked by one three weeks ago. I left the hospital only today."

With sudden interest, I asked: "Three weeks ago? Were you sitting in the square?"

"Yes, I was. The most absurd thing. I was sitting in the square, dying for a smoke. No matches! After ten minutes or so, a gentleman passed with some old hag. He was smoking. I go up to him, touch him on the sleeve and ask in my most polite manner: 'Can you oblige me with a light?' And what do you think? The madman stoops down, picks up something, and the next moment I am lying on the ground with a broken head, unconscious. You probably read about it in the newspapers."

I looked at him and asked earnestly: "Do you really believe you met up with a lunatic?"

"I am sure of it."

Anyhow, afterwards I was eagerly digging in old back numbers of the local paper. At last I found what I was looking for: A short note in the accident column.

UNDER THE INFLUENCE OF DRINK

"Yesterday morning, the keepers of the square found on a bench a young man whose papers show him to be of good family. He had evidently fallen to the ground while in a state of extreme intoxication, and had broken his head on a nearby brick. The distress of the prodigal's parents is indescribable."

The seeker of truth naturally asks, "What really happened?" The police, of course, investigate situations such as this one in order to determine who is *telling the truth.* "Someone must be lying" or "Someone is twisting the truth to fit his or her own needs." It is difficult for most of us to accept the view that all may be telling the "truth." We might see things differently if we imagine that each one of the individuals (including the interviewer) comes to the situation with a different *perspective,* and therefore sees a *different reality,* and although some of these perspectives may be closer to "physical reality" than others, all of them probably capture at least one part of that reality, and none of them is able to capture the whole of it.

The story is called "Point of View," and in a sense, a perspective is a point of view, placing observers at various angles in relation to events and influencing them to see these events from these angles. By its very nature, then, a point of view, or perspective, limits what the observer sees by allowing only one side of what is "out there" to be seen.

There is no way that any individual can see all aspects of any situation simultaneously. One must pull out certain stimuli and totally ignore other stimuli. One must also put the stimuli pulled out into a larger context so that what is seen makes sense. That is what perspectives do: they *sensitize* the individual to parts of physical reality, they *desensitize* the individual to other parts, and they help the individual *make sense* of the physical reality to which there is sensitization. Seen in this light, a perspective is absolutely basic to the human being's everyday existence, since it is needed to make sense out of what is seen. Yet, because of perspective, the human being cannot encounter physical reality "in the raw," directly, since whatever is seen can only be *part* of the "real situation."

Perspectives are made up of words—it is these words that are used by the observer to make sense out of situations. In a way, the best definition of perspective is a *conceptual framework,* which emphasizes that perspectives are really interrelated sets of words used to order physical reality. The words we use cause us to make assumptions and value judgments about what we are seeing (and not seeing).

Reality, for the individual, depends on the words used to look at situations. If we examine the story by Averchenko in this light, it becomes obvious that the differences between actors' viewpoints depend on the words they used to *see.* The woman uses "Othello," "married," "black hat," ("which suits me"), "pale, dark-haired fellow," all of which reveal that in that situation she was "seeing" according to a perspective associated with a woman concerned with her attractiveness. Her husband, fearful of his money, uses these words: "fifteen hundred rubles," "diamond earrings," "accosts," "deserted," "gets hold of your arm." In both cases, and in the other cases too, certain aspects of the situation were pulled out, emphasized, and integrated, according to each person's *perspective,* or conceptual framework. And in each case, the conceptual framework led to various value judgments and assumptions by the actor in the situation.

A college education, in many ways, is an introduction to a variety of perspectives, each telling us something about what is going on around us. Sociology, psychology, history, humanities, art, George Orwell, Machiavelli, Freud, James Joyce, and Malcolm X—each represents a perspective that we might adopt as our own, integrate with others we have, or forget entirely after our final exam. Each perspective is a different approach to "reality," and each, therefore, tells us something but cannot include everything.

It seems that the most difficult aspect of "perspective" to grasp is that perspectives cannot capture the whole physical reality. It is probably because we want so desperately to know that what we believe is true that we cannot face the fact that whatever we know must be seen only as a truth gained from a certain *perspective*. We cannot, for example, even agree totally on what a simple object is. One day in the middle of winter, I went outside and picked up something from the ground and brought it to class. I asked, "What is this?" The answers were snow, a snowball, ice crystals, frozen water, something you are showing us to make some point, something little boys use to frighten little girls, the beginning of the world's biggest snowman, molecules, dirty snow, a very interesting shape to draw, the symbol of cold weather. Of course, my response was, "What is this really?" And, of course, the response by them was that it is all of these things, and probably many, many more things. Indeed, whatever that physical reality was is interpreted by people in many ways, depending entirely on the perspective they use to see it. No one of these perspectives could ever claim to have grasped the true essence of that which was brought in from outside. And even if we might try to claim that all of these perspectives together capture the object completely, we would be missing the point: Perspectives are almost infinite, thus we can never claim to have found all the possible perspectives on anything.

Human beings are limited by their perspectives; they cannot see outside of their perspectives. Yet, perspectives are vitally important: They make it possible for human beings to make sense out of what is "out there."

Perspectives must be judged by individuals according to their usefulness in interpreting situations that arise. Perspectives should not be thought of as true or false (as we might be tempted to do) but as helpful or useless in understanding. We accept or reject various perspectives in our education based on whether or not they make sense to us; that is, do they help us understand people or situations we encounter? The more useful a perspective is, the more apt we are to regard it as truth, but truths today have a habit of becoming "just *his* opinion" tomorrow, and we find ourselves giving up older perspectives for newer, more useful ones.

NEW PERSPECTIVES MEAN NEW REALITIES

Many are familiar with *The Autobiography of Malcolm X*. Malcolm is a good example of an individual whose life situations brought about very definite changes in perspectives and thus opened up whole new worlds for him. With each perspective came a new reality. In seventh grade, for instance, he was elected class president, and in looking back, he reports:

> And I was proud; I'm not going to say I wasn't. In fact, by then, I didn't really have much feeling about being a Negro, because I was trying so hard, in every way I could, to be white. . . . I remember one thing that marred this time for me: the movie "Gone With the Wind." When it played in Mason, I

was the only Negro in the theater, and when Butterfly McQueen went into her act, I felt like crawling under the rug. (Malcolm X and Haley, 1965:31-32)*

Malcolm remembers his perspective changing in school:

It was then that I began to change—inside. I drew away from white people. I came to class, and I answered when called upon. It became a physical strain simply to sit in Mr. Ostrowski's class. Where "nigger" had slipped off my back before, wherever I heard it now, I stopped and looked at whoever said it. And they looked surprised that I did. (p. 37)

Then in New York:

"Man, you can't tell him nothing!" they'd exclaim. And they couldn't. At home in Roxbury, they would see me parading with Sophia, dressed in my wild zoot suits. Then I'd come to work, loud and wild and half-high on liquor or reefers, and I'd stay that way, jamming sandwiches at people until we got to New York. Off the train, I'd go through that Grand Central Station afternoon rush-hour crowd, and many white people simply stopped in their tracks to watch me pass. The drape and the cut of a zoot suit showed to the best advantage if you were tall—and I was over six feet. My conk was fire-red. I was really a clown, but my ignorance made me think I was "sharp." My knob-toed, orange-colored "kick-up" shoes were nothing but Florsheims, the ghetto's Cadillac of shoes in those days. . . . And then, between Small's Paradise, the Braddock Hotel, and other places—as much as my twenty- or twenty-five dollar pay would allow, I drank liquor, smoked marijuana, painted the Big Apple red with increasing numbers of friends, and finally in Mrs. Fisher's rooming house I got a few hours of sleep before the "Yankee Clipper" rolled again. (p. 79)

Malcolm has been seeing the world from the perspective of zoot suits, reefers, conk, Cadillac of shoes, but he is suddenly exposed to a new perspective, which opens up a new world to him:

When Reginald left, he left me rocking with some of the first serious thoughts I had ever had in my life: that the white man was fast losing his power to oppress and exploit the dark world; that the dark world was starting to rise to rule the world again, as it had before; that the white man's world was on the way down, it was on the way out. (p. 162)

Because of this new perspective, Malcolm X becomes sensitive to things in his world he never really saw before. His past takes on a new meaning, and the many situations that took place between blacks and whites in his past are seen differently. He joins the Black Muslims, and he becomes a great leader in that movement. At the height of his activity in that movement, the words he preaches reflect his perspective:

*From *The Autobiography of Malcolm X,* by Malcolm X, with the assistance of Alex Haley. Copyright © 1964 by Alex Haley and Malcolm X. Copyright © 1965 by Alex Haley and Betty Shabazz. Reprinted by permission of Random House, Inc., New York, and the Hutchinson Publishing Group, London.

> No *sane* black man really wants integration! No *sane* white man really wants integration. No *sane* black man really believes that the white man ever will give the black man anything more than token integration. No! The Honorable Elijah Muhammed teaches that for the black man in America the only solution is complete *separation* from the white man! (p. 248)

And, finally, Malcolm's perspective changes once more, as a result of a pilgrimage he makes to Mecca. As his perspective changes, the world around him becomes transformed:

> It was in the Holy World that my attitude was changed, by what I experienced there, and by what I witnessed there, in terms of brotherhood—not just brotherhood toward me, but brotherhood between all men, of all nationalities and complexions, who were there. And now that I am back in America, my attitude here concerning white people has to be governed by what my black brothers and I experience here, and what we witness here—in terms of brotherhood. The *problem* here in America is that we meet such a small minority of individual so-called "good," or "brotherly" white people. . . . (p. 368)

Malcolm X's autobiography is an excellent description of an individual undergoing profound changes in *perspective*. His story is not unique, but what is happening is probably more obvious to us in his story than it would be in many others.

Not only do we all undergo *basic* change in our perspectives many times throughout our lives, but our perspectives change from situation to situation, often many times during the same day. Few of us have one perspective that we can apply to every situation we encounter. Perspectives are situational: In the classroom my perspective is that of teacher/sociologist; in my home it becomes father or husband; on a fishing trip it changes to "seasoned fisherman." Each situation calls forth a different role, which means a different perspective. Some roles we play may have more than one perspective we can use (there are many different *student* perspectives we might draw on depending on the situation we encounter), and some perspectives may apply to more than one role we play (for example, a Christian may apply his or her perspective as a Christian to a number of roles). Perspectives are a complex matter.

Perspectives are not perceptions but are guides to our perceptions; they influence what we see and how we interpret what we see. They are our "eyeglasses" we put on to see. Figure 1-1 summarizes the meaning of perspective.

A perspective, then, by its very nature, is a bias, it contains assumptions, value judgments, and ideas, it orders the world, it divides it up in a certain way, and as a result it influences our action in the world. A father and his son see each other from at least two perspectives (one the father's, the other the son's) and thus define a situation that affects them both (e.g., the use of the car) in two very different ways. Neither is necessarily wrong or in error, although they may certainly disagree. A candidate for president of the United States may see the society as in need of change and promise all kinds of possibilities, but once that person is in office, his or her perspective will change and his or her behavior will be affected. It is not, as may ap-

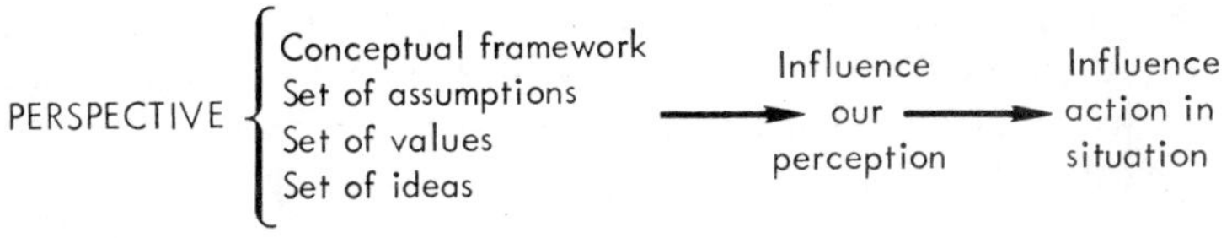

PERSPECTIVE {
Conceptual framework
Set of assumptions
Set of values
Set of ideas
} ⟶ Influence our perception ⟶ Influence action in situation

FIGURE 1–1

pear to us, that the new president is dishonest, but rather that the definition of the situation has changed because that person now sees the world from the perspective of president, not candidate.

IS THERE A "BEST" PERSPECTIVE?

Are all perspectives equally "good," or can one argue that one perspective is "better" than another? Is, for example, a son's perspective "better" than his father's? Is an artist's perspective "better" than a scientist's?

Whenever any two things (such as perspectives) are compared, there has to be agreement on criteria for comparison. So, for example, Martha is "better" than Marsha if we agree that the criterion is I.Q. and can agree on how it should be measured. One painting is "better" than another if we use "capturing physical reality" as a criterion for comparison and can agree on how to measure "capturing physical reality."

Some perspectives are therefore "better" than others. All are not equal. To judge which is "better," however, a standard of comparison must be established. Some people, for example, would argue that the best perspective is the one that conforms closest to Holy Scripture or the one that comes closest to the "American creed." Thus, atheism is not a good perspective in the first case, and for most of us, a racist perspective is not good in the second case.

Most of us are probably interested in using perspectives that *accurately describe* what is "really" happening in the world around us. Certainly, in the world of scholarship accurate description is one of the most important measurements of a "good perspective." A good perspective gives us insight, clearly describes reality, helps us find the truth. Most scientists, natural and social, make a claim that their perspectives are better than common-sense ones because there is a disciplined control of personal bias. The fruits of science do indeed support the fact that the scientific perspective is superior to the vast majority of perspectives that deal with the natural and social worlds. If given a choice between a scientific perspective and a nonscientific perspective examining exactly the same question, it would be unusual for me to opt for the latter, since it is clear to me that scientific perspectives are usually more reliable than nonscientific ones in accurately answering questions about the natural and social world. It depends a great deal, however, on the nature of the question asked.

Science is far from accurate in answering a number of important questions, and scientists are unable to deal with whole layers of reality that other perspectives deal with. Even in the natural and social worlds that the scientist does examine, there are realities that go unnoticed and are not even looked for, realities too difficult to examine scientifically. To claim that the perspective of science is better than any others because it is more accurate is not a just claim for all questions.

The problem of the "best" perspective is confounded when we try to determine the most accurate scientific perspective. Although scientists share a scientific perspective, they differ in what they focus on in reality, and it would be very difficult to establish criteria for judging which one of the sciences captures reality the best. This could be done, but probably to no good purpose. It is best to understand scientific perspectives as each focusing on a different aspect of the natural and social world, each helping us more clearly understand that aspect. Comparing scientific perspectives—indeed, comparing all perspectives—is a difficult task, but it is not impossible if criteria are *carefully* established.

CONCLUSION

It may be beneficial to summarize this chapter by simply restating the basic points and by listing some examples of perspectives.

1. Perspectives are points of view—eyeglasses, sensitizers—that guide our perceptions of reality.
2. Perspectives can further be described as conceptual frameworks, a set of assumptions, values, and beliefs used to organize our perceptions and control our behavior.
3. The individual judges perspectives according to their usefulness for himself or herself.
4. The individual has many perspectives. Perspectives arise in interaction and are role-related.
5. Some perspectives can be considered better than other perspectives if we can agree that "better" means more accurate and if we can measure accuracy—a difficult task. In science some may be more accurate than others, but it is probably more correct to argue that each *focuses* on a different aspect of reality.

Perspectives can be thought to differ according to how formal they are. We, of course, may be constantly using our perspectives of male, female, student, lover, buyer, music freak, friend, or amateur counselor. It would be helpful perhaps to distinguish these from more formal, organized perspectives such as Christian, American, sociologist, psychologist, historian. Further, we could distinguish scientific perspectives from the nonscientific, and then subdivide scientific perspectives. The following list graphically illustrates the diversity of perspectives an individual may use to examine reality. It is not meant to be all-inclusive, only suggestive of the diversity of perspectives available.

1. Some informal everyday perspectives:
     student
     daughter
     mother
2. Some formal perspectives—nonscientific:
     stamp collector
     artist
     poet
     black
     American
     Christian
3. Some formal perspectives—scientific:
     biologist
     physicist
     chemist
     astronomer
     psychologist
     anthropologist
     economist
     sociologist
4. Some perspectives within sociology:
     Marxist
     Parsonian
     Symbolic interactionist
     Weberian
     Durkheimian
     Systems theory
     Exchange

Any one individual is made up of several of these kinds of perspectives and may enter any one of them in a situation. Indeed, once in the situation, the individual can change perspectives or even find that the initial perspective is being transformed as he or she interacts with others. A person may in a single day be student, daughter, mother, artist, black, American, Christian, biologist, sociologist, Marxist, and Parsonian. In each perspective a different world will be seen, and perhaps a new way of looking at old things will be revealed.

This book is an attempt to systematically examine one perspective in social science. It is an unusual perspective, different from most other social sciences. For some it may seem like common sense. That is because we will recognize that its ideas explain so well what we all do in the situations we encounter. Yet most of us do not in fact think about people in the way that this perspective does. We have been exposed to psychology, sociology, anthropology, and the various other "traditional" perspectives for too long to be easily swayed by a perspective that describes us in a very different way.

You are invited to give this perspective a chance. It is limited and far from perfect, but so too are all perspectives. It promises much, as you will undoubtedly recognize.

REFERENCES

AVERCHENKO, A.
  "Point of View."
MALCOLM X and ALEX HALEY
  1965 *The Autobiography of Malcolm X.* New York: Grove Press. Copyright
       © 1965 by Alex Haley and Betty Shabazz. Reprinted by permission of
       Random House, Inc., New York, and the Hutchinson Publishing Group,
       London.

2
THE PERSPECTIVE
OF SOCIAL SCIENCE

Immanuel Kant (1724–1804) was an important philosopher whose work included a noble attempt to deal with the conflict between religion and science. Kant, a believer in religion, observed the assault of reason and science on traditional religious belief as well as the feeble attempts of religious thinkers to defend their ground through the tools of rational argument. He was critical of these attempts to defend the metaphysical world through reason, for he felt it was an impossible task and therefore a waste of time.

He argued that there are two worlds of reality: a world of *phenomena* and a world of the *noumena*. The world of phenomena is the world we can experience with our senses; it is open to scientific and rational investigation. Science observes the world of phenomena—the natural world—and reason orders these observations. The world of noumena is above scientific investigation; it cannot be approached by empirical observation since it is not physical/empirical. Although many people have attempted to approach this world through reason, they have failed. Kant states in the Preface to the second edition of *The Critique of Pure Reason:*

> We find, too, that those who are engaged in metaphysical pursuits are far from being able to agree among themselves, but that, on the contrary, this science appears to furnish an arena specially adapted for the display of skill or the exercise of strength in mock-contests—a field in which no combatant ever yet succeeded in gaining an inch of ground, in which, at least, no victory was ever yet crowned with permanent possession. (Kant, 1952:6)

Those who use reason or science, or both, to understand some things are engaged in "mock-contests," never "gaining an inch of ground." Further he states, "Now there are objects which reason *thinks* . . . but which cannot be given in experience, or, at least, cannot be given so as reason thinks them" (p. 7). Kant is saying that although we can *think* the world of the noumena, reason and science, limited to the world of phenomena, cannot be used to investigate it. In a sense, Kant then is arguing that science is a *perspective,* sensitizing the investigator to part of the world, the natural, phenomenal world, but that science is unable to sensitize us to another world, nor should we use it to try.

One of the reasons that Kant is important to us here relates to how he applied this philosophy to an understanding of the human being. Physical objects such as plants, livers, wastepaper baskets, dogs, and tape recorders are clearly in the world of phenomena and therefore subject to scientific investigation, and God, heaven, angels, and the devil are clearly noumena. But in which world does the human being belong? If we are in the world of phenomena, we are physical, we are part of the natural universe, we can be investigated and fully understood through the tools of science. If we are noumena, however, then we are beyond science, not understandable as part of the natural physical universe. Kant argues that we are both; we are phenomena, subject to the laws of nature, open to science, and "subject to natural necessity"; that is, our behavior is subject to natural cause. On the other hand, we are also noumena, the "human soul," at least in part, containing a will that is *free.* The human being is conceptualized here as both *passive* in that individuals are caused, shaped, and driven by forces beyond their control, and individuals are also *active,* controlling, shaping, acting, free.

We will not describe here Kant's other insights in relation to this issue, but it is important to underline the fact that science, by its very nature, is empirical and investigates the phenomenal world, and at least according to Kant's framework, it cannot deal with part of that which we call *human.* For social *scientists,* the investigation of the human being takes the form of proving whatever information we can gather about those aspects of the human being that are subject to natural causation. And the greater our attempt to be scientific, the greater will be our focus on those aspects of the human being to which Kant referred as phenomenal—those qualities of the human being that lend themselves to scientific measurement. We *risk,* however, the danger of concluding that all of the human being can be, at least theoretically, captured or measured scientifically and that what we have already been able to learn gives us a good representation of the human being rather than a selective or biased one.

SOCIAL SCIENCE AS A PERSPECTIVE

It is maintained here that social science is a *perspective.* Since its beginning it has attempted to apply the tools of science to understanding the human being. As a perspective, it has made certain assumptions, the most important being that the human being is phenomenal, caused, open to scientific measurement, and not an active agent in relation to his or her environment—not self-determining or free. As social scientists, we assume causality in social life, and our goal is (perhaps must be) to uncover that causality.

Peter Berger (1963) clearly presents the problem of finding a place for freedom in social science. After showing vividly how human beings are controlled, imprisoned, caused, shaped, and molded by a multitude of social forces, he turns the argument around and attempts to eke out some room for human freedom. Before trying to determine how that freedom is possible, however, he discusses freedom and science, and in so doing develops an argument almost identical with Kant's:

> Freedom is not empirically available. More precisely, while freedom may be experienced by us as a certainty along with other empirical certainties, it is not open to demonstration by any scientific methods. If we wish to follow Kant, freedom is also not available rationally, that is, cannot be demonstrated by philosophical methods based on the operations of pure reason. . . . the elusiveness of freedom with regard to scientific comprehension does not lie so much in the unspeakable mysteriousness of the phenomenon . . . as in the *strictly limited scope of scientific methods.* An empirical science must operate within certain assumptions, one of which is that of universal causality. Every object of scientific scrutiny is presumed to have an anterior cause. An object, or an event, that is its own cause lies outside the scientific universe of discourse. Yet freedom has precisely that character. For this reason, no amount of scientific research will ever uncover a phenomenon that can be designated as free. Whatever may appear as free within the subjective consciousness of an individual will find its place in the scientific scheme as a link in some chain of causation. . . .
>
> In terms of social-scientific method, one is faced with a way of thinking that assumes a priori that the human world is a causally closed system. The method would not be scientific if it thought otherwise. Freedom as a special kind of cause is excluded from this system a priori. In terms of social phenomena, the social scientist must assume an infinite regress of causes, none of them holding a privileged ontological status. If he cannot explain a phenomenon causally by one set of sociological categories, he will try another one. If political causes do not seem satisfactory, he will try economic ones. And if the entire conceptual apparatus of sociology seems inadequate to explain a given phenomenon, he may switch to a different apparatus, such as the psychological or the biological one. But in doing so, he will still move within the scientific cosmos—that is, he will discover new orders of causes, but he will not encounter freedom. There is no way of perceiving freedom, either in oneself or another human being, except through a subjective inner certainty that dissolves as soon as it is attacked with the tools of scientific analysis. (Berger, 1963:122–24)*

One is reminded of the cocktail party where the bright new college graduate with one sociology course and one psychology course under his belt is impressing

*Excerpt from *Invitation to Sociology,* copyright © 1963 by Peter L. Berger. Reprinted by permission of Doubleday & Company, Inc., New York, and Penguin Press, Harmondsworth, Middlesex, England.

everyone with how much he understands about human behavior. The conversation goes something like this:

> "That's silly. You're not free to do anything," he brags.
> "Of course, I am. I decide what I believe and where I go," the innocent citizen responds.
> "Take the girl you're with here tonight. Did you freely choose to bring her?"
> "Of course."
> "Aha." (I've got you, he says to himself.) "You are attracted to her because she is in the 'right' social class. She reminds you of your mother. She is approximately at your own level of physical attractiveness." Etc., etc., etc., etc.
> "Wow!"

Most of us are amazed at the predictability of human behavior and at all the social and psychological causes of behavior that social scientists have been able to amass. But Berger's point must be reiterated: "Freedom as a special kind of cause is *excluded* from this system." It is one of science's central assumptions. The purpose of science is to isolate cause, not freedom, so it must, in the end, be considered as excluding some things about the human being. This is not, of course, to criticize science, it is merely to try to isolate its limits as a perspective.

Social scientists seem to be becoming increasingly aware of the fact that social science is a *perspective,* that it makes certain assumptions, that it sensitizes and desensitizes the investigator, that it has a certain conceptual framework (e.g., "empirical," "cause," "independent variable," "dependent variable," "measurement," etc.), and that it can never reveal the whole truth about the human being.

Indeed, social science might even lead us to a misleading or even false picture of the human being. Charles Hampden-Turner argues this in his thoughtful book *Radical Man* (1970). He describes social science as a *perspective* and then concludes that it is clearly a biased one by its very nature: It is consistently a politically *conservative* one, and it must inevitably lead the social scientist to take a conservative view of the human being, systematically ignoring a host of important human qualities. Hampden-Turner (1970:1-15) takes the position that the social-scientific perspective by its very nature:

a. *Concentrates on the repetitive, predictable, unvariable aspects of the human.* In a sense, social science assures a "compulsive, obsessive, and ritualistic" human subject, rather than recognizing the centrality of creativity and novelty to human life.

b. *Concentrates on "visible externalities,"* that which is "exposed to the general gaze," rather than the subjective world of dreams, philosophies, and the whole mental life of those whose physical movements we observe.

c. *Concentrates on the various parts of the person,* analyzing the parts in order to understand the whole. In a sense, "the human is indivisible" and "we are left with the same problems as all the king's horses and all the king's men."

Hampden-Turner criticizes the scientific perspective on other grounds, too, but the point that he makes for our discussion here is that social science is a perspective, and what emerges from it is a picture of the human being that is far from objective and "value-free." That perspective may indeed be as conservative and biased as Hampden-Turner describes it, or it may be less so—on the other hand, it may be even more biased than any of us realize. The treatment of social science as a perspective is only now being investigated seriously, so it is difficult to know the nature of its bias. But it does indeed appear that in order to be scientific we have to focus on those aspects of the human that are more open to measurement. It is important to recognize that there are qualities left untouched because of our scientific search, even qualities that are measurable but not perfectly open to our contemporary instruments of investigation.

Social science is a perspective; it is an important approach to understanding the human being; it has produced much that has helped us predict, control, improve, and even mess up the condition of the human being. It is not complete, for no perspective can be complete, and it is a bias, but it is a most important perspective for understanding, as witnessed by its results over the past two hundred or more years.

Within social science there are, of course, many perspectives (we might call these subperspectives), and each one is thought unique in its approach to the human being. Each one pulls out some aspects of reality, emphasizing those, and in a sense ignores other aspects of reality picked up by other social sciences.

Sociology as a Perspective

Sociology focuses on social structure in its analysis. Human beings are "caused" by their positions in various social structures, by expectations held by others: They play roles developed over time; they are more or less controlled by their place in the stratification systems in society; and they internalize their cultures through being socialized by various socialization agencies. One of the best descriptions of the sociological perspective is Peter Berger's Chapter 4 in *Invitation to Sociology* (1963:66-92). He sees behavior as resulting from three important social forces: social controls, social stratification, and institutions. Every organization we are in exerts social controls, we are ranked in social stratification systems that largely determine our "life chances" and "life styles," and we are subject to societal patterns (institutions) created by the "dead hand of the past." Berger's description is vivid, and one is caught up in the power of the sociological perspective. It is a perspective that views the human being as shaped and controlled by outside forces, by forces relating to social structure. Berger closes the chapter with a picture of society as prison:

> Finally, we are located in society not only in space but in time. Our society is a historical entity that extends temporally beyond any individual biography. Society antedates us and it will survive us. It was there before we were born and it will be there after we are dead. Our lives are but episodes in its majestic

march through time. In sum, society is the walls of our imprisonment in history. (p. 92)

In Chapter 5 Berger continues this picture. He borrows from three perspectives in sociology: role theory (our roles and identities are created, maintained, and changed by society), the sociology of knowledge (our truths are shaped by the social worlds we interact with), and reference-group theory (our roles, identities, ideas, and actions are shaped by the social worlds we identify with, even those we are not part of). Each one of these emphasizes how we are socialized to accept the prison of society.

The two chapters are entitled "Sociological Perspective—Man in Society" and "Sociological Perspective—Society in Man." Berger's point is that humans live *within* a massive reality—society—developed historically, regarded by us as legitimate, telling us what to do and what to think, and shaping our behavior through a variety of mechanisms. More than that, however, Berger emphasizes that we, in a sense, "agree" to this imprisonment precisely because the society has penetrated us through socialization; we have, in a real sense, *become* what society has demanded. Social structure and socialization, both powerful and determining forces, are the two critical concepts in understanding the nature of the sociological perspective. He concludes Chapter 5:

> Society not only controls our movements, but shapes our identity, our thought and our emotions. The structures of society become the structures of our own consciousness. Society does not stop at the surface of our skins. Society penetrates us as much as it envelopes us. Our bondage to society is not so much established by conquest as by collusion. . . . The walls of our imprisonment were there before we appeared on the scene, but they are ever rebuilt by ourselves. We are betrayed into captivity with our own cooperation. (p. 121)

Although some sociologists have come to question this deterministic position in sociology, it is difficult to deny its dominance both historically and in contemporary sociology. And in a way, this *must* be the case if sociology is to create for itself a place in the scientific community. The whole purpose of sociology must be to isolate the important social regularities and to determine social *cause*. Its whole conceptual framework aims at this. It is different from other perspectives in social science, such as psychology, since it focuses on social structural variables as cause. Sociology is a useful perspective since it does help explain a part of human behavior. As a perspective, however, it can only sensitize us to a part of the picture, and it is really up to other social-scientific perspectives to help us understand the other parts.

Psychology as a Perspective

Psychology is also a social-scientific perspective, and in some ways it is similar to sociology. It is a science, often attempting to borrow even more directly the tools developed in natural science. More than sociology, it has relied heavily on the controlled laboratory experiment (indeed, some psychologists will define a perspective as scientific only if the controlled laboratory experiment is the norm), and it has usually considered the human being wholly in the world of phenomena, moved by natural laws, created, shaped.

Because there are many schools of psychology (each can be called a perspective), there are differences between psychologists. Psychologists, however, like sociologists, seem to share certain assumptions, ideas, and concepts, sensitizing the investigator to certain aspects of the human being while neglecting others. Let us emphasize again, that it is not a fault; it is a limitation of every perspective, and there seems to be no way to escape it: Perspectives are absolutely essential for understanding, but by their very nature they do not capture the whole of reality.

The threads of the psychological perspective are not always clear, and there is always a danger that someone who is not himself or herself a psychologist will mistake the perspective. However, it seems that all schools of psychology emphasize the following:

1. The *individual* organism, shaped by various combinations of heredity and environment, social and nonsocial.
2. An underlying belief that a person's performance at any point is tied to previous experience. This can be labeled a *predispositional* orientation. For example, in psychoanalysis this means that very early childhood training causes one to act later on in a certain manner; in learning theory previous conditioning causes behavior; in gestalt psychology it may be the person's conceptual framework or cognitive structure developed in the past that is all-important.
3. An attempt to explain behavior in relation to the *organism:* Change is explained in relation to change *in* the organism; stability of behavior is due to the stability *in* the organism.
4. A focus primarily on personality *traits,* developed over time, such as "self-image," "attitude," "response pattern." In examining an individual, the psychologist will consider these developed traits as they influence action in a situation. The traits are often conceptualized as the individual's "personality."
5. Behavior is *not* situational or structural but personal and trait-related, even though social situations might influence traits over the long run.

It should be emphasized here that the psychological perspective differs significantly from the sociological. Although both emphasize studying human behavior, one (psychology) focuses on the individual organism and how it is shaped, the other (sociology) on social structure and how people are shaped by their positions in various social structures. In psychology, cause for change is in what happens to or within the organism, whereas in sociology cause for change is in changes in the social structure, in changes in the person's position in that structure or the person who is changing social structures.

In both cases, the focus is on the human being's behavior being caused by forces beyond the individual's own will. The individual is conceptualized as passive in relation to these forces; that is, we are shaped, we are not actively shaping our behavior or our environment as individuals. By taking a scientific perspective, social science has focused on those aspects of the human being molded by the biological, physical, and social world. The purpose of social science has been to try to identify those forces.

Erich Fromm (1973) is critical of some scientists for creating this passive human organism who responds to stimuli, is driven by unconscious forces, and is shaped by animalistic instincts. He writes:

> In spite of the great differences between instinctivistic and behavioristic theory, they have a common basic orientation. They both exclude the *person*, the behaving man, from their field of vision. Whether man is the product of conditioning, or the product of animal evolution, he is exclusively determined by conditions outside himself; he has no part in his own life, no responsibility, and not even a trace of freedom. Man is a puppet, controlled by strings—instinct or conditioning. (1973:70–71)

There are, of course, exceptions to a deterministic and passive view of human beings in both sociology and psychology. Fromm is one such example in psychology, as are perhaps "humanistic" psychologists such as Rogers and Maslow. Certainly, some of the insights of Max Weber would be one example in sociology. However, it is by far the passive, created, caused human being who has dominated most of both sociology and psychology in the nineteenth and twentieth centuries. And that seems perfectly understandable since the goals have been to examine the human as part of the natural universe, governed by laws as are all other phenomena in that universe. A liberal education in social science seems to create an image of the human being as determined in nature, as are all other living organisms. Indeed, other social science perspectives (such as anthropology, geography, and economics) do not seem to question this image, but on the contrary, to reinforce it. We will not examine all these various perspectives, but it will be beneficial to look at traditional social psychology briefly.

The Perspective of Social Psychology

Of all perspectives in social science, social psychology is the most difficult to describe. Some would argue that it is not a perspective at all, but a conglomeration of topics and studies with little unity. Others will argue that it is a discipline in its own right, with roots in both psychology and sociology, but with its own distinct history and subject matter.

Elliot Aronson, an important contemporary social psychologist, defines the field as the study of social influence, "the influences that people have upon the beliefs or behavior of others." (1984:6) Aronson calls his book *The Social Animal,* and what he means is that we are social in the sense that we are influenced by others.

By far the most important concept investigated in social psychology has been attitudes and attitude change. An attitude is usually conceptualized as a person's set of beliefs and feelings toward an object that predisposes the person to act in a certain manner when confronted by that object (or class of objects). Studies have usually attempted to examine how attitudes are formed and changed through the influence of other individuals. Attitudes, it has been assumed, are useful traits to study because they lead to behavior. To change behavior, therefore, the strategy implied in social psychology has been to change one's attitudes. Although the usefulness of studying attitudes as predictors of behavior is increasingly being questioned by critics, it is still seen by most social scientists as one of social psychology's most useful concepts. For most people, attitudes are fascinating to study, and they seem to most of us to be basic to our action in real situations. Nothing seems so important to many people as knowing how to change such attitudes as prejudice toward blacks, sexist attitudes toward women, or narrow-minded attitudes toward cultures different from our own. Many, especially social psychologists, believe that attitudes are important and that attitude change is possible. It is, in a sense, an optimistic view of the future, implying that we can improve the world through changing people's attitudes. And nothing seems to be more appropriate to this view than an understanding of social psychology, which has focused much of its efforts on attitudes and attitude change.

Social psychology is also the study of how other people influence our *behavior.* Conformity, obedience, power, leadership, and attraction are some of the exciting topics covered in the field of social psychology. Interpersonal communication, group decision making, and propaganda are also important. The key to the perspective seems to be, as Aronson states, interpersonal influence, the importance of the social situation in influencing attitudes and/or behavior. The human being is conceptualized as a "social animal" in the sense that he or she conforms to the expectations of others in interaction.

There is a great similarity between the perspective described as social psychology and the sociological and psychological perspectives discussed earlier. Social psychology attempts to uncover the causes of human behavior by isolating forces in the social environment that create individual attitudes and behavior. A person is determined both by attitudes (developed socially) and by various social forces in the situation encountered. The emphasis placed on the *social* and on the importance of the *situation* distinguishes social psychology from other perspectives in psychology, and the focus on the reactions of the *person* to the social (without emphasizing social structure, position, role, and the like) tends to distinguish it from sociology. These distinctions, however, are far from crystal clear, and there is a great deal of overlap, leading some to suggest that there is little that distinguishes the field of social psychology from other social sciences.

The origins of social psychology, to a large extent, were in gestalt psychology, an important perspective in psychology first developed in the late nineteenth and early twentieth centuries. Gestalt psychology emphasized the central importance of *perception* in human behavior: The human being acts according to how the situation is perceived. Gestalt psychologists have attempted to isolate various principles of perception in order to better understand how the individual organizes the stimuli he or she confronts. Gestalt psychology as such is entirely psychological in its orientation, but because of the work of some gestaltists—especially Solomon Asch and Kurt Lewin—a social dimension was added to the framework, which influenced greatly the direction of social psychology.

It was Lewin's field theory especially that laid the foundation for much of social psychology. The gestaltists' focus on perception is expanded in Lewin's social psychology to an emphasis on cognitions, beliefs, attitudes, and perceptions. Lewin's social psychology, heavily influenced by its gestalt foundations, emphasized the *social situation,* the forces at work on the individual in a social situation as well as the individual's perception of and attitudes toward those forces. Lewin sees the individual within a "field," within an interrelated set of forces (past, present, and future). This whole emphasis on the person's *cognitive world* (perception, attitudes, beliefs, and so on) and also the emphasis placed on *situational* variables are probably the most distinguishing qualities of social psychology, and both are very much the result of gestalt psychology and the field social psychology of Lewin.

Social psychology has other important roots and themes (such as sociology, learning theory, psychoanalysis, group dynamics), but I have tried here to highlight the most prominent ones. Social psychology today is going in a number of directions and will be perhaps increasingly difficult to characterize as a perspective in the future. It has several subperspectives, each with its own conceptual framework, assumptions, and so forth, including exchange theory, cognitive theory, cognitive stages theory, and group dynamics.

Social Psychology within the Discipline of Sociology

The perspective of social psychology just described should be understood along the following lines:

1. It developed from both psychology and sociology, but primarily from psychology. Its practitioners have gotten their training primarily from psychology.
2. Because it has importance to understanding the human being as a social being, its ideas and research have been very useful in sociology.
3. This social psychology sees the human in the same general way as other social sciences. As a perspective, it defines us as shaped, molded, created. Other people shape us in group life, and our attitudes, developed socially, influence our acts in relation to stimuli we encounter. If we integrate social psychology with the other social sciences we have examined, a very strong case against an active, self-determining, "free" human being is made.

There are, however, two other social psychologies more difficult to describe, both found in the discipline of sociology.

One is not really distinguishable from sociology in general. Sociology is often divided into "macrosociology," or the study of large-scale organized life, such as society, institutions, social class, and so on, and "microsociology," the study of interaction, small-group life, and socialization. The latter is what some refer to as social psychology, drawing from all the classical sociologists as well as a large number of research studies. Social psychology in sociology focuses on the social nature of the human being, the centrality of socialization, and the various socialization agents (family, school, religion, peer groups, and so on) in society. It also examines the links between society and the individual—for example, the types of personality qualities developed in various types of societies.

A second social psychological tradition within sociology is called "symbolic interactionism," which is the topic of this book. No perspective in sociology has influenced our understanding of interaction, socialization, and the social nature of the human being as much as this perspective. It is quite different from all the other perspectives we have looked at in this book. Its roots are different from the other tradition, social psychology in psychology, as are its views of the human being. It is a social-scientific perspective, and as such, it is a science, but it takes a more critical approach to science, and its image of the human being is less deterministic. Chapter 3 is an introduction to symbolic interactionism, and each chapter after that will discuss one aspect of the perspective in some depth.

REFERENCES

ARONSON, ELLIOT
    1984 *The Social Animal.* San Francisco: W. H. Freeman & Company Publishers.
BERGER, PETER
    1963 *Invitation to Sociology.* Garden City, N.Y.: Doubleday. Copyright © 1963 by Peter L. Berger. Reprinted by permission of Doubleday & Company, Inc., New York, and Penguin Press, Harmondsworth, Middlesex, England.
FROMM, ERICH
    1973 *The Anatomy of Human Destructiveness.* New York: Holt, Rinehart & Winston. Copyright © 1973 by Erich Fromm. Reprinted by permission of Holt, Rinehart & Winston.
HAMPDEN-TURNER, CHARLES
    1970 *Radical Man.* Cambridge, Mass.: Schenkman.
KANT, IMMANUEL
    1952 *The Critique of Pure Reason.* (1781) Trans. J.M.D. Meiklejohn. *The Great Books of the Western World.* Ed. Robert Hutchins. Chicago: Encyclopaedia Britannica. Copyright © 1952 by Encyclopaedia Britannica, Inc.

3
SYMBOLIC INTERACTIONISM AS A PERSPECTIVE

INTRODUCTION: FOUR CENTRAL IDEAS

Symbolic interactionism is a perspective in social psychology that is especially relevant to the concerns of sociology. Instead of focusing on the individual and his or her personality characteristics, or on how the social structure or social situation causes individual behavior, symbolic interactionism focuses on the *nature of interaction,* the dynamic social activities taking place between persons. In focusing on the interaction itself as the unit of study, the symbolic interactionist creates a more active image of the human being and rejects the image of the passive, determined organism. Individuals interact; societies are made up of interacting individuals. People are constantly undergoing change in interaction, and society is changing through interaction. Interaction implies human beings acting in relation to each other, taking each other into account, acting, perceiving, interpreting, acting again. Hence, a more dynamic and active human being emerges, rather than an actor merely responding to others.

The second important idea distinguishing this perspective is related to the first. The human being is understood as acting in the *present,* influenced not by what happened in the past, but by what is happening *now.* What we do in any given situation is primarily a result of what is going on in that situation, not what we bring to that situation from our past, not our position in the class structure, and not some attitude we were taught long ago. The past, of course, enters into action as we recall it in the present and apply it to the situations at hand. Interaction takes place now: What we do now is linked to that interaction.

Third, interaction is not simply what is happening be<u>tween</u> people, but <u>also</u> what is happening *within* the individual. Human beings are thought to act in a world that they *define*. We act according to the way we define the situation we are in, and while that definition may be influenced by others we interact with, it is also a result of our own definition.

Finally, symbolic interactionism describes the human being as more unpredictable and "<u>active</u>" in his or her world than other perspectives do. Indeed, many symbolic interactionists argue that the human being is "free" to some extent in what he or she does. We all *define* the world we act in; part of that definition is *our own:* It involves conscious choices, we direct ourselves accordingly, we assess our actions and those of others, and we redirect ourselves.

These ideas are not difficult to understand. You have no reason to believe them at this point, since the perspective has not yet been explained. However, they are the broad outline, and we will go back to them again and again in the chapters that follow.

PERSPECTIVE, ATTITUDES, AND BEHAVIOR

To further clarify the perspective of symbolic interactionism, it should be pointed out that "perspectives" and not "attitudes" (as defined by other social psychologists) are thought to be an integral part of the human being. Here is why.

First of all, an attitude is tied to an object or a class of objects, usually in the external environment. Its stimulus is the object "out there." Supposedly, the appearance of the objects will bring forth the attitude, and the attitude will have at least some effect on the behavior. On the other hand, a perspective is attached to interaction and to various groups with which the individual identifies. Individuals interact with many others, individuals take on many perspectives; therefore, any given object can be defined in a number of ways, not one. We play many "roles," each role having another perspective, and each role placing us around certain others. Thus, we cannot predict how any given individual will define an object in his or her situation—it all depends on the interaction and the perspective used. A person I see in a situation may be a black, a teacher, a male, an artist, a scholar, a liberal, and upper class, but what I focus on and how I act will depend on how I define the situation, and my definition, in turn, will be determined by which perspective I use to define it. Any one of the individual's characteristics may or may not be important in that situation. I may, for example, be prejudiced against artists, but that may not be important.

The point is that by focusing on perspectives and not attitudes, the symbolic interactionist describes a picture of the human being *interacting, defining, acting in the present,* and *active.* Attitudes, on the other hand, suggest things that belong to the person, were developed in the person's past, and cause an unthinking response to a stimulus.

The second difference between attitudes and perspectives is that attitudes tend to be regarded as relatively fixed and difficult to change, part of one's personality, and usually consistent with other attitudes. The image of the human is one of a consistent whole organism, responding in situations according to his or her traits. An attitude is a call to response, a determinant of behavior, encouraging consistent action by the organism in a multitude of situations. Perspectives, on the other hand, are conceptualized as dynamic and changing, guides to interpretation and then to action, undergoing change during interaction, and not necessarily consistent in the same person. Behavior becomes unpredictable to a great extent; even if we know the person's perspectives before entering a situation, we do not know beforehand which one will be chosen by the person, nor can we predict how it will change in interaction. And even if we know the perspective used, we still cannot know exactly how the individual will define the situation. Clearly a more dynamic actor is perceived when we use the concept "perspective" rather than "attitude."

REFERENCE GROUPS AND PERSPECTIVES

The complex and dynamic nature of the human being's perspectives is the subject of an excellent article by Tamotsu Shibutani. Shibutani, first of all, describes perspectives in much the same way Chapter 1 of this book describes them. "A perspective is an ordered view of one's world—what is taken for granted about the attributes of various objects, events, and human nature. It is an order of things remembered and expected as well as things actually perceived, an organized conception of what is plausible and what is possible; it constitutes the matrix through which one perceives his environment" (1955:564). It allows us to see a dynamic changing world as "relatively stable, orderly, and predictable." It is "an outline scheme defining and guiding experience." Shibutani likens a group's perspective to culture (as Robert Redfield defines it) consisting of the "conventional understandings, manifest in act and artifact, that characterize societies." And, Shibutani continues, these understandings are the "premises of action." Perspectives/culture are dynamic, defined and redefined through interaction, a "product of communication." The individuals guide themselves by taking on the perspectives of those with whom they interact, the societies with which they communicate.

Reference groups, to Shibutani, are simply those groups whose perspectives the individual shares. For each individual there are several. Reference groups are groups the individual may belong to ("membership groups"), but social *categories* such as social class, ethnic group, or community may also be reference groups. Reference groups can even be future groups, for instance, "philanthropists who give for 'posterity'" or environmentalists who are concerned with unborn generations. They can be civilizations or groups from our distant past, as evidenced by many people's interest in the ancient Greeks or the American revolutionaries or the early Christians.

Shibutani calls reference groups "societies" or "social worlds." The individual has many societies, each one held together through communication and culture/perspectives. Our modern mass society is characterized by a multitude of these social worlds, each one sharing a perspective/culture, and each one held together through some form of interaction/communication. Sociologists are part of a social world, for example, and are held together by journals, conventions, and correspondence. My family is a social world and it is held together through face-to-face interaction. America is a social world, held together through television, newspapers, economic and political activities, advertising, travel, geographic mobility. Blacks constitute a social world in all probability, and they are held together, for example, through magazines, newspapers, those who travel between communities, and shared music. Shibutani summarizes the complexity of the individual—one's many perspectives and social worlds—in the following statement:

> One of the characteristics of life in modern mass societies is simultaneous participation in a variety of social worlds. Because of the ease with which the individual may expose himself to a number of communication channels, he may lead a segmentalized life, participating successively in a number of unrelated activities. Furthermore, the particular combination of social worlds differs from person to person; this is what led Simmel to declare that each stands at that point at which a unique combination of social circles intersects. The geometric analogy is a happy one, for it enables us to conceive the numerous possibilities of combinations and the different degrees of participation in each circle. To understand what a man does, we must get at his unique perspectives—what he takes for granted and how he defines the situation—but in mass societies we must learn in addition the social world in which he is participating in a given act. (1955:567)*

Shibutani is telling us a great deal about the human being and society. Human beings identify with a number of social worlds (reference groups, societies), learn through communication (symbolic interaction) the perspectives (symbolic/conceptual frameworks, culture) of these social worlds, and use these perspectives to define or interpret situations that they encounter. Individuals also perceive the effects of their actions, reflect on the usefulness of their perspectives, and adjust them in the ongoing situation. They do not passively respond, nor are their actions determined by attitudes or environmental stimuli.

It seems, then, that to know what an individual believes about a class of objects through an attitude survey may be highly irrelevant when encountering those objects in a real situation. We must instead begin to understand how one defines the situation, the reference group one identifies with in that situation, the perspective one draws on, and how one's role, reference groups, and/or perspectives undergo change in the situation in interaction with others. Figure 3-1 shows the model that is slowly being developed. This model is the beginning of our explo-

*Reprinted from "Reference Groups as Perspectives," by Tamotsu Shibutani in *The American Journal of Sociology,* by permission of The University of Chicago Press. Copyright © 1955 by The University of Chicago.

Interaction ⟶ Role ⟶ Reference group ⟶ Perspective ⟶
                              identified

Definition of ⟶ Action ⟶ Interpretation ⟶ Alter role,
the situation   and judgment   reference group,
                                                           perspective

FIGURE 3-1

ration into the symbolic interactionist perspective. It conceptualizes the human as more complex, less predictable, more contradictory, more situational, more dynamic, and less passive than do all the other social-scientific perspectives considered thus far.

GENERAL HISTORICAL BACKGROUND
OF SYMBOLIC INTERACTIONISM

Symbolic interactionism is usually traced back to the work of George Herbert Mead (1863-1931), who was a professor of philosophy at the University of Chicago. Mead wrote many articles, but much of his influence on symbolic interactionists comes through the publishing of his lectures and notes by his students, as well as through interpretation of his work by various other sociologists, especially one of his students, Herbert Blumer.

Herbert Blumer is probably the most important integrator and interpreter of the symbolic interactionist perspective. I once asked one of my professors in graduate school for some advice in what to read in order to gain a good background in symbolic interactionism. She replied: "Well, you know, everything that has ever been written on symbolic interactionism has been written by Herbert Blumer." At the time I laughed at the remark and tried to disregard it, but as I worked through the literature, I realized how true her statement was. It is not that Blumer is the only good symbolic interactionist, but his work probably represents the best interpretation and integration of the writings of others, and at the same time, it pulls out the social implications and unique insights of the perspective.

It is not only Mead whom Blumer draws from, and who pioneered symbolic interactionism. The perspective goes back to the work of John Dewey, William James, W. I. Thomas, and Charles Cooley, to name a few. Blumer, writing primarily in the 1950s and 1960s, integrated much of their work. In addition M. H. Kuhn, Arnold Rose, Norman Denzin, Gregory Stone, Alfred Lindesmith, Anselm Strauss, Jerome Manis, Bernard Meltzer, and Tamotsu Shibutani, among others, have made contributions to this perspective by integrating the work of the earlier writers and showing some of its theoretical and empirical applications. Symbolic interactionism has also inspired other perspectives, such as labeling theory in the study of deviance, Erving Goffman's dramaturgical perspective, and probably Harold Garfinkel's ethnomethodology. Figure 3-2 illustrates the development of the symbolic interactionist perspective.

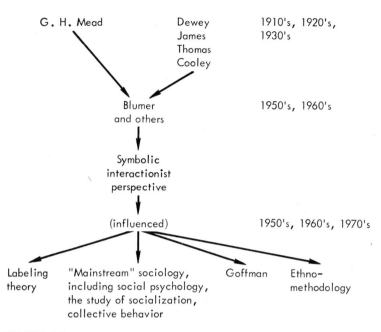

FIGURE 3-2

One way of understanding the general position of the symbolic interactionist perspective is to summarize the major influences on G. H. Mead, its principal founder. (The following draws from Strauss, 1964, and Desmonde, 1957.) There were three such influences, each one being central to all the symbolic interactionists since:

1. The philosophy of pragmatism
2. The work of Charles Darwin
3. Behaviorism

Mead and Pragmatism

Mead is part of that school of philosophy known as pragmatism. The ideas of this school are especially important to Mead's approach to understanding the nature of truth. As we shall see, this becomes a very important foundation for the whole perspective of symbolic interactionism. Basically, four ideas are important here:

1. *Truth is possible for the human being only through the individual's own intervention.* That is, it essentially does not "come to us" from things around us; things do not tell us what they are. Human beings interpret all things. We never see reality "in the raw"; nothing for humans ever "speaks for itself."
2. *Knowledge for the human being is judged on its usefulness.* This is a simple but very important principle. Many people are familiar with the pronounce-

ment: "People see what they want to see and remember what they want to remember." This is the pragmatist idea too. However, what we *want* to remember is that knowledge that we can *use*. We remember what *works* for us in the situations we encounter. Perspectives, facts, definitions, ideas—all are judged by the individual in terms of application. In a sense every situation is a test for our ideas: If they work (help us achieve our goals) we keep them; otherwise, we alter them.

3. *Objects we encounter are defined according to their use for us.* Not only is knowledge judged by use, we also see *things* in our environment according to their use. What things mean to us depends on how we intend to use them. The world out there is defined according to how it fulfills our needs at any given moment. Any object has a multitude of uses, and it can thus be defined in a multitude of ways. A wastebasket is "something to throw waste in," "something to sit on," "something to draw," "something to pound," "something to use to store corn in," "something to practice our basketball skills with"—the definition depends entirely on the person's goals in the situation. Objects do not in effect exist for the human being apart from the many *uses* the human has for them. Of course, we ignore that which we do not use.

4. *Understanding about the human being must be inferred from what he or she does.* The pragmatic approach to knowing about the human being is the same as the behaviorist approach in this sense: It is from *human action* that we can empirically observe that we are able to understand the human organism. It is from what we see people *do* that we can come to understand society and the group. However, the action that we can see always has *meaning* to the actor. We *think* about what we do. We *interpret* our action and that of others. Unlike the behaviorist in psychology, the pragmatist regards this covert, thinking action to be an essential part of the investigation of the human being. We must try to understand it in a number of ways; if we ignore it, we miss the essence of human action.

Mead and Darwin

Mead was inspired and influenced by the work of Charles Darwin. Darwin's work, of course, helped to revolutionize the study of biology through its contribution to the theory of evolution. Darwin was a naturalist. He believed that we must try to understand this world that we live in without appealing to supernatural explanation. God may, of course, exist, but nature should be understood on its own terms, as subject to natural laws. So too, Mead argued, should we regard the human being in naturalistic terms. If we are free, if we are unique, if we possess qualities different from other animals, then these must be understood in natural rather than supernatural terms. Mead's whole approach to truth, self, mind, symbols, and the other quite difficult and abstract concepts in his perspective is naturalistic: It tries to understand them as part of the qualities developed by the human being as part of nature, part of our heritage in the animal kingdom.

Of course, Mead was also heavily influenced by Darwin's theory of evolution. Humans are animals, social animals, evolved from other forms, and like all other animals, they are unique. Our uniqueness can be traced not to individual isolated qualities but to a combination of several that together form a qualitative difference, unexplainable by just the sum of the individual traits. Human uniqueness relates to the ability to reason and to communicate symbolically with oneself and with others. It is difficult to isolate exactly what traits came together to make this possible, but a highly developed brain, heavy reliance on socialization, and the ability to make subtle and sophisticated sounds seem to be very important.

The ability to reason and use symbols, according to Mead, changes the human being's relationship with nature. In a sense, it turns around evolution. The human is the only organism that is able to *understand* the forces working in nature, making it possible for humans to alter those forces in some cases, and certainly to adjust to them through building, inventing, discovering. This makes the human not passive in nature, but *active*—to some extent in control of his or her own evolution.

Darwin was also influential in his emphasis on an evolutionary, dynamic universe rather than a static one. All of nature is a process, all "things" in nature should be thought of as constantly in a state of change. To Mead and to the symbolic interactionists, everything about the human being is considered as *process*, rather than as stable and fixed. Indeed, one of the most important criticisms of symbolic interactionism is that it deemphasizes structure too much, giving the false impression that everything is always changing. However, by emphasizing *process,* a view of human beings and society emerges that is unique in social sciences. Symbolic interactionists contend, for example:

1. The *individual* is not a consistent, structured personality as much as a dynamic, changing actor, never "becoming" anything, but always "in the state of becoming," unfolding, acting. The individual is not socialized but is always in the process of socialization; the individual is not set or fixed but constantly undergoing change in the process of interaction.
2. *Society and the group* is conceptualized *not* as something static "out there," influencing us, but entirely as an interaction process. Society is individuals in interaction, dynamic, with patterns emerging and constantly being changed or reaffirmed over time. What people call "society" and "the group" are patterns we infer from the interaction process.
3. The individual is characterized as possessing a *mind* and a *self,* but both are conceptualized as process, not as static entities. The person does not possess a mind so much as a minding process, meaning an ability to converse with self and an ability to pull out stimuli selectively from the environment, assess their significance, interpret the situation, judge the action of others and self, and so on. All of this means an active, dynamic conversation is taking place within the organism in interaction with others.
4. The human has many *selves,* each related to the interaction he or she is involved with, and each constantly being changed in the process of interaction. When the symbolic interactionist argues that the individual possesses a self, he or she is really saying that the individual has selfhood, that one treats oneself as an object, and that, as with other objects, a constant redefinition is taking place in interaction with others.
5. *Truths,* ideas, attitudes, perceptions, and perspectives are all conceptualized as process, being judged and changed dynamically by the organism in relation to what is being observed. People are not brainwashed and conditioned so much as constantly testing and reassessing their truths. Truth is arrived at through interaction, and it is also transformed in the process of interaction.

Mead and Behaviorism

Thus Darwin and his biology combine with the ideas of pragmatism to form the basis of Mead's ideas. There is one more influence, however. It is the influence of those who have come to be called behaviorists in psychology.

Behaviorism influenced Mead in two ways. One was a positive influence: Humans should be understood in terms of their behavior, not in terms of *who* they are. The behaviorists believed that the only scientifically legitimate way for understanding all animals, including humans, was through their behavior.

However, Mead was more influenced in a negative way. James B. Watson, a psychologist who became one of the important founders of behaviorism in the United States, was actually a student of Mead and Dewey at the University of Chicago, but he rejected the pragmatists in favor of a behaviorism that ignored all behavior except that which can be seen. Mind action, so central to Mead and the other pragmatists, was rejected. Throughout his academic life, Mead reacted to this kind of science, believing that without an understanding of mind, symbols, self, and so on, human behavior cannot be understood for what it is. To measure overt behavior alone without trying to understand covert, "minded" behavior was to ignore the central qualities of the human being; it was to treat humans identically with all other things in nature, as physical organisms. Mead was a behaviorist, but a *social behaviorist,* arguing that as we observe overt action we must always consider what is going on in terms of definition, interpretation, meaning.

SUMMARY

This chapter has introduced the perspective of symbolic interactionism. It set forth a number of ideas that will weave themselves throughout the rest of the chapters. Here is a brief summary of those ideas:

1. Symbolic interactionism focuses on *interaction* rather than on personality or social structure. It also focuses on *definition,* the *present,* and the human as an *active* rather than passive participant in the world.
2. Humans are thought to be heavily influenced by their *perspectives,* which are always dynamic, guiding (not determining) influencers. Humans are much less influenced by attitudes developed in their past because they do not simply respond to their world, they define and interpret it.
3. Perspectives are learned, altered, transformed, and replaced in interaction. Each actor has many perspectives, each one associated with a reference group or society.
4. A society is individuals in interaction, communicating, developing a common, shared perspective. The individual is not thought to be a product of society so much as an actively involved actor in its development.
5. Symbolic interactionism as a perspective was highly influenced by the work of George Herbert Mead, by the integrating work of Herbert Blumer, and by pragmatism, Darwin, and behaviorism.

6. Pragmatism, a school of philosophy of which Mead is an important part, emphasizes that the human intervenes in determining what is real, knowledge is judged by the individual according to its usefulness, objects too are defined according to their use, and humans must be understood through what they do in the world.

7. Darwin influences Mead in seeing the human as part of nature, evolved yet unique, and as always changing.

8. Mead, like the behaviorists, focuses on human behavior, but he goes further in calling for as full an understanding of mind behavior as of overt behavior.
covert

A CONTRAST WITH OTHER PERSPECTIVES

Charles K. Warriner (1970:1-13) highlights these same themes, but in a historical manner. The question of the human's passive or active nature has traditionally been part of society's ideology—the question of human freedom has rarely been tackled from an objective perspective. Yet the question, "[What is] the relation of man to society and of society to man?" is probably "the most fundamental, the most frequently recurring" one we have dealt with, and the answer to this has had the "most extended implications" for our history. Do humans create society, or are we passively shaped by it? Traditional social science, in its attempt to take the lead from natural science, has built the human within the walls of society. Yet, after centuries of debate and after much research in social science, only one truth clearly emerges, according to Warriner: human beings and human society are interdependent, they come into being together, "man has become human only as social systems have come into being; society develops only as man becomes human." The traditional biological and social-scientific views Warriner labels "stable-man" views, the human having a "permanent nature," "inborn or learned." The human is born, is shaped, and as an adult, is directed. According to stable-man views, human action is caused by human nature or nurture, the individual always acting according to earlier influences. Warriner's diagram of this sequence is shown in Figure 3-3. The cause of human behavior is always related to earlier influences, and stability is assumed for the human personality. This stable-man point of view, Warriner argues, is tied to a

FIGURE 3-3*

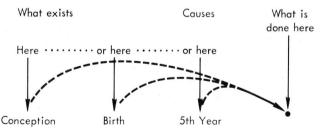

*From Charles K. Warriner, *The Emergence of Society*. Copyright © 1970 by the Dorsey Press. Reprinted by permission of the Dorsey Press, Homewood, Illinois.

"physicalist," "deterministic and mechanistic," nonsocial/nonmentalist view of the world that dominates science and philosophy.

In reaction, Warriner describes another view, which he calls "the emergent-human view of man," emphasizing "immediate situational factors" as cause, "examining the social and 'spiritual'" characteristics of human beings, and accepting "indeterminacy and probability" in dealing with causes of human action. This theory regards the human as an "actor rather than as a being, treats man's acts as symbolic in character rather than primarily physical, and views interaction as the basic social and psychological process from which personalities and societies emerge, through which they are expressed, and by which they are maintained as continuities." Human beings are now to be understood as social, interactional, and symbolic by their very nature. Those who see only the physical, who measure only that which is directly observable, miss the whole essence of the human being. Our uniqueness is in

> the symboling process, in the capacity of man to see things not as they are but as they have been or might be in the future, in the capacity of man to use sound and marks on paper as conventional signs and thus to communicate with others, in the capacity of man through these functions to create worlds that never existed in physical reality. (Warriner, 1970:9-10)

CENTRAL CONCEPTS OF SYMBOLIC INTERACTIONISM

In the following chapters, the central concepts of the symbolic interactionist perspective will be examined, with an emphasis on their complex interrelationships. Mead focuses on three concepts: *mind, self,* and *society*. Bernard Meltzer (1972: 11-25), in a great summary article, lists the following: *society, self, mind,* and the *act*. There is little question that a good understanding of these concepts might give one the essence of the symbolic interactionist perspective, but these concepts should be developed systematically and carefully. In order to examine these central concepts, I have added several others and have put them into an order that seems logical.

Some symbolic interactionists may be impatient with the chapters that follow. The overriding strategy, however, is *not* to present all the concepts at once but to build patiently from a simple beginning and finally, in the closing chapters, to lay out a highly complex and interrelated set of concepts.

We turn first to the symbol.

REFERENCES

DESMONDE, WILLIAM H.
    1957 "George Herbert Mead and Freud: American Social Psychology and Psychoanalysis." In ed. Benjamin Nelson, *Psychoanalysis and the Future,* pp. 31-50. New York: Psychological Association for Psychoanalysis.

MELTZER, BERNARD N.
1972 *The Social Psychology of George Herbert Mead.* Kalamazoo: Center for Sociological Research, Western Michigan University. By permission of Bernard Meltzer.
SHIBUTANI, TAMOTSU
1955 "Reference Groups as Perspectives." *American Journal of Sociology* 60:562–69. By permission of The University of Chicago Press. Copyright © 1955 by The University of Chicago. All rights reserved.
STRAUSS, ANSELM
1964 *Introduction to* On Social Psychology *by George Herbert Mead.* Chicago: The University of Chicago Press.
WARRINER, CHARLES K.
1970 *The Emergence of Society.* Homewood, Ill.: Dorsey Press. By permission of the Dorsey Press.

4
THE MEANING
OF THE SYMBOL

We walked down the path to the well-house, attracted by the fragrance of the honeysuckle with which it was covered. Someone was drawing water and my teacher placed my hand under the spout. As the cool stream gushed over one hand she spelled into the other the word water, first slowly, then rapidly. I stood still, my whole attention fixed upon the motions of her fingers. Suddenly I felt a misty consciousness as of something forgotten—a thrill of returning thought; and somehow the mystery of language was revealed to me. I knew then that "w-a-t-e-r" meant the wonderful cool something that was flowing over my hand. That living word awakened my soul, gave it light, hope, joy, set it free! There were barriers still, it is true, but barriers that could in time be swept away.

I left the well-house eager to learn. Everything had a name, and each name gave birth to a new thought. As we returned to the house every object which I touched seemed to quiver with life. That was because I saw everything with the strange, new sight that had come to me. . . .

I learned a great many new words that day. I do not remember what they all were; but I do know that *mother, father, sister, teacher* were among them—words that were to make the world blossom for me, "like Aaron's rod, with flowers." It would have been difficult to find a happier child than I was as I lay in my crib at the close of that eventful day and lived over the joys it had brought me, and for the first time longed for a new day to come. (Helen Keller, 1954:36–37)

We take for granted the fact that we use language. We rarely think about what it would be like without language. Only when we consciously attempt to examine

---

*Excerpt from *The Story of My Life* by Helen Keller. Copyright © 1902, 1903, 1905 by Helen Keller. Reprinted by permission of Doubleday & Company, Inc.

language objectively do we realize how central it is to what the human being is. Helen Keller, both blind and deaf, was not able to use language for a good part of her childhood because she was unaware of words, unaware that humans can respond to a reality outside the physical reality, to a reality uniquely human—a social/symbolic reality that opens up for human beings behavioral possibilities that other organisms do not have. Indeed, it is due to the world of symbols and language that the human is not passive in nature and does not respond to physical stimuli as other organisms do. The symbolic interactionist perspective takes the use of symbols and relates it to all that is human. The symbol is, in a way, the central concept of the whole perspective.

What is the nature of the human being? Are we by nature evil? Selfish? Good? Hungry for knowledge? What? Borrowing from Warriner's (1970) argument, whatever we are, whatever "human nature" is, is highly dependent on society. This statement refers to two human characteristics in a sense. One is that we become violent, selfish, peaceful, or loving, owing in large part to the society. But also we are, in our very nature, social beings, dependent on society for all our most basic human qualities, such as conscience, language, the ability to reason. However, Warriner also emphasizes that the nature of human society is highly dependent on the nature of the individual, both in the sense that individuals shape society, and in the sense that individuals—highly complex, intelligent, creative, and flexible—are necessary for society to exist. It is the nature of the *symbol* that makes this interdependence most clear. Each individual depends on society for symbols; without other people each individual would be without a symbolic life and all the things that symbols make possible. But the relationship is also reversed: Complex human society demands and depends on human symbolic life—symbolic communication and the ability to think and to solve problems—which results, in turn, in the individual's ability to conform, question, reject, or alter society's direction. Society makes us, but we, in turn, make society. The key to this interdependence is our symbolic life. The purpose of this chapter will be to explain this relationship through focusing on the nature of the symbol and the importance of the symbol for understanding the uniqueness of the human being. It will focus on the fact that our symbols not only are social and allow for the sharing of culture and the continuation of society but also assure the active human being.

There are several important terms for us to consider as we examine the meaning of the symbol.

THE NATURE OF REALITY

To begin with, we must consider further the nature of "reality" for human beings. Since, as we have pointed out, the human sees the world through perspectives, developed socially, reality is *social,* and what we see "out there" (and within ourselves) is developed in interaction with others. We interpret the world according to *social* definitions. It is important to emphasize, however, that social scientists (including symbolic interactionists) operate from the assumption that a physical objective reality does indeed exist independent of our social definition, that our social definitions do respond, at least in part, to something "real" or physical. Although there are some who question even this assumption, most of us would indeed agree to some *objective reality* existing out there. Symbolic interactionists sometimes call this reality "the situation as it exists." The point, however, is that we do not respond to this reality directly. We define the situation "as it exists" out there, and that definition is highly influenced by our social life. We are not like billiard balls responding directly to other billiard balls, nor are we like rats responding to physical stimuli. Someone may push us physically, and we must respond physically in the sense that our bodies give way to the push, but we also immediately *interpret* that act and decide on a line of action. At first our physical bodies respond to other physical bodies, but immediately we socially define that reality, putting that action into a working context (e.g., Why did he push? Did he mean to be aggressive? Is he bigger than I am?), and we define the act accordingly.

In addition to a physical objective reality and a social reality, each individual, because he or she sees the world uniquely, has an *individual, personal reality*. The nature of this individual reality will be made clearer later on in this book. However, for now it is important to realize that this personal, somewhat unique approach to reality that each of us develops does not arise in a vacuum: It arises from and is based on the social realities that we develop in interaction with others.

Importance of a Socially Defined Reality

Howard Becker (1953), in an interesting and comprehensive study of marijuana users, done before marijuana became such a popular part of many social worlds in America, illustrates the central importance of a social definition of reality, even the reality that we *feel* inside our own bodies. His point: To identify the effects of marijuana as good and pleasurable is a matter of socialization; it is, in a real sense, a result of social interaction, a social reality. In conclusion, Becker writes:

> This analysis of the genesis of marihuana use shows that the individuals who come in contact with a given object may respond to it at first in a great variety of ways. If a stable form of new behavior toward the object is to emerge, a transformation of meanings must occur, in which the person develops a new conception of the nature of the object. This happens in a series of communicative acts in which others point out new aspects of his experience to him, present him with new interpretations of events, and help him achieve a new conceptual organization of his world, without which the new behavior is not possible. Persons who do not achieve the proper kind of conceptualization are unable to engage in the given behavior and turn off in the direction of some other relationships to the object or activity. (1953: 242)

The fact that others are responsible for defining what is real is one of the central ideas in sociology today and need not be documented extensively here. However, another very fascinating study worth mentioning was done by Mark Zborowski (1952). He points out that pain is a "physiological phenomenon [but] acquires specific social and cultural significance . . ." (p. 17). His research examined patients' definitions of their pain in order to show that what they saw and felt was related to their group life. His major point is that people define pain differently, give it a different meaning, and react to it differently according, at least in part, to their ethnic group membership, which is a social definition. There is no reason to believe that some ethnic groups actually experience more physical pain than others, yet some groups complain more than others, some groups respond to the physical pain itself and are thankful for immediate relief, while other groups tend to interpret pain as representing something more serious; they are not relieved just with pain killers, but need assurance about their future health. It seems that for human beings even something as immediate and physical as pain is defined in interaction with others.

The importance of socially defined reality to the human is even more obvious when we look beyond our own bodies. Every day we encounter countless physical objects. To make sense out of them, the human actor must isolate, identify, and catalogue them. How do we do that? To a great extent it is done by society; we come to identify and classify our world according to what we learn from others in interaction.

OBJECTS AS "SOCIAL OBJECTS"

Objects may exist in physical form, but for the human being, they are pointed out, isolated, catalogued, interpreted, and given meaning through social interaction. In the symbolic interactionist perspective, we say that objects for the human being are really *social objects*. This concept is very important in the symbolic interactionist perspective, for, as we shall see, it will become an integral part of every chapter in this book.

First, we begin with objects "as they are." Objects may exist in physical form, but for the human being they are seen not "in the raw," but only through a perspective of some kind. We learn what things are and what they are good for. Objects are pointed out, isolated, catalogued, named, interpreted, and given meaning as we interact with others. Children want to know, "What's that?" The newcomer to football wants to know, "What are they doing now? What is a 'down?' What is a 'huddle?'" And a student at college for the first time wants to know, "What is a G.P.A.? What is a graduate assistant? What is sociology?" We ask. We watch. We are told. But, in the end, we learn from each other what things are in the world. This is why objects are called *social* objects by the symbolic interactionist.

Objects in nature are, of course, responded to by both human and nonhuman organisms. Bernard Meltzer (1972:22–23) describes Mead's thesis that all organisms must single out certain things around them to respond to, since only certain things are important to their survival. Other stimuli become largely irrelevant. (A tree, grass, a human, and acorns are all different things to a cow, a squirrel, a beaver, and a cat.) Objects in the physical world act as stimuli for animals, leading to specific responses. The same object (e.g., grass) will lead to different responses depending on which species is involved. For the human being, however, all objects in nature are not fixed stimuli but are *social objects* constantly changing as they are defined and redefined in interaction. "Objects consist of whatever people indicate or refer to" (Blumer, 1969:68). Objects are given importance by us not through fixed biological patterns (as is the case in most other animals) but according to what others around us decide to give importance to. And each object changes for the human, not because *it* changes, but because people change their definition. The meaning, says Blumer, "is not intrinsic to the object" (p. 68).

But how do we define these social objects? We give them *names,* but more important, we learn what they are good for, how they are *used.* Social objects are defined according to their *use* for the people involved in a situation. Meaning "arises from how the person is initially prepared to act toward it" (Blumer, 1969: 68-69). A chair becomes "something to sit in." A desk is "something to write on." A flower is "something to smell." A podium is "something to speak from." In each of these cases, however, the object changes as its use for us changes, as we change the meaning it has for us. Chairs are also something to stand on, to store things on, to draw, to put side by side in order to sleep on, and so forth. A desk is something to sit on or stand on, to collate papers on, to represent our prestige to others with, to hide something in, and so forth. A flower is also something to give to a loved one or someone in the hospital, something to send to a person in mourning, something to decorate our yard, something to draw, something to extract medicine from, something to use to attract bees. A podium is also something to represent our authority, something to store notes in, something for children to play with. Objects change for us precisely because our use for them changes. Blumer supplies some excellent examples: "A tree is not the same object to a lumberman, a botanist, or a poet; a star is a different object to a modern astronomer than it was to a sheepherder of antiquity; communism is a different object to a Soviet patriot than it is to a Wall Street broker" (p. 69). Most physical objects have almost an infinite number of possible uses, thus they have almost an infinite number of social meanings, and each physical object constitutes, therefore, a multitude of social objects.

This view of objects is one that goes back to pragmatism, which was briefly discussed in Chapter 3. Between objects out there and the individual's overt response is a perspective—a definition, a meaning—socially derived.

Mead, Blumer, and other symbolic interactionists see objects as defined by "a line of action" one is about to take toward them. When I see a horse out there, I see something I am about to ride, mount, pet, run from, eat, sell, buy, or use to teach my children that animals are their friends. To say we see according to a line of action we are about to take toward something is the same as saying we organize our perception of objects according to the use they have for us.

A social object then is *any object in a situation that an actor uses in that situation. That use has arisen socially.* Other objects are ignored. However, as action unfolds, the individual may change his or her use, notice new objects, ignore objects used initially, and so on. The actor *acts* toward objects, socially defined, of use to him or her in a particular situation.

Social objects include anything. Consider the following examples:

1. Physical natural objects—a tree, a flower, a rock, or dirt can become social objects in a situation.
2. Human-made objects—a radio, a fork, a piece of paper, a computer terminal—can become social objects in a situation.
3. Animals are sometimes used as social objects by the individual.
4. Other people are social objects—both individually and in groups, we define other people as important to the situations we are in. We develop lines of action toward them, and we "use" them (not necessarily selfishly). You are someone I ask for a date one day, ask to marry, marry, live with, get angry with, share my cares with, and so on.
5. Our "past" is a social object, as is the "future." We *use* these to work through situations.
6. Our "self" is a social object (as we shall emphasize in Chapter 6).
7. Symbols are social objects. We create and use symbols to communicate and represent something to others and to our self.
8. Ideas and perspectives can be social objects.

Anything can become a social object for the human actor. Whatever we use is a social object to us in a given situation. Our use defines it, and almost always that use has arisen socially. "It" changes, as our use for it changes.

SYMBOLS—A CLASS OF SOCIAL OBJECTS

This is a chapter about symbols. But what are symbols? Simply, symbols are one class of social objects. Some social objects are symbols, some are not. Like all social objects symbols are used and are defined according to their use. *Symbols are social objects used to represent* (or "stand in for," "take the place of") whatever people agree they shall represent. A bolt of lightning stands for the wrath of God, two fingers in the air stands for victory (or peace, or loyalty to the Cub Scouts, or rebellion toward the adult world), the word "m-a-n" stands for approximately one half of the human race (or all of the human race).

Words, of course, are symbols, but so are many objects that people may make into symbols (like the cross). Indeed, most human action is regarded as symbolic, as representing something more than what is immediately perceived. A clenched fist, for example, may represent the fact that the other person is about to take a swing at us.

Many social objects are not used to represent something else and are therefore not symbols. A flower is used for drugs, for smelling, for picking, for food. However, if I use it to represent my love for you, it becomes a symbol. The same physical object (a chair, for example, or lightning, or a picture on the wall), therefore, can be a purely social object to some and a symbol to others. And for still others that object does not exist because it goes unnoticed, serves no useful function in their world.

It is very difficult to distinguish objects that are symbols from other social objects. Indeed, some, such as Herbert Blumer, argue that all social objects are symbolic—that is, each social object *stands for* a line of action we may take toward it. The distinction between a symbol and social objects, however, goes beyond just representation. Symbols represent, but they are also *used for communication* between actors or within the actor. Through symbols we are able to communicate to others and interpret other's communications. Through symbols we are also able to communicate to our self (to think) about our world. A horse is just a social object until I make it into something to represent and communicate skill, prestige, wealth, or happiness to others. The word "horse" is a word-symbol, used specifically to represent a certain animal as I communicate to others and to myself.

Symbols then are social objects used by the actor for representation and communication.

SYMBOLS ARE SOCIAL, MEANINGFUL, AND SIGNIFICANT

Symbols are *social.* They are defined in interaction, not established in nature. People make them, and people agree on what they shall stand for. Some call symbols *"conventional"*: They represent something else only because of convention, only because of common agreement.

Symbols are *meaningful*. That is, the users *know* what they represent. They involve an understanding rather than a simple response to their presence. When we say that symbols "represent" something to the user, we are actually saying that they stand in for something else, and that the user understands that relationship. A symbol is "any object, mode of conduct, or word toward which men act *as if it were something else.* Whatever the symbol stands for constitutes its *meaning*" (Shibutani, 1961:121). For instance, Shibutani gives us the example of a colored piece of cloth, what we call a "flag."

> A flag is a symbol for a nation. The piece of colored cloth often evokes patriotic sentiments and plays an important part in the mobilization of millions of men for war. Seeing someone treat the flag with disrespect can arouse the most violent emotional reactions, for men often regard the piece of cloth as if it were the nation with which they identify themselves. . . . Soldiers risk their lives on battlefields to save a flag from falling into the hands of the enemy; the cloth in itself is of little value, but what it stands for is of great importance. (1961:120–21)

Symbols are *significant.* By this Mead means that symbols are meaningful not only for the actor who receives them but also to the *user.* The user of symbols uses symbols *intentionally,* not by mistake. "What is essential to communication is that the symbol should arouse in one's self what it arouses in the other individual" (Mead, 1934:149). The person who uses symbols does so for the purpose of giving off meaning that he or she believes will make sense to the other. Symbols are not an individual act, therefore, but, by their very nature, are social, are meaningful to more than one. A crying infant does not at first use symbols to communicate to parents, although the parents do see the act of crying as important, interpret it, and respond. Crying becomes symbolic only when its meaning is understood by the one who produces it, the infant. Then, as the infant intentionally communicates through crying, there is a request for a response by the other, and we can begin to speak of symbolic behavior between child and parents. Symbols, then, because they are meaningful to the actor, are used *purposively* to give off meaning to others. Sheldon Stryker describes the process by which a small child comes to share meaning:

> The early activity of the child will include random vocalization. Eventually, too, he will imitate sounds others make. Others respond to the initially random vocalization by selecting out particular sounds and responding to these. They respond to the imitated sounds as well by acts which contain the adult meanings of these sounds. For the child, the correspondence between sound and meaning will be initially vague, but in the process of interaction over time the correspondence will become more pronounced. So, for example, the child may use the sound "ba" to refer to any approximately round object and, having played this game with daddy, may be led to roll any such object—ball, orange, egg—around the floor. The response of parent to the rolling of an egg—especially an uncooked one—will soon make clear that an egg is not a "ba" and thus is not to be rolled on the floor. In the course of time, child and parent will come to agree on what is and is not a ball, and thus a significant symbol will have come into existence. A sound, initially meaningless to the child, comes to mean for the child what it already means for the adult. (1959:116)

Symbols then are social objects intentionally used to represent and communicate. It is the actor's *aim* to use them. There is a purpose, and symbols selected are used as a means to that purpose. Without intention, the actor may be communicating, but we do not call it symbolic.

Bernard Meltzer (1972:12–13), borrowing from Mead, contrasts significant symbols with the clucking of a hen or the barking of a dog. He argues: Communication is "nonsignificant" as with the crying infant, or "nonmeaningful" in the sense that the actors do not understand the meaning of the other's act or of their own. A hen clucks and chicks respond. "This does not imply, however, that the hen clucks *in order* to guide the chicks, i.e., with the *intention* of guiding them." A dog barks; the bark acts as a cue for a response by a second dog. There seems to be little evidence that each thinks, "What does he mean by that?" or, "How should I respond to that?" or, "If I run away now, he'll think I'm chicken, so I'd better fight." Meltzer points out: "Human beings on the other hand, respond to one another on the basis of the intentions or meanings of gestures. This renders the gesture *symbolic,* i.e., the gesture is a symbol to be interpreted. . . ." Miller (1973:86–87) contrasts significant symbols with the dance of the bees:

First of all, the dance is not learned; it is committed impulsively. Second, there is no evidence that the dancer intends to evoke responses by other bees. Should there be no others present, it will perform the dance anyway; and if others are present but do not "obey the request," the dancer does not perform the dance again, as if to say, "I have told you once, why aren't you on your way?" There is no evidence, in short, that the dancer intends anything by its gesture or that it is in the least aware of the behavioral consequences of its behavior.

Examples of symbols are everywhere. The more we examine our world, the more it is transformed from a purely physical world to a fully symbolic world. Let me emphasize:

1. Words are symbols—they stand for something; they are meaningful; they are used by actors to represent physical objects, feelings, ideas, values. They are used for communication. Their meaning is social.
2. Our acts often are symbols. Whatever we do is often meant to give off some meaning, to communicate with others. We tell each other in what we do what we think, feel, see, what our intentions are, what is coming next. Acts are not symbolic if they are not intentional, or if they are not meant for anyone else. Let me give you some examples of acts as symbolic:

   Writing an outline of my lecture on the blackboard (symbolic of "This is important" or "I care that you understand")

   Looking into someone's eyes as he or she talks

   Walking out in the middle of a lecture

   Gunning a car engine at the corner

   Winking

   Kissing

   Looking at a watch as someone talks to you

   Each one of these is not simply an "act"; it is symbolic. Each person is telling the other something, each is meant for communication of meaning. Acts, for most of us most of the time, stand for much more than we physically sense directly. They are symbolic; they represent more.
3. Many *objects* can take on a symbolic quality. We can agree that the red star shall represent a certain political philosophy; a Cadillac, status; a diamond, luxury; long hair, rebellion.

Finally, symbols are *arbitrarily* associated with what they represent. That is, there is nothing inherent in the association. It is not the same as a black sky "representing" a coming storm, or a fever "representing" illness. The meaning of symbols is not found in nature, but only through arbitrary designation by people. People create symbols, and they, not nature, designate that something shall stand for something else. The fact that two fingers in the air means peace is arbitrary—it could just as well be a thumb in the air, a hand closed over our head, a black mark on our forehead.

Symbols are obviously very complex, and there is a lot of room for misunderstanding. No two people will ever agree on the exact meaning of any symbol. No one can know exactly what someone else means. Sometimes we mean one thing and others take it for something else. Sometimes we do not mean to communicate, but others think we are (as, for example, when students walk out in the middle of a lecture). Sometimes even though we do not intend to communicate, others, because they are sensitive to symbols, pick up a twinkle in our eye, a nervous twitch, a frown, and they accurately interpret what we are thinking. Perfect symbols are hard to find; but symbols saturate our every move. Their ambiguity does not take away from their importance. Indeed, as Hugh Duncan (1968:7) writes, "perhaps it is the ambiguity of symbols which makes them so useful in human society."

SUMMARY

Language is a special kind of symbol. More than any other symbol, it can be produced at will, and it can represent a reality that other symbols cannot. Before we look at language, let us summarize what has been said about social objects and symbols:

1. Social objects result from interaction and they are defined according to their *use.*
2. Many social objects are not symbols, for their use is not in communication; they represent lines of action but nothing more.
3. Some social objects are symbols. They are *used* for representation and for communication between people.
4. Symbols can be physical objects, human acts, or words.
5. Symbols are significant, meaningful, conventional, and arbitrary.

LANGUAGE

Not only are words symbols, but without words other symbols would not exist. Symbols—acts, objects, words—have meaning to us only because they can be described through using words. Meaning involves understanding what symbols stand for. All symbolic acts and all objects that are symbolic are defined using words. Words, then, as one kind of symbol—are in fact the most important kind and make possible all others.

> *The key and basic symbolism of man is language.* All the other symbol systems can be *interpreted* only by means of language. It is the instrument by means of which every designation, every interpretation, every conceptualization, and almost every communication of experience is ultimately accomplished. What is not expressed in language is not experienced and has no meaning; it is "beyond" the people. . . . Fundamentally, the spoken *word,* or its equivalent or functioning counterpart in the languages that do not have "words," is the only all-inclusive and basic medium of communication. There are, of course, other forms of conveying messages interpersonally, which express ideas, emotions, intents, or directives: laughter, . . . gestures, facial

expressions and postures; . . . especially, writing. But these *other* signs, signals, expressions, and marks, and all other symbolic systems relate to words, imply words, are translations, substitutes, adjuncts, or supplements of words. . . . Bereft of their relation to, and interpretation in terms of, language they would be meaningless. Thus, for example, among us the raucous guffaw means "You're a fool!!"; the wave of an arm by an acquaintance means "Hello"; the green light at the intersection means "Go!"; the nod and wink means "Come on"; the beckoning gesture means "Come!"; the Civil Defense siren means "Be on the alert!"

When a people have reached the stage of literacy in their language development, they have *writing* or written language. . . . These, in various combinations, make possible the recording and perpetuation of meanings and their transmission across space and time. But speech always precedes writing. In societies like our own, communication by language is further facilitated and extended by mechanical means of transmitting either speech or writing, such as postal service, printing in its multiple uses, telegraph, telephone and teletype, radio, photography, motion pictures, and television. These are sometimes referred to as secondary symbolic systems. (Hertzler, 1965:29-31)*

Hertzler defines language as "a culturally constructed and socially established system . . . of standardized and conventionalized . . . symbols, which have a specific and arbitrarily determined meaning and common usage for purpose of socially meaningful expression, and for communication in the given society (p. 30). Language is made up of *words,* each one having meaning alone and also having meaning when combined with others in a standardized way, according to certain established rules. Roger Brown refers to the "miracle of language": "Fewer than one hundred sounds which are individually meaningless are compounded, not in all possible ways, to produce some hundreds of thousands of meaningful morphemes, which have meanings that are arbitrarily assigned, and these morphemes are combined by rule to yield an infinite set of sentences, having meanings that can be derived" (1965:248). It is a *symbolic system,* defined in interaction, and used to describe to others and to ourselves what we observe, think, and imagine. Language describes all other social objects, all that people point out to each other in interaction. Language is used to *refer to* or *represent* a part of reality.

Words as Categories

Words are really categories, used to *refer* to a class of objects that are distinguishable to the human being. To say that words refer to something else is to say that they *represent,* "they take the place of" their referent. And to say they refer to a "class of objects" means that they rarely refer to a single object. Roger Brown uses the example of the word "larger," a symbol that stands for a difference in size. Not only can it describe the difference between two specific objects (a single cat and a single rat), but it can be applied to all cats and rats, and indeed to all objects. The word can be applied to a host of things once its meaning is grasped by the per-

*From *A Sociology of Language* by Joyce O. Hertzler. Copyright © 1965 by Random House, Inc. Reprinted by permission of the publisher.

son. If words did not refer to some general category, humans would need a huge increase in the number of their words, and the real value would be lost. Each concrete object would need a name, and its similarity to and differences from other concrete objects would be lost to us. That specific object named Charles Mole is a "man," a "teacher," an "American," a "father," a "moral person." Each of these words is a category that tells us what Charlie has in common with other objects and what some of his differences are. Without words Charles Mole would be Charles Mole to us and nothing more (and he would be a physical object, not "Charles Mole"). Our ability to categorize and transfer past experiences to new situations depends on this generalizing capacity—this contrasts with the nonsymbolic world of most other organisms, where they must learn specific responses to specific stimuli in order to "know" what to do.

SUMMARY

It is now easier to understand what *perspectives* are. Perspectives are a *set of symbols.* We approach reality with the symbol; we see according to our *symbolic framework.* Recall that perspectives (i.e., symbols) arise in interaction with others and in our social worlds (or reference groups). Our symbols are therefore our guides to what we see, what we notice, how we interpret—as well as what we miss—in any situation.

Figure 4-1 illustrates the point that human interaction gives rise to such things as social objects, symbols, language, and perspectives, which, in turn, lead to an interpretation of a situation and, ultimately, action in it.

We are really saying more, however. Interaction is a dynamic process: As it progresses over time our definitions may also change, and our interpretation and action will be affected. Social objects, symbols, language, and perspectives are also dynamic and not static "things"; they arise in and are transformed through interaction.

FIGURE 4-1

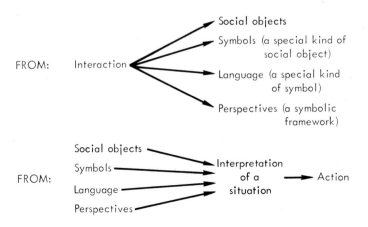

HUMANS AND "INFRAHUMANS"

Infrahumans (the term Mead uses to label presymbolic infants and nonhuman animals) are not symbolic, do not define social objects in interaction, do not use symbols or language as we defined it above, and do not use perspectives to define the reality they respond to. Infrahumans—at least the vast majority of them—seem to have a passive relationship with their environment. Behavior is usually instinctive (biologically programmed) or learned through imitation and experience. There is communication among many infrahumans, but it is what might be called a conversation of *nonmeaningful* gestures, where the act of one organism becomes a cue for the response of the other. "There the beginning of the act of one is a stimulus to the other to respond in a certain way, while the beginning of this response becomes again a stimulus to the first to adjust his action to the oncoming response" (Mead, 1934:144-45). Meltzer borrows a good illustration from Mead:

> Two hostile dogs, in the pre-fight stage, may go through an elaborate conversation of gestures (snarling, growling, baring fangs, walking stiff-leggedly around one another, etc.). The dogs are adjusting themselves to one another by responding to one another's gestures. (A gesture is that portion of an act which represents the entire act; it is the initial, overt phase of the act, which epitomizes it, e.g., shaking one's fist at someone.) Now, in the case of the dogs the response to a gesture is dictated by pre-established tendencies to respond in certain ways. Each gesture leads to a direct, immediate, automatic, and unreflecting response by the recipient of the gesture (the other dog). Neither dog responds to the *intention* of the gestures. Further, each dog does not make his gestures with the intent of eliciting certain responses in the other dog. Thus, animal interaction is devoid of conscious, deliberate meaning. (1972:12-13)

Infrahumans may have highly complex instinctive behavior, their learning through imitation may be extensive, and their communication may be important, but so far as we know, symbols, social objects, perspectives, and language (as we have defined these things) are not part of their worlds.

It is true that humans have taught chimpanzees symbols—even written words (languages)—and most recently, even how to combine the words. As far as we know, however, although chimps may have *potential* for language, they do not produce it through interaction with each other in nature in the sense that humans do. The evidence is far from complete, and we may indeed find other animals who use symbols as we have here described, but thus far that does not seem likely.

The evidence supporting the use of symbols by dolphins and whales seems most convincing (and exciting). The dolphin's intelligence, memory, problem-solving ability, interaction, sounds, and complex social behavior all seem to support the fact that dolphins, and whales as well, may be symbol users. Robert Stenuit makes the following case for dolphin language, and it is a very attractive one. (Although this quotation is long and not absolutely necessary for understanding, it is fascinating and I encourage you to read it.)

In 1962 Dr. John Dreher, a Californian acoustics expert turned cetologist, was conducting research on the Pacific gray whale on board the research ship *Sea Quest*. Across a channel south of San Diego he submerged a complex experimental device consisting of a series of aluminum poles, cables, hydroplanes, and so on. Suddenly, five hundred yards away from the barrier, he noticed a group of five dolphins who were heading straight towards it. As soon as the underwater microphones were connected, they relayed to the loudspeaker the grinding of the dolphins' sonars. The signals were evenly spaced, evidently just routine emissions. At a distance of four hundred yards the dolphins stopped and appeared to gather together, all emissions ceasing. Then one dolphin broke away from the group and, as a scout might do, came along to inspect the obstacles by sonar, closely, methodically, from left to right. He returned to the waiting group and the microphones transmitted what seemed to be a general discussion. The reconnaissance of the "scout" and the "group discussions" were repeated three times. Then the majority, or perhaps the leader, apparently decided that the strange poles were harmless, for the group resumed its course and quietly passed through.

Puzzled by this story, Dr. Jarvis Bastian, a psychologist at the University of California, recently decided to conduct a similar experiment in the laboratory. The best approach, he thought, would be to place two dolphins in a predicament where they would be forced to employ a system of vocal communication, that is, talk to each other, in order to extricate themselves. If they managed to find a way out, then the demonstration would be complete.

Using a male and a female dolphin, Buzz and Doris, he set about to make clear to them, step by step, exactly what he wanted from them.

First he showed each of them two underwater levers to push. The levers controlled two mechanisms for distributing mackerel; to obtain the reward they had to push the lever on the right when a continuous light came on, and the lever on the left when the light was flickering. Up to this point, it was child's play.

For the second stage he introduced a new rule. When the light, either continuous or intermittent, came on, Doris, on her side of the pool, was to wait until Buzz had pushed the correct lever on his side. If she was the first to push, no fish. Still no problems. After a few attempts, it was child's play again.

But for the third stage of the experiment Dr. Bastian separated the two dolphins by a curtain so arranged that they could still hear each other quite well, but could no longer see either each other or the other's light.

What would happen when Bastian gave Doris a signal which was invisible to Buzz, and which she could not answer herself before Buzz had released his own lever? And how would Buzz know which was the correct one?

Bastian switched on the continuous light opposite Doris. Doris waited as instructed, but she was heard to give a sound signal. Buzz immediately pushed the right-hand lever, the correct one, then Doris too pushed her lever and she received her fresh fish.

Bastian repeated the experiment fifty times, and on the basis of Doris's information, Buzz reacted correctly forty-eight times.

Scientific literature today is filled with similar examples and so are the stories of fishermen, sailors and whalers. The evidence is so abundant that it is becoming impossible to deny that dolphins and other toothed cetaceans possess a complex language and also a complex social organization.

During a recent expedition in the Antarctic, a Norwegian whaling fleet received a radio call for help from a deep-sea fishing fleet. A band of several thousand killer whales had arrived in the fishing area and was so thoroughly decimating the fish that the fishermen no longer saw a scale. Killer whales (Orcinus orca) are very large—twenty feet and longer—and very voracious cousins of the dolphin.

The whalers sent out three boats, each equipped with a harpoon gun. One of them fired a single shot, and the harpoon with its explosive head wounded or killed a whale. Within half an hour all cetaceans had completely disappeared from the surface of the sea around the gun boats, but they remained just as active and voracious around the fishing-boats. Now the fishing-boats and gun boats were identical, both types being converted World War II corvettes. They had the same silhouette above the water, the same hull, the same engine, and therefore, made the same noise; the only difference was a small harpoon gun on the bow.

Obviously the wounded whale, or other whales who had witnessed the incident, had immediately spread the alert, described the danger and even specified the dangerous zones.

The fishermen, the whalers and later the cetologists of Oslo's Whaling Institute concluded from this that killer whales possess sufficient intelligence to establish immediately the relation of cause to effect between the harpoon gun and the wound suffered by one of them; they have a sufficiently clear and discriminating eyesight, a sufficient power of observation and sufficient capacity to distinguish, among almost identical ships, those which were made dangerous by a small additional contraption on the bow from those which were harmless; that they possess the means of communicating not only precise information and descriptions, but also recommendations; that these are transmitted to all and received by all and that the spreading of their danger warnings is rapid, pervasive and 100 per cent efficient.

One could also, it would seem to me, conclude from this story that the cetaceans who first spread the alert showed a marked spirit of organization and altruism and that their solidarity, at least from this point of view, is on a level with that of the human tribe. But above all, and this is most exciting, the messages transmitted here do not emanate at all from the old stock of instinctive answers built up and shared from time immemorial. No, they deal with an unexpected peril coming from a modern object totally alien to their known environment. One may deduce also that the "culture" or at least the stock of information used by certain cetaceans, far from stagnating or progressing with the slowness shown by other mammals (who, since the invention of firearms have not learnt to distrust them), builds up rapidly, perhaps daily, through contact with new situations. We can deduce from all this that certain Odontoceti display an almost human ability to adapt and improvise. (1972: 55–58)

Evidence is still being sought to determine if symbol use exists in nonhuman animals. The symbolic interactionist, by and large, sees the human as unique in nature, and unique precisely because of symbol use. If, however, it is established that other animals use symbols too, then this fact will in no way detract from the perspective; indeed, our understanding of both the human and other symbol-using animals will be greatly increased. However, if other animals do indeed use symbols in the sense defined here, it must be established that (1) the symbols are *developed socially,* through interaction, (2) the symbols are not universally agreed on within the species but are arbitrarily established by and changed through interaction of users, and (3) a language of sounds or gestures exists that is meaningful and that includes rules allowing for combining the sounds or gestures into meaningful statements. To be symbolic means that the organism not only rotely learns responses to cues (as a dog may do from its master), but that the organism *actively creates and manipulates symbols* in interaction with others. Leslie White summarizes the critical differences between humans and other animals in this concise statement:

> The man differs from the dog—and all other creatures—in that *he can and does play an active role in determining what value the vocal stimulus is to have, and the dog cannot.* As John Locke has aptly put it, "All sounds (i.e., in language) ... have their signification from the arbitrary imposition of men." The dog does not and cannot play an active part in determining the value of the vocal stimulus. Whether he is to roll over or go fetch at a given stimulus, or whether the stimulus for roll over be one combination of sounds or another is a matter in which the dog has nothing whatever to "say." He plays a purely passive role and can do nothing else. He learns the meaning of a vocal command just as his salivary glands may learn to respond to the sound of a bell. But man plays an active role and thus becomes a creator: Let x equal three pounds of coal and it does equal three pounds of coal; let removal of the hat in a house of worship indicate respect and it becomes so. This creative faculty, that of freely, actively, and arbitrarily bestowing value upon things, is one of the most commonplace as well as *the* most important characteristic of man. Children employ it freely in their play: "Let's pretend that this rock is a wolf."
>
> The difference between the behavior of man and other animals then, is that the lower animals may receive new values, may acquire new meanings, but they cannot create and bestow them. Only man can do this. (1940: 456-57)

One of the best ways to understand the nature of the symbol is to contrast it with the nonsymbolic approach to environment that characterizes other animals. Such a contrast is one of the themes in a book by Ernest Becker (1962:15-22). He makes the point that a symbolic approach to one's environment is a *qualitatively* different one from other nonsymbolic approaches. The human is unique in nature, or borrowing Warriner's term, humans are *emergent* in nature precisely because of the symbol.

How Animals Approach Environment

Ernest Becker describes four basic approaches to environment by animals. In the first type the organism responds directly to a stimulus. The stimulus controls the action; there is total passivity on the organism's part. The second type is the conditioned response, where the organism is trained to make an association. The organism can learn to respond to a stimulus since it has learned that the stimulus is *associated* with something else of importance. The third approach to environment is the ability of some animals to make relationships in the visual field and to act. The animal is not trained but seems to make the association by itself. Becker describes this approach:

The best example of it is the chimp who uses a stick to knock down a banana, suspended out of reach. He sees a relationship between two objects in his visual field, and swings the stick to bring down the banana. The crucial difference between this behavior and that of Pavlov's dog is that, for the chimp, the relationship between banana and stick is something he establishes himself. It results from an alertness to a problem situation. The equation is not built into the chimp by an experimenter, in step-by-step fashion. There is some masterful autonomy here that is absent in the simple conditioned reflex. It is not easy for an animal to relate itself to two or more things in the environment. A dog, for example, seeing food through a picket fence, will detour to a gate twenty feet down the fence to get to the food on the other side. He has seen a relationship between the open gate and getting the food. But a hen, seeing the same food and the gate as well, does not establish any relationship, and runs helplessly back and forth directly in front of the food, watching it through the pickets. (1962:17–18)

The final type is symbolic action: response "to an arbitrary designation for an object, a designation coined by him alone, that stands for the object." Becker explains:

The word "house," for example, has not intrinsic qualities within itself that would connect it with an object, since someone else may use "casa" or "maison" or "dom." Unlike Pavlov's dog, man *creates* the relationship between stimuli. . . . Symbolic behavior depends, of course, upon the ability to create identifiable word sounds that become object representations of infinite degrees of subtlety—from "minnow hook" to "minestrone." (1962:18–19)

Becker emphasizes that the differences in the four approaches are qualitative differences, not just a matter of degree. Each one seems to be critical in the kinds of responses possible. Symbol use provides the most flexible and *active* approach precisely because the organism has a mind to deal with the environment, whereas in the other approaches to environment, organisms are tied to simple reflex, to conditioning, or to seeing relationships in the immediate environment only.

Symbols versus Signs

Symbols are often described by distinguishing them from *signs*. Ernest Becker (1962) points out that the difference is that the organism does not give meaning to signs and does not reflect on them, but instead habitually responds to them. Signs *may* indeed be associated with something else—for example, the flap of a beaver's tail may act as a sign to other beavers of approaching danger—but not necessarily: The flap of the tail probably calls forth an immediate response from the beavers without their making any association. Signs are not arbitrary or conventional, nor do they arise in interaction, nor is there any meaning assigned through words. But signs are responded to because they are produced in one's physical presence and lead to an unthinking response. They must be *sensed,* and the receiver has no *choice* in response.

Humans do not often respond to signs. We are so highly symbolic that if we are trained to respond to a word or object without reflection, in another situation or with another group that same word or object will most likely take on a different meaning and be transformed into a symbol. To the new recruit the word "attention" may act as a sign. It is associated without reflection with an officer, with danger, with a certain act, and the response is probably made without reflection. The sign acts as a cue that leads to a response. Yet the sign "attention" is transformed when the officer leaves the room and the servicemen may play at "attention," making fun of the whole matter. We are so thoroughly symbolic that our most habitual behavior is transformed as we move from situation to situation, from group to group, from context to context. We act in our worlds according to interpretations of objects in a context, rather than through specific responses to specific stimuli, cues, or signs.

Even "signs" in nature become profoundly complex and symbolic and do not exist for us at all in any pure sense. Most other animals, it seems, respond only to signs, cues, and stimuli.

This symbolic nature that is ours is profoundly significant of what humans are capable of. It is basic to almost everything we are. Even if other animals do indeed use symbols as described here, few will be found to depend on them as humans do, and probably none will be found whose central qualities are traceable to symbol use. The contrast with the rest of the animal kingdom, be it comfortable for you or uncomfortable, should not be disregarded as unimportant. Kenneth Burke (1966:4-5) illustrates this contrast through the interesting example of a wren. He reports how the mother wren was able to get all the baby wrens out of the nest except for one. Nothing seemed to work:

> Then came the moment of genius. One of the parent wrens came to the nest with a morsel of food. But instead of simply giving it to the noisy youngster, the parent bird held it at a distance.

Slowly the baby was teased out of the nest. The parent pushed, and through obtaining the needed leverage on the baby, whose balance was shaky, was able to push it out. Pure genius, Burke announces. But, on the other hand, the wren is not now able to write a dissertation on "The Uses of Leverage," nor can this be shared throughout the wren kingdom so that others too can try it. Three important points to note, according to Burke, are:

1. The ability to describe this method in words would make it possible for all other birds to take over the same "act" of genius, though they themselves might never have hit upon it.
2. The likelihood is that even this one wren never used this method again. For the ability to conceptualize implies a kind of *attention* without which this innovation could probably not advance beyond the condition of a mere accident to the condition of an invention.
3. On the happier side, there is the thought that at least, through lack of such ability, birds are spared our many susceptibilities to the ways of demagogic

spellbinders. They cannot be filled with fantastic hatreds for alien populations they know about mainly by mere hearsay or with all sorts of unsettling new expectations, most of which could not possibly turn out as promised.

REFERENCES

BECKER, ERNEST
    1962 *The Birth and Death of Meaning.* New York: Free Press. Copyright ©
    1962 by The Free Press of Glencoe, a division of The Macmillan Company. By permission of The Macmillan Company.
BECKER, HOWARD S.
    1953 "Becoming a Marihuana User." *American Journal of Sociology* 59:235–42.
BLUMER, HERBERT
    1969 *Symbolic Interactionism: Perspective and Method.* Englewood Cliffs, N.J.: Prentice-Hall. Copyright © 1969. Reprinted by permission of Prentice-Hall, Inc.
BROWN, ROGER
    1965 *Social Psychology.* New York: Free Press.
BURKE, KENNETH
    1966 *Language as Symbolic Action.* Berkeley: University of California Press.
DUNCAN, HUGH DALZIEL
    1968 *Symbols in Society.* New York: Oxford University Press.
HERTZLER, JOYCE O.
    1965 *A Sociology of Language.* New York: Random House. Copyright © 1965 by Random House, Inc. Reprinted by permission of the publisher.
KELLER, HELEN
    1954 *The Story of My Life.* Garden City, N.Y.: Doubleday. Copyright © 1902, 1903, 1905 by Helen Keller. Reprinted by permission of Doubleday & Company, Inc.
MEAD, GEORGE HERBERT
    1934 *Mind, Self and Society.* Chicago: University of Chicago Press. Copyright © 1934 by The University of Chicago. All rights reserved. Reprinted by permission of The University of Chicago Press.
MELTZER, BERNARD N.
    1972 *The Social Psychology of George Herbert Mead.* Kalamazoo: Center for Sociological Research, Western Michigan University. By permission of Bernard N. Meltzer.
MILLER, DAVID L.
    1973 *George Herbert Mead: Self, Language and the World.* Chicago: University of Chicago Press.
SHIBUTANI, TAMOTSU
    1961 *Society and Personality: An Interactionist Approach to Social Psychology.* Englewood Cliffs, N.J.: Prentice-Hall. Copyright © 1961. Reprinted by permission of Prentice-Hall, Inc.
STENUIT, ROBERT
    1972 *The Dolphin: Cousin to Man.* New York: Bantam Books. By permission of Robert Stenuit.

STRYKER, SHELDON
1959 "Symbolic Interaction as an Approach to Family Research." *Marriage and Family Living* 21:111–19. Copyright © 1959 by the National Council on Family Relations, St. Paul, Minnesota. Reprinted by permission.

WARRINER, CHARLES K.
1970 *The Emergence of Society.* Homewood, Ill.: Dorsey Press. By permission of the Dorsey Press.

WHITE, LESLIE A.
1940 "The Symbol: The Origin and Basis of Human Behavior." *Philosophy of Science* 7:451–63. Copyright © The Williams & Wilkins Co., Baltimore.

ZBOROWSKI, MARK
1952 "Cultural Components in Responses to Pain." *Journal of Social Issues* 8:16–30.

5
THE IMPORTANCE
OF THE SYMBOL

Imagine a world without symbols, without language, or without social objects. Our actions would be fixed, we would *respond* to stimuli, not to meaning. We would not problem solve, reflect, imagine, recall the past at all, or teach others anything other than simple responses learned through imitation. We would not be able to depend on culture for our action but would have to rely instead on instinct and/or simple learning. Understanding would cease, worlds outside our immediate physical space would not exist for us, and so much that is abstract—goodness, love, God, freedom, life and death—would not be examined at all and would not exist as a reality for us. Certainly communication with each other would not contain anything like concepts but would be confined to simple "nonmeaningful" gestures.

It is difficult to imagine a world without symbols, since the human world is so overwhelmingly symbolic at its very core. Very few cases of non-symbol-using humans appear in history, and the few that do are incomplete studies making generalizations difficult. Symbol use by the human begins at a very early age, first through understanding others' symbols, then through intentional symbolic expression.

The symbolic interactionist emphasizes that all that humans are can be traced to their symbolic nature. Our world is a symbolic one: We see, we think, we hear, we share, we act symbolically. Symbols are critical for the human precisely because (1) they are *our reality,* (2) they *make our complex group life possible,* and (3) they *make the human being possible.* The purpose of this chapter will be to explore each of these points in detail in order to show more fully the implications that symbol use has for the human.

SYMBOLS AND SOCIAL REALITY

The human acts within a world of social objects. That is, we act not toward a world out there but rather toward a world defined by others through symbolic communication. We share with others a definition of the world and its objects. Objects are transformed from physical stimuli responded to automatically into objects socially constructed. Each time we interact with others we come to share a somewhat different view of what we are seeing. We see what is out there in a new light. As we interact we develop a perspective as to what is real and how we are to act toward that reality. This interaction that gives rise to our reality is *symbolic*—it is through symbolic interaction with each other that we give the world meaning and develop the reality toward which we act. "Meaning . . . arises out of the social interaction that one has with one's fellows" is the way Blumer (1969:2) expresses this simple principle.

Whenever there is interaction between persons, there is meaning shared, and this meaning is symbolic in nature and is the reality toward which we act. Humans do not respond to a physical reality but to a symbolic one. Here lies the first important function of symbols.

> Man operates within an *ideational framework*—that is, a body of ideas of interpretations and analyses, which he has developed, and by means of which his observations of the universe and all that it contains, as well as his reactions to it, become meaningful. He can be said to live in a world of ideas. But it is within and by means of the *linguistic framework* that the ideationally established world exists and operates. Language is the means and mode of man's whole mental existence. (Hertzler, 1965:42)*

Kenneth Burke (1966:5) writes that our reality in the world at this split moment is nothing other than what we have learned from a "clutter of symbols about the past combined with whatever things we know mainly through maps, magazines, newspapers, and the like about the present." Whatever we experience *now* is seen through the symbols we use to see, and our ability to tie the present to a bigger picture depends on symbols. Burke concludes:

> To meditate on this fact until one sees its full implications is much like peering over the edge of things into an ultimate abyss. And doubtless that's one reason why, though man is typically the symbol-using animal, he clings to a kind of naive verbal realism that refuses to realize the full extent of the role played by symbolicity in his notions of reality. (1966:5)

*From *A Sociology of Language* by Joyce O. Hertzler. Copyright © 1965 by Random House, Inc. Reprinted by permission of the publisher.

"A person learns a new language, and as we say, gets a new soul . . . He becomes in that sense a different individual." (Mead, 1934:283)

SYMBOLS AND HUMAN SOCIAL LIFE

Human social life depends on symbols. It is through symbols that individuals are socialized, coming to share the culture of the group and coming to understand their roles in relation to the others. We do not know much through instinct; we do not learn simply by imitation or experience. Each individual learns how to act through symbols and thus becomes part of society through symbols:

> This does not happen by instruction, at least not in the pre-school years; nobody teaches him the principles on which social groups are organized, or their systems of beliefs, nor would he understand it if they tried. It happens indirectly, through the accumulated experience of numerous small events, insignificant in themselves, in which his behaviour is guided and controlled, and in the course of which he contracts and develops personal relationships of all kinds. All this takes place through the medium of language. And it is not from the language of the classroom, still less that of courts of law, of moral tracts or of textbooks of sociology, that the child learns about the culture he was born into. The striking fact is that it is the most ordinary everyday uses of language, with parents, brothers and sisters, neighbourhood children, in the home, in the street and the park, in the shops and the trains and the buses, that serve to transmit, to the child, the essential qualities of society and the nature of social being. (Halliday, 1978:9)

Recall Shibutani's "Reference Groups as Perspectives": It is through symbolic communication that we come to share culture, and it is through this communication and resulting culture that social worlds (groups, societies) are able to continue. Culture, a very important part of every society, is learned through symbols, and it is itself symbolic.. We share ideas, rules, goals, values (all symbolic), and these allow us to continue to interact cooperatively with others. Figure 5-1 summarizes the importance of symbols to our ongoing social life:

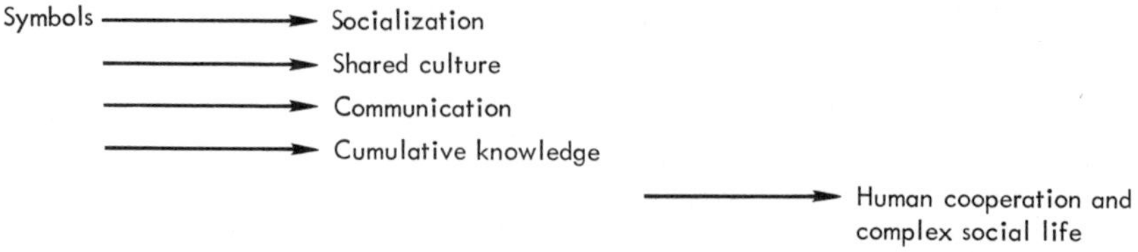

FIGURE 5-1

We seem to grasp almost intuitively the central importance of symbols for our group life. We set up rules (symbolic) to be taught (usually through written or spoken *words*) to newcomers entering an already established group. We assure that the ideas we have developed are somehow shared and that what takes place is fully understood (has the right meaning) to the newcomer. That is true for college-orientation week, where students learn new rules, abbreviations, course names, teacher names, buildings, and requirements for graduation. It is true of the poker club, which must, during breaks in the action, teach the rules, the meanings, the taboos, the appropriate language, the proper betting to the newcomer. Both the college and the poker club know that without some shared reality their very existence may be at stake. And if we look at the group situation from the standpoint of the newcomer, he or she wants to understand the *meanings* attached to all the various acts—to learn immediately the shared reality in order to operate within the group.

Indeed, as Ralph Ross emphasizes, the words *community* and *communication* show an immediate similarity:

> They emphasize commonness, togetherness. People gather or live *together* for certain purposes, and they *share* meanings and attitudes; the first presupposes the second, for without communication there is no community. Community depends on shared experience and emotion, the communication enters into and clarifies the sharing. Forms of communication like art and religion and language are themselves shared by a community, and each of them contains and conveys ideas, attitudes, perspectives, and evaluations which are deeply rooted in the history of the community. (1962:156-57)

But there is much more. Groups have histories, and often a long history means a very large corpus of knowledge. It is by means of symbols that the past is recorded—knowledge and wisdom are not lost but are cumulative. We can reflect and build on them—each interaction need not start from scratch. Joyce Hertzler (1965: 50-51) states that language is "the major vehicle whereby we transmit—that is, impart or send and receive—our factualized experience . . . to others across space and time . . . from one individual, one area, one generation, one era, one cultural group to another." Complex ongoing societies depend heavily on this function of symbols.

In summary, symbols are important to both social reality and social life. Social reality is created in *symbolic* interaction, and social life depends on symbols for socialization, mutual understanding, and cumulation of knowledge.

SYMBOLS AND THE INDIVIDUAL

Reality is symbolic. Society depends on the symbol for its continuation. More than this: The human being comes to act "human" only because he or she takes on symbols. We all may be born with certain prerequisites for acting like others in our species, but it is through the taking on of symbols that we come to act and look human.

It is essential for us to appreciate the central role that the symbol plays for the individual. The symbol, and especially language, transforms the human being from a weak, helpless, unintelligent, simple organism to one whose complexity, flexibility, and intelligence brings about a uniqueness in nature. To gain an understanding of what symbols mean for the individual we will briefly examine nine very basic functions of symbols and/or language.

Naming, Memorization, Categorizing

Through calling something a name we have identified it, "marked it out," "distinguished" it, and we are able to "store" it for later application. We can recognize similar objects and call them by that name. Naming an object allows us to apply it to another situation without its immediate physical presence. We can identify individual objects that we have never seen before because we have learned their names, 'that is, what they "are." The name can be stored in memory and purposely recalled in a multitude of situations. It might be possible that memory can exist without language (for example, other animals may be able to recall pictures), but language allows for a much more complex, efficient memory system, one that can be more easily activated, whose parts can be more easily interpreted, transferred, and isolated. As Hertzler puts it: "The words of language, functioning as categories of experienced reality, not only facilitate more precise analysis, but also aid in the comparison of one portion of experiential data with other portions." (1965:41)

Related to the naming function, of course, is categorizing. Language is the tool the individual uses to make order out of experience. Language is used to discriminate, to generalize, to make ever so subtle distinctions in one's environment. The world is literally divided up by means of the language we use.

> Language has to interpret the whole of our experience, reducing the indefinitely varied phenomena of the world around us, and also of the world inside us, the processes of our own consciousness, to a manageable number of classes of phenomena: types of processes, events and actions, classes of objects, people and institutions, and the like. (Halliday, 1978:21)

Perception

Language guides us through what our senses experience. It constitutes the individual's *perspectives,* and thus it serves the function of alerting the individual to some parts of the environment and not to others. "A language, once formed, has a self-contained organization somewhat like mathematics, and it previsages possible experience in accordance with accepted formal limitations. . . . perception is limited by each language; men put what they perceive into preexisting linguistic categories." (Shibutani, 1961:122)

Thinking

Hertzler calls language "our means of thinking." Thinking can be conceptualized as symbolic interaction with one's self. Thinking is talking to oneself; it is an activity, a constant, ongoing process. Almost every moment, the individual is thinking in this sense—according to Blumer, constantly modifying reality through an "interpretive process." When we act alone we are usually engaged in self-communication; when we are with others we engage in symbolic interaction—we communicate with, we give off meaning to, others, but because symbols by their nature are understood by their user, there must be a simultaneous communication with ourselves in all social encounters. To get others to understand us, we must understand ourselves, which demands that we symbolically interact with ourselves as we communicate with others. We are thus constantly engaged in active thinking, often without realizing that we are doing it. Thinking is so central to all we do that it, like language itself, is taken for granted unless pointed out to us.

Deliberation and Problem Solving

Deliberation is a type of thinking, but it is more "deliberate" and conscious self-communication than the constant, ongoing thinking just described. It occurs most often when a problem is presented, when the situation requires analysis before action. It involves an attempt to consciously manipulate one's situation. The individual views self as an object in the situation, holds back action, analyzes, engages in lengthy discussion with self as action unfolds. In a sense, there is no difference between deliberation and the thinking described in the preceding paragraph, for the difference is really a matter of the degree of consciousness and the degree that one holds back overt action until the situation is fully understood. In fact, it is useful to understand almost all human behavior—but especially social behavior—as involving more or less conscious deliberation. Life can be thought of as a multitude of problems confronting the individual, each one calling for handling and solving, and each one demanding at least some deliberation. Each time we interact with someone else, "problems" are presented to us: how to understand the other, how to make ourselves understood, how to influence the other, how to avoid or get to know the other, how to work together or successfully dominate or successfully resist domination. Every time we enter a situation, working through that situation is a problem that demands decisions on our part. Deliberation means we analyze situations (sometimes very rapidly), interpret the ongoing action (our own and others'), consider alternative plans of action, rehearse our acts before we commit ourselves to overt action, and recall past situations that may be applicable. Problem solving in any situation is an evolving process, so that what we do at any one point can be analyzed at a later point, possibly leading to a new strategy or a new line of action. Deliberation as described here, as well as the ongoing thinking described above, is an integral part of human action and depends fully on the manipulation of *symbols*.

Transcendence of Space and Time

Problem solving and reflection involves transcending the immediate. Hertzler (1965:53-54) states that language

> enables men to overcome the limited time-and-space perceptions of the subhuman creatures. It is, in fact, man's means of mentally breaking through the space-time barrier. . . . he is also able to inhabit simultaneously the past

(through legend, traditions, and formal records), the present and the future (by means of declared ideals, projections, anticipations, plans and programs).

Language allows individuals to understand worlds they have never seen; it allows them to see the future before it occurs and to integrate past, present, and future. For example: I "know" ancient Greece without having been there, and I have a strong notion of what America will become in twenty years. I also believe that America's unjust treatment of minorities *today* is a result of a painful *history* of racism, and I also see today's policies as having some impact on a more just society *tomorrow.* The individual is guided in social situations by recalling the past, and by looking to the future, immediate and distant. When an individual acts, others outside the immediate situation may be the most important influences, the struggles of societies the individual has never had any contact with may be his or her most important inspiration, and what is going on "in the next room" outside the immediate field of vision and hearing may be perceived to be most influential on the individual's future. Language allows the individual to break out of the present and immediate stimulus environment and adds immeasurably to the factors that influence action.

Transcendence of One's Own Person

Not only do symbols allow individuals to leave the immediate space-and-time environment but also they allow them to leave their own "bodies," to get outside of their selves and imagine the world from the perspectives of others. This very important human quality, which symbolic interactionists refer to as "taking the role of the other," allows us to understand others, to manipulate them, to sympathize with them, to love them. It allows for human beings' understanding of each other's ideas, since the more we are able to see things from the perspective of the people with whom we communicate, the more we are able to truly "see" what other people are saying. It is through language that we come to understand other people, their perspectives, their perceptions, their feelings, and their behavior. This ability to take the role of the other, itself dependent on our symbolic nature, is so central to human social life that its nature and its importance will be the subject of Chapter 8.

Abstract Reality

Language also allows the human being to imagine and perceive a reality beyond the concrete. Only through language can we establish objects like God, love, freedom, truth, good and evil, afterlife, and a host of other abstract objects that are so much an integral part of our existence. A reality beyond physical reality is open only through words and the manipulation of words into ideas. The concrete world of our senses is transformed by language into a reality not possible to non-symbol users. Hertzler puts it nicely:

> By means of conceptualization, [the human] is able to develop and live in the abstract world of intellectual experience—the world of ethical, aesthetic,

evaluational, teleological, spiritual, and supernatural considerations. . . . "goodness" as an ethical aspect, or "beauty" as an aesthetic characteristic, are not inherent in the event or the object; they are nonexistent, except in so far as we "perceive" and "conceive" them in terms of words. With language, we can wrestle with such perplexing questions as "truth" and "error," "right" and "wrong," "existential" and "transcendental." Words can stand for such abstractions as electricity, force, justice, time, space, future, deity—ideas which cannot possibly be represented by any visual picture. (1965:55)

Because human beings are symbol users and are able to create an abstract world, human beings can thus imagine goals, ideals, values, and morals that themselves become important motivating factors in human behavior. To die for "my country," to work for "freedom," to try to end "poverty" show a kind of motivation impossible to any except symbol users. This means that the human potential is limited only by human imagination. As long as we believe, for example, that "love" and "goodness" and "equality" are worth working for, we can constantly try to guide our behavior toward those ends. And if we believe that "materialism" or "destruction of others" or "power over others" is important, it becomes a guide to behavior. But symbols by their very nature open up a wide range of behavior possibilities. In a sense, no action is "unnatural" to us, since symbols allow for virtually any possibility.

Creativity

The symbolic interactionist emphasizes the central importance of language in creating the active rather than passive person. It is through thinking with symbols that each individual is able to create his or her own world beyond the physical, develop highly individual interpretations of reality, and respond uniquely to that reality. Language arises from society, yet it is the tool that the human can use to think about and challenge that society. The key is not so much the symbol as it is *symboling,* the *manipulation of symbols* by active persons, defining and redefining their social situations. Give the child an understanding of certain *words,* and it is impossible to control fully how these words will be combined and recombined. This is the magic of language. To teach "love your country," and to teach "hate other countries" is to create the possibility in students of deciding to hate their country and love other countries. To teach a child what "little" means, what "big" means, what "in a little while" means is to invite from him: "No, I'll go to bed in a *big while.*" Every sentence is, in a sense, a creative act. To manipulate the words we learn from interaction (society) is to be individual, active, and shaping, not passive and conforming.

Self-direction

Language allows the human being to exercise self-direction. Our communication with ourselves is a form of giving orders: Cooperate! Rebel! Listen! Get away! Run! Walk! Turn right! Work harder! Sleep! Think! Any control that we have over ourselves (and the symbolic interactionists claim it is considerable) comes through symbolic interaction with ourselves, through telling ourselves what is going on, what alternatives there are, and what line of action to take. The decision to conform and cooperate as well as the decision to rebel are both a matter of the individual's deciding through symbolic interaction with self what to do.

The importance of the symbol for the individual can best be summarized by combining all of these contributions to the individual into a single central point: The human being, because of the symbol, does not respond passively to a reality that imposes itself but actively creates and recreates the world acted in. Humans name, remember, categorize, perceive, think, deliberate, problem solve, transcend space and time, transcend themselves, create abstractions, create new ideas, and direct themselves—all through the symbol.

Ernst Cassirer describes the human as discovering

> a new method of adapting himself to his environment. Between the receptor system and the effector system, which are to be found in all animal species, we find in man a third link which we may describe as the *symbolic system*. This new acquisition transforms the whole of human life. As compared with the other animals man lives not merely in a broader reality; he lives, so to speak, in a new *dimension* of reality. There is an unmistakable difference between organic reactions and human responses. In the first case a direct and immediate answer is given to an outward stimulus; in the second case the answer is delayed. It is interrupted and retarded by a slow and complicated process of thought. (1944:24–25)

SUMMARY

There is probably no better summary of the central importance that symbolic interactionists give to symbols than that of S. Morris Eames (1977:40–41):

> Pragmatic naturalists conceive of humans as a part of nature. Although they share many organic processes with other animals in their life in nature, humans emerge above the animals in certain forms and functions. For instance, humans can construct symbols and languages, they can speak and write, and by these means they can preserve their past experiences, construct new meanings, and entertain goals and ideals. Humans can make plans and by proper selection of the means to the ends carry them through. They can write poetry and novels, compose music and painting, and otherwise engage in aesthetic experiences. They can construct explanatory hypotheses about the world and all that is in it, of electrons, protons, and neutrons, and solar systems far away. They can dream dreams, concoct fantasies, erect heavens above the earth which entice their activities to far-off destinies, and they can imagine hells which stimulate fears of everlasting torture. The emergent functions of symbolic behavior make it possible for humans to transcend parts of their immediate undergoing and experiencing and to know that death and all that it entails is a part of organic life.

Figure 5–2 summarizes this chapter and integrates it with the previous chapter.

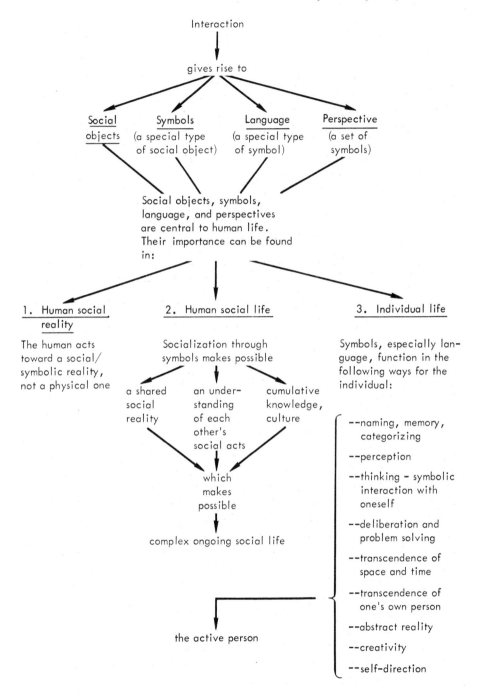

FIGURE 5-2

REFERENCES

BLUMER, HERBERT
    1969 *Symbolic Interactionism: Perspective and Method.* Englewood, Cliffs, N.J.: Prentice-Hall, Inc. Copyright © 1969. Reprinted by permission of Prentice-Hall, Inc.
BURKE, KENNETH
    1966 *Language as Symbolic Action.* Berkeley: University of California Press.
CASSIRER, ERNST
    1944 *An Essay on Man.* New Haven: Yale University Press.
EAMES, S. MORRIS
    1977 *Pragmatic Naturalism.* Carbondale, Ill.: Southern University Press.
HALLIDAY, M. A. K.
    1978 *Language as Social Semiotic.* Baltimore: University Park Press.
HERTZLER, JOYCE O.
    1965 *A Sociology of Language.* New York: Random House. Copyright © 1965 by Random House, Inc. Reprinted by permission of the publisher.
MEAD, GEORGE HERBERT
    1934 *Mind, Self and Society.* Chicago: University of Chicago Press. Reprinted by permission of The University of Chicago Press. Copyright © 1934 by The University of Chicago. All rights reserved.
ROSS, RALPH
    1962 *Symbols and Civilization.* New York: Harcourt Brace Jovanovich.
SHIBUTANI, TAMOTSU
    1961 *Society and Personality: An Interactionist Approach to Social Psychology.* Englewood Cliffs, N.J.: Prentice-Hall. Copyright © 1961. Reprinted by permission of Prentice-Hall, Inc.

6
THE NATURE
OF THE SELF

Thus far, our emphasis has been human beings coming to understand their world through interaction. We indicate objects to each other, we share meanings, we create symbols as we interact with each other. Bernard Meltzer (1972:11) points out that everything ultimately comes back to society, to interaction. In fact, Meltzer feels that Mead's book *Mind, Self and Society* (1934) should really be entitled *Society, Self and Mind* since individuals are always born into a society, and that is what gives them such human characteristics as self and mind. Of course, this was also the point in Chapter 5: Our symbols, which are so central to what we are, arise from inter-action. The human is so thoroughly social that society provides our most basic ele-ments: symbols, self, and mind.

SELF AS A SOCIAL OBJECT

There are many views of self in philosophy and social science, and few are either clear or consistent. The term "self" is used in so many different ways in our every-day speech that it is often hard to pin down what we mean by it.

In the symbolic interactionist perspective, "self" has a very specific meaning, not perfect but very usable. As Rosenberg (1979:6-8) points out, this meaning is different from so many other meanings that are popular today. For example, it does not have the same meaning as Freud's "ego." It does not mean the "real" person, nor the "productive person," nor "the total person."

For the symbolic interactionist, the self is an *object* that the actor acts toward. Many—including Mead—attempt to treat the self as both object and subject, but this becomes almost a hopeless swamp, especially at an introductory level. The self should simply be understood as a *social object which the actor acts toward*. The self does *not* act as a subject; symbolic interactionists normally say that the *actor* or *person* acts; sometimes toward the environment out there, sometimes toward his or her internal environment, the "self." It is more complicated than this; but this is a good beginning for understanding.

When we say that the self is a social object, we are saying (first) of all that an individual comes to *see* self in interaction with others. One's self, like all else, is pointed out and defined socially. The individual comes to see self as a separate object because in interaction with others he or she is pointed out and defined. "You are Andrew," "You are a nice person," "You are a boy," "You are Mom's favorite person." You are, in essence, Andrew, an object, a thing like the chair, the telephone, the mouse, and the doorknob. And, like all these things, it takes others in interaction to point out to Andrew that he is a separate object and to give him some kind of understanding of himself. The individual becomes an object to himself or herself because of others. "In the beginning he is quite unable to make a distinction between himself and the rest of the world" (McCall and Simmons, 1966:207). Not only does society make possible our symbols and our ability to think but it makes possible the self.

George Herbert Mead emphasizes the social nature of the self in *Mind, Self and Society*. He asks:

> How can an individual get outside of himself experientially in such a way as to become an object to himself? . . . [It is through] the process of social conduct or activity in which the given person or individual is implicated. . . . The individual experiences himself as such, not directly, but only indirectly, from the particular standpoints of other individual members of the same social group. . . . [he] becomes an object to himself just as other individuals are objects to him or in his experience. . . . it is impossible to conceive of a self arising outside of social experience. (1934:138–40)

The self, then, is an object, social in origin, and an object that undergoes change like all other objects: in interaction.

Not only does the self arise in interaction with others, but, like all social objects, it is defined and redefined in interaction. The self is really a process like all other social objects, constantly changing as the individual interacts with others. How I view myself, how I define myself, the judgment I have of myself are all highly dependent on the social definitions I encounter throughout my life. Peter Berger (1963:106) refers to this view of the self as radical in the sense that the self "is no longer a solid, given entity that moves from one situation to another. It is rather a process, continuously created and recreated in each social situation that one enters. . . . man is not *also* a social being, but he is social in every respect of his being that is open to empirical investigation."

The self as a social object arises in childhood through interaction with parents and other individuals, and it constantly undergoes change as the individual interacts with others in various situations. A true transcendental self, the "true, authentic person" is not assumed here. "Hey, Charlie, who are you really?" does not make sense in this context. Charlie's "true self" is what he defines as his true self at that point in interaction. What we see ourselves as results from our interaction with other people—indeed, the fact that we see ourselves as objects at all is a result of our interaction. That is the meaning of the statement, the self is social. Stryker sums up nicely:

> the human organism as an object takes on meaning through the behavior of those who respond to that organism. We come to know what we are through others' responses to us. Others supply us with a name, and they provide the meaning attached to that symbol. They categorize us in particular ways—as an infant, as a boy, et cetera. On the basis of such categorization, they expect particular behaviors from us; on the basis of these expectations, they act toward us. The manner in which they act toward us defines our "self," we come to categorize ourselves as they categorize us, and we act in ways appropriate to their expectations. . . . as the child moves into the social world he comes into contact with a variety of persons in a variety of self-relevant situations. He comes, or may come, into contact with differing expectations concerning his behavior and differing identities on which these expectations are based. Thus he has . . . a variety of perspectives from which to view and evaluate his own behavior, and he can act with reference to self as well as with reference to others. In short, the socialization process as described makes possible the appearance of objectivity. (1959:116)

Stryker here ends up his description of the self with the word "objectivity." Socialization makes possible the fact that the individual is able to get outside of himself or herself and look back at the self objectively, as an object like all the objects defined in interaction. Mead makes a very big point of this ability to get outside of one's self, to take the perspective of the other, and as we shall see in the description of the development of the self in children, it is through "taking the role of the other" that the self emerges.

STAGES OF "SELF" DEVELOPMENT

The central meaning of the social nature of the self can be appreciated with a brief review of four stages in "self" development that each individual goes through, all related to interaction with others. The first three stages are drawn from the work of George Herbert Mead, and the last is suggested by Shibutani.

The Preparatory Stage

The earliest stage of the self is referred to as the *preparatory stage*, with an almost primitive self emerging, a presymbolic stage of self. Mead probably did not explicitly name this stage, but he implied it in various writings (Meltzer, 1972:15). The child acts as the adult does. The child imitates the others' acts toward other objects and toward himself or herself as object. The parent may push the chair and so may the child. The parent may point to the child as object, the child may also point to self. The parent may say "Dad" and the child may imitate "da." But the interaction, so long as it is only imitation, lacks meaning, lacks a symbolic understanding. The person as object can really emerge only when objects take on some meaning, that is, when objects are defined with words. When Andrew realizes that he is Andrew, separate and distinct from others, someone represented with a name and described with word qualities, then a symbolic self emerges. That is why Mead refers to this first stage as preparatory; it is purely imitation, and social objects, including the self, are not yet defined with words that have meaning.

The Play Stage

The second stage, referred to by Mead as the *play stage*, comes early in the individual's development, during the acquisition of language. For most children language comes very early and meaning arises early, really making the preparatory stage insignificant in terms of length of time. The child, learning language, is now able to label and define objects with words that have shared meaning, so objects originally acted toward because of imitation now are acted toward according to the meaning shared in interaction with others. The self is pointed out and labeled by the significant others. "Hi, Andrew!" (Hey, Andrew stands for this object: *me, myself*) "Good boy!" (Hey, *me* is good.) "Are you sleeping?" (Am *I* sleeping?) "Go play!" (She is telling *me* to play.) As others point us out to ourselves, we see ourselves. We become social objects to ourselves. Others point us out, they give us names. The "creation of self as social object is an identification of that object. . . . Identification involves naming. Once an object is named and identified a line of action can be taken toward it" (Denzin, 1972:306). Our names, as well as various pronouns and adjectives, are used to identify "me" in relation to others. Susan, girl, baby, good, you, she, pretty, slow, funny, bad, wise, Christian, honest: That's *me*!

During this play stage, the child assumes the perspective of certain *individuals*, whom Mead refers to as "significant others," those individuals who take on importance to the individual, those whom the individual desires to impress; they might be those he respects, those he wants acceptance from, those he fears, or those with whom he identifies. Significant others are usually role models, who "provide the patterns of behavior and conduct on which he patterns himself. It is through interaction with these role models that the child develops the ability to regulate his own behavior" (Elkins and Handel, 1972:50). For the child, role models are most likely parents but can also be other relatives, TV heroes, or friends. As the child grows older, the significant other possibilities increase greatly and can be a whole number of individuals, including Socrates, Jesus, mom, wife, son, the Six Million Dollar Man, the boss, the president of the United States, and Elvis Presley. Whoever our significant others are at any point in our lives, they are important precisely because their views of social objects are important to us, including, and especially, our view of our selves as social objects. The concept of significant others recognizes that "not all the persons with whom one interacts have identical or even compatible perspectives, and that, therefore, in order for action to proceed, the individual must give greater weight or priority to the perspective of certain others. . . . others occupy high rank on an 'importance' continuum for a given individual" (Stryker, 1959: 115). To the small child significant others are responsible for the emergence of the self; the child comes to view self as an object because of significant others. In a sense, I fail to see myself without my awareness that these significant others see me.

The reason Mead calls this second stage the *play* stage is that the child assumes the perspective of only one significant other at a time. In this stage individuals are incapable of seeing themselves from the perspective of many persons simultaneously. The child segregates the significant others, and the view of self is a segmented one. The self is a multitude of social objects, each one defined in interaction with a single other. Play refers to the fact that *group* rules are unnecessary, that the child and a single other are necessary for controls at any single point in time. The child needs to guide self, needs to see self, needs to judge self from the view of only one individual at a time in order to be successful at play. Play is an individual affair, subject to the rules of single individuals. Mead's play stage is a time when the child takes the roles of significant others—father, Superman, mother, teacher—and acts in the world as if he or she were these individuals. In taking the role of these others the child acts toward objects in the world as they act, and that includes acting toward self as they do. This stage is the real beginning of the self as social object.

The Game Stage

The third stage is the *game stage*. The "game" represents organization and the necessity of assuming the perspectives of several others simultaneously. Cooperation and group life demand knowing one's position in relation to a complex set of others, not just single others. They demand taking on a group culture or perspective. This stage is, to Mead, the adult self, a self that incorporates all one's significant others into one "generalized other." The self becomes more a unitary nonsegmented self, changing in interaction but not radically changing each time another significant other is encountered. The child puts together the significant others in his or her world into a whole, a "generalized other," "them," "society." The self matures as our understanding of *society* matures: It is the other side of the coin. Interaction with others brings us face to face with *their* rules, *their* perspectives, and it also brings us *their* perspective of self, and the self becomes an object defined not only by the individual (play stage) but also by *them* (game stage).

The play antedates the game. For in a game there is a regulated procedure, and rules. The child must not only take the role of the other, as he does in the play, but he must assume the various roles of all the participants in the game, and govern his action accordingly. If he plays first base, it is as the one to whom the ball will be thrown from the field or from the catcher. Their organized reactions to him he has embedded in his own playing of the different positions, and this organized reaction becomes what I have called the "generalized other" that accompanies and controls his conduct. And it is this generalized other in his experience which provides him with a self. (Mead, 1925:269)

The development of a generalized other by the individual is really the internalization of society as the individual has come to know it, society's rules and perspectives become the child's, and society's definition of self becomes the individual's. "In one sense socialization can be summed up by saying that what was once outside the individual comes to be inside him" (Elkins and Handel, 1972:53). Meltzer emphasizes the central significance of internalizing a generalized other:

Having achieved this generalized standpoint, the individual can conduct himself in an organized, consistent manner. He can view himself from a consistent standpoint. This means, then, that the individual can transcend the local and present expectations and definitions with which he comes in contact. An illustration of this point would be the Englishman who "dresses for dinner" in the wilds of Africa. Thus, through having a generalized other, the individual becomes emancipated from the pressures of the peculiarities of the immediate situation. He can act with a certain amount of consistency in a variety of situations because he acts in accordance with a generalized set of expectations and definitions that he has internalized. (1972:16-17)

The Reference Group Stage

Mead does not always make it clear if the individual has just one generalized other or several. It seems that what begins as one increasingly becomes several. Shibutani (1955) makes this explicit, emphasizing what amounts to a fourth stage of self, the *reference group stage,* a stage that seems especially characteristic in an industrial urban "mass society."

The individual interacts with many different groups and thus comes to have several reference groups (social worlds or societies), and he or she shares a perspective, including a perspective on the *self,* with each of them. If he or she is to continue to interact successfully with a reference group, then that perspective must, at least temporarily, become the individual's generalized other, used to see and direct the self in that group. The distinction between a perspective and a generalized other that an individual borrows from a group to see and guide the self is blurred.

This notion is highly consistent with the definition of social objects discussed in Chapter 4: Social objects are defined in interaction and change in the process of interaction and as the people with whom we interact change. The self as a social object has these identical qualities. In interaction with students I define my self one way, with my family another, with sociologists another, and with male friends another. Think of your life: Your self changes as you interact with friends, family, salespeople, strangers at a party. In each case, our view of self is somewhat different, and it is always undergoing change. William James points this out nicely:

> Properly speaking, *a man has as many social selves as there are individuals who* *recognize* him and carry an image of him in their mind. To wound any one of these images is to wound him. But as the individuals who carry the images fall naturally into classes, we may practically say that he has as many different social selves as there are distinct *groups* of persons about whose opinion he cares. He generally shows a different side of himself to each of these different groups. Many a youth who is demure enough before his parents and teachers, swears and swaggers like a pirate among his "tough" young friends. We do not show ourselves to our children as to our club-companions, to our customers as to the laborers we employ, to our own masters and employers as to our intimate friends. From this there results what practically is a division of the man into several selves; and this may be a discordant splitting, as where one is afraid to let one set of his acquaintances know him as he is elsewhere; or it may be a perfectly harmonious division of labor, as where one tender to his children is stern to the soldiers or prisoners under his command. (1915: 179–80)

THE SELF AS AN EVERCHANGING SOCIAL OBJECT: A SUMMARY

Let us try to bring some central ideas together here. The small child, before the language-play stage, has only a primitive self, indeed a preself. Then the child assumes the perspectives of significant others, then of a generalized other, and finally of several reference groups, in each case entering into a new stage of the self. At the point where the individual reaches the reference group stage, there seems to be a consistent social self related to a single generalized other, but there is also a multitude of social selves, each relating to one of the individual's social worlds. The individual as an adult defines the self as social object at any point in relation to his or her:

1. Significant others, alive or dead, imaginary or real, from the past or in the present, and physically present or physically distant
2. Reference groups, alive or dead, imaginary or real, from the past or in the present, and physically present or physically distant

The self rests on other people, both individuals and reference groups. To some extent we have several distinct selves, but because our interaction overlaps, because our significant others and reference groups probably form a relatively consistent whole, our self is not as segmented as might have been implied in this discussion.

Let me give some examples of the social nature of the self as well as its complexity. A president of the United States may use various individuals, groups, and categories of people for his definition of self, including, for example, "the Republican party," "the American people," "the corporate rich," "the 1776 revolutionaries," "a small group of loyal advisors," "black people," Thomas Jefferson, Hubert Humphrey, Mao Tse-tung, his or her spouse, their children, or the unknown soldier. Whoever's perspective is assumed in the definition of the president's self will be critical to how the president acts. If Ivan matters and Ivan defines the president as one who cares about human beings, then in the presence of Ivan (or even away from Ivan) the president will define his self as "one who cares" and will guide his behavior accordingly. It is much more complex, but we will better understand self-definition and its consequences later in this chapter. Or take the example of Felix the freshman: mom, dad, girl friend, President Buick, Ernest Hemingway, the Rolling Bones, the alienated generation, the business world, Johnny Cash, the Harwood football team—each will influence how Felix defines himself and how he acts. If it is the alienated generation that constitutes his reference group, then he will act in relation to the college authorities as a noncooperative and distant role player.

It should be emphasized that the individual may or may not use people in his or her presence as significant others or reference groups. If people in the present situation are not important, then their perspective is not important and their definition of self is also not important. They are not significant others or reference groups. Thus the poor teacher is often the one whose reference group does not include the students, and the "moral" person may be the one who rejects the standards of those who are *immediately* around him or her doing things people (significant others, reference groups) elsewhere consider immoral.

THE SELF AS OBJECT

We have stated that the self is an object, a social object. It is a thing, like other things pointed out and shared in interaction. As Blumer emphasizes (1962:181), the importance of the self as object cannot be understated: It means that the individual can *act* toward himself or herself as he or she acts toward all other people. In a sense the individual has an additional person to act toward in the situation. Since we sometimes judge other people, so we can also judge our self. Since we can talk to others, so we can also talk to our self. Since we can point things out to our self about other people, so we can actually point things out to our self about self. We can direct others; so we can direct our self. When we say that selfhood means that the person is object we mean that the actor can act toward his or her self. "The individual achieves selfhood at that point at which he first begins to act toward *himself* in more or less the same fashion in which he acts toward other people. . . . It is still he who is doing the responding, even though he is also the object *toward* which he is responding" (McCall and Simmons, 1966:54). Herbert Blumer emphasizes the central importance of the self to symbolic interactionism:

> The key feature in Mead's analysis is that the human being has a self. This idea should not be cast aside as esoteric or glossed over as something that is obvious and hence not worthy of attention. In declaring that the human being

has a self, Mead has in mind chiefly that the human being can be the object of his own actions. He can act toward himself as he might act toward others. Each of us is familiar with actions of this sort in which the human being gets angry with himself, rebuffs himself, takes pride in himself, argues with himself, tries to bolster his own courage, tells himself that he should "do this" or not "do that," sets goals for himself, makes compromises with himself, and plans what he is going to do. That the human being acts toward himself in these and countless other ways is a matter of easy empirical observation. To recognize that the human being can act toward himself is no mystical conjuration. (1962:181)

To truly appreciate the importance of the self we should break down the different actions that the individual can take toward it. These actions fall into three general categories: We can talk to it, we can see it, and we can direct it. It is important to describe each of these acts in turn.

THE IMPORTANCE OF THE SELF: SELF-COMMUNICATION

One of the central functions of the self is to serve as an object of symbolic interaction. In a real sense the human is a society in miniature, for as the individual communicates with himself or herself, he or she becomes a subject and an object in communication. Because of the self, humans are able to think, to point things out to themselves, to interpret a situation, to communicate with themselves in all of the diverse ways they are able to communicate with all other humans. "The possession of a self," Blumer concludes, "provides the human being with a mechanism of self-interaction with which to meet the world—a mechanism that is used in forming and guiding his conduct" (1966:535). Mead points out that "the essence of the self . . . is cognitive: it lies in the internalized conversation of gestures which constitutes thinking, or in terms of which thought or reflection proceeds" (1934:173). To think is to speak to one's self, to point things out, to reflect, to carry on conversation with that social object called the self, in identically the same manner as one speaks to others, except that, in most cases, conversation with one's self is silent.

Without the self, the human would also not be able to communicate with others, for it is only because the human can simultaneously give off meaning to other people and understand (through communication with self) what he or she communicates, that effective communication with others can take place. Meaning takes more than one: the person who communicates meaning to self and simultaneously gives off meaning to the other, and the person for whom communication is meant. "From Mead's point of view . . . only humans can self-consciously and purposively represent to themselves that which they wish to represent to others: this, for Mead, is what it means to have a self and what it means to be human" (Elkins and Handel, 1972:50). "What is essential to communication," Mead states, "is that the symbol should arouse in one's self what it arouses in the other individual" (1934:149).

All other action we take toward the self depends on this first action. The fact is that all of the action we take involves this symbolic communication. It then is really the most important action of all, since it makes all others possible.

THE IMPORTANCE OF THE SELF: SELF-PERCEPTION

When we communicate to the self, we analyze or define the situations we act in. We indicate to the self information about all objects in the situation: other people, tools, the clock, for example. We also indicate to the self information about the self in the situation. The fact is that selfhood means that the individual is able to *see self in situation,* and is able to consider that object as he or she acts. We look at the world in relation to self. We assess how others affect us, and how we affect them. Hickman and Kuhn point out that the self "anchors" us in each situation, since unlike other objects, the self is present in all situations. The self serves as the basis from which a person "makes judgments and subsequent plans of action toward the many other objects that appear in each situation" (Hickman and Kuhn, 1956:43). This is a very critical and not very much discussed point: Selfhood allows us to examine situations and how they affect us and to determine the kind of action we might take by imaginatively testing proposed action first on its effects on the self, that object we seem to know the best. When I engage in conversation I engage in a self-interaction that attempts to assess the other's image of me and how I am acting in relation to the other. As I hold my loved one close to me I try to assess not only her activity but my own activity—if, for example my action in relation to her is appropriate, tender, or beastly. How I assess my self in each of these acts described will lead me to adjust my acts accordingly.

The human being then has a number of ideas *about* self, and these ideas affect what he or she does in a particular situation. Sometimes self-perception is called the individual's "self-concept." For example Rosenberg (1979:ix) describes the self-concept as the "totality of the individual's thoughts and feelings with reference to himself as an object." It is what we *see* as we look at our self. It is our "picture" of our self. Indeed, this picture involves not only what we see but also what we *want* to see, or an "idealized self." (Rosenberg, 1979:38) Without any question, what we think we *are* and what we think we *want to be* influences what we do and are thus important parts of our "self-concept."

> It is plain that we can never attain an adequate grasp of the self-concept without taking account of man's extraordinary tendency to visualize himself as other than what he is, to construct in imagination a picture of what he wishes to be. No one can see himself as bad or good, admirable or contemptible, except with reference to the standards he has set for himself. (1979:45)

Self-Judgment as an Aspect of Self-Concept

Part of what we think of our self involves a judgment. This is sometimes called "self-esteem." The self is something we see and judge, evaluate, like or reject, love or hate. We may feel good as we look at our self; we may feel bad. Good boy! Bad boy! Stupid! Klutz! Beautiful! Wow! Ugh! Charles Cooley emphasizes this aspect of the self in his description of "looking-glass self." He states:

> As we see our face, figure, and dress in the glass, and are interested in them because they are ours, and pleased or otherwise with them according as they do or do not answer to what we should like them to be; so in imagination we perceive in another's mind some thought of our appearance, manners, aims, deeds, character, friends, and so on, and are variously affected by it.
>
> A self-idea of this sort seems to have three principal elements: the imagination of our appearance to the other person; the imagination of his judgment of that appearance; and some sort of self-feeling, such as pride or mortification. (1970:184)

"He sees that I am talking a lot. He likes that about me. I like me too." "She sees me walking toward her slowly and deliberately. She thinks I'm cool. Yes, I'm cool!" "I must appear to them to be skillful at this game. They hate me for it, for I threaten them. Maybe I shouldn't be so showy. I don't like this aspect of me!" What we think of ourselves and what we *feel* about ourselves, like all else about the self, results from interaction: Self-judgment is a result, to a high degree, of judgment by others. Shibutani describes the interrelationship of self-judgment and interaction in this manner:

> Like other meanings, sentiments toward one-self are formed and reinforced in the regularized responses of other people. Through role-taking a proud man is able to visualize himself as an object toward which others have feelings of respect, admiration, or even awe. If others consistently address him with deference, he comes to take it for granted that he deserves such treatment. On the other hand, if someone is consistently mistreated or ridiculed, he cannot help but conclude that others despise him. If a person is always ignored, especially in situations in which others like himself are given attention, he may become convinced that he is a comparatively worthless object. Once such estimates have crystallized, they become more independent of the responses of other people. (1961:434-35)

And, it is important to reiterate, it is not all people we interact with whose perspective we assume in judgment of self, but our significant others and reference groups.

> Since men are socialized creatures whose perspectives develop through communication, the criteria by which they evaluate themselves are cultural. Standards differ from one reference group to another. In the social worlds that make up American society there are an amazing variety of attributes of which people are proud or ashamed: their speaking voices, the straightness of their teeth, their ancestry, their muscular strength, their ability to fight, the number of books they have read, the number of prominent people they know, their honesty, their ability to manipulate other people, the accessories on their automobiles, or their acquaintance with exotic foods. Each person sees himself from the standpoint of the groups in which he participates, and what-

ever he believes will impress his audience becomes a source of pride. (Shibutani, 1961:436)

Of all the propositions derived from symbolic interactionism, this one—the relation
between the judgment of others and self-judgment—has been the most empirically
supported and has been the subject of the most studies. In a sense it is the easiest to
study precisely because within the symbolic interactionist perspective it comes
closest to a simple causal relationship in the traditional scientific sense.

The fact that self-judgment is highly related to the judgment of others has
many implications in real life. A whole theory of deviance, called labeling theory, is
developed from this simple beginning. If we look for the most important principle
of labeling theory, it is this: The individual's self-judgment and identity are shaped
in interaction, and this principle has all kinds of consequences for further action. A
circular process is developed from action by others, to self-judgment, to action by
person, to reaction by others. Deviance, like many other things about us, results
from the judgment of others, which eventually becomes the judgment we have of
self. The self is dependent on others, and if others are powerful and are significant
to us in some way, then our assessment of our selves will also be shaped and our behavior will be affected. There seems to be little question that self-assessment arises
from our interaction with others, but what we must consider is this question: To
what extent does the individual, in interaction with the self, come to shape his or
her own judgment apart from interaction with others? The symbolic interactionist
would probably argue that our self-judgments, like all else concerning the self, can
come, in differing degrees, from our reference groups and significant others not in
our immediate situation, from those with whom we are immediately interacting,
and from a self-judgment the individual works out in active self-interaction.

Erving Goffman (1959:14-60) describes the situation where the individual's
judgment of self is almost completely in the hands of other people who have very
great control over the physical and social environment the individual is in. He calls
these instances total institutions, institutions that are apart from the wider society,
isolated, where for a length of time the individual's life is in an enclosed, regimented
space. Prisons, mental hospitals, the army, and some religious orders are examples.
Goffman describes the process by which the total institutions systematically (but
not always intentionally) manipulate the individual's world so that the individual
comes to redefine self—to reject or question the conceptions of self brought in from
the outside, which resulted from interactions in various social worlds. One is, in a
real sense, redefined at first through "a series of abasements, degradations, humili-
ations, and profanations of self." Isolation itself, as well as the dispossession of
property and loss of one's name, contributes to the pattern. Individuals may be
stripped of privacy and also the ability to present themselves to others in the way
they choose. For example, clothes, cosmetics, haircuts are all restricted. A host of
other acts that the individual is forced to perform, such as the constant use of "sir,"
asking permission, and figuratively bowing to those in authority, all operate to bring
about a "mortification of self." New self-judgments slowly replace the old ones.

Gradually, any positive self-judgments depend on the authorities and on the actions they wish to support. To obey passively becomes action rewarded with praise and approval, so a positive self-judgment, as it becomes more and more dependent on authorities, is tied to obedience. This whole process depends on (1) isolation from significant others and reference groups outside the institution, (2) total control of the individual's environment by a few powerful individuals, and (3) constant interaction within a social world whose perspective is assumed, including perspective on self.

This model, although extreme and not usual for most of our lives, still serves to sensitize us to a multitude of situations where people do have power and do indeed manipulate self-judgments. Parents, teachers, and peers do this to each child. Sometimes the judgments of these others are highly consistent and lead the individual to totally reject self or fully love self. More often, significant others and reference groups are inconsistent and the judgment of self is to some extent a continuously changing process. The "brain-washing" of Patricia Hearst or the example of the "Moonies" seem to follow the model of the "total institution": isolation, control of environment, limited interaction with outsiders, rejection of self-judgments developed elsewhere, and assumption of alternative perspective. It may be hypothesized that those members of society who lack the material or intellectual resources necessary to determine their own lives may have selves that are consistently mortified by authorities and may have judgments of selves that are more likely to be shaped and manipulated. It seems that freedom may exist for all of us but that it is a matter of degree, with one important ingredient, an ability to take an active rather than a passive role in self-definition and self-judgment. And this ability demands a complex social world, not manipulated by a few, where self-definitions and judgments remain a constant process and where the individual participates in forming self-judgments and does not just passively respond to others.

Identity as an Aspect of Self-Concept (socially established)

The self then is an object toward which we direct communication and an object we see and think about in situations. Part of this "self-conception" involves judgment; part of it also involves *identity*. We call social objects names, and this allows us to identify and classify them in a world of a multitude of social objects. So too do we give our selves a name. Our identities are simply the names that we call our self. Gregory Stone (1962:93) describes identity as the perceived social location of the individual: where one is "situated" in relation to others," who one tells the self one is, what one "*announces*" to others that one is.

Identities, Peter Berger (1963:98) says, are "socially bestowed, socially maintained, and socially transformed." Thus, defining self, like all the other actions the individual takes toward his or herself, is carried out in interaction with others. As others label me, so I come to label myself. The names given us become our names, and our names are our definitions of "who we are" in relation to those we interact with. And if the identities are regarded as good by others, we too will probably regard them as good. That is how identities and self-judgment are interrelated. Self-judgment is related to both what we do (our action) and who we "are" (our identities).

The identities are labels used not by all others but by the reference groups and significant others of the individual. And these identities become central to us over time as our interaction reconfirms them over and over. Further, as Stone points out, not only do we, of course, learn from others who we are, not only do we announce to our *self* in communication who we are, but also we announce to those we interact with who we are. Thus interaction is a two-way process by which others identify us and by which we influence others to identify us in ways we desire.

The central importance of identity to the individual is the subject of a great deal of theoretical and empirical work at the State University of Iowa. Much of this work has been done or inspired by Manford Kuhn. Kuhn developed the Twenty Statements Test (TST), which simply asks the individual to answer the question, Who am I? with twenty statements. The answers to the question tell the researcher the central identities or self-definitions of the person (boy, Christian, Smith, student, and so forth). As one would expect, as the person identifies his or her self, there is almost always a simultaneous identification of reference group. The instructions for the TST are as follows:

> There are twenty numbered blanks on the page below. Please write twenty answers to the simple question "Who am I?" in the blanks. Just give twenty different answers to this question. Answer as if you were giving the answers to yourself, not to somebody else. Write the answers in the order that they occur to you. Don't worry about logic or "importance." Go along fairly fast, for time is limited. (Kuhn and McPartland, 1954:70)

C. Addison Hickman and Manford Kuhn (1956:43-44) describe their view of self that is operationalized by the Twenty Statements Test:

> There is nothing mystical about this self. It consists of the individual's attitudes (plans of action) toward his own mind and body, viewed as an object. We may think of it as consisting of all the answers the individual might make to the question "Who am I?"

Probably "identity" would be more correct than "self," since the answers to the questions are core names with which the individual labels self. As Stone (1962:93) emphasizes, identities are *social locations,* and individuals will usually answer a question like "Who am I?" by identifying themselves in groups or in social categories. "I am a woman," is a valid social category in that it refers to the fact that women constitute an important reference group, that in the individual's relations with others she sees this as an important identity, and she *believes* others also regard it as such. Several hypotheses can be made on the basis of the order in which subjects list their identities, the degree to which the order changes over time, or the relationship between identities and such things as age, sex, social class, and marital status.

One example of how the TST was used in empirical research is a study by Richard Brooks (1969). The TST is used to measure one of the variables in the study: the degree to which one identifies with major social institutions in society. Brooks attempts to distinguish political extremists in American society. He hypothesizes that those who are committed to either political radicalism or right-wing conservativism will differ significantly in their identification with major institutions in society—identified conservatives will respond on the TST with more references to family, occupational and economic institutions, church and religious institutions, and political and civic organizations than will the radicals. Brooks found support for his hypothesis in 254 respondents. Identification with major institutions was significantly more common among the conservatives. Brooks concludes from this that right-wingers view themselves *within* societal institutions, while radicals are more likely to view themselves as acting against or toward them.

The importance of self-identification, of course, is in the consequences it has for the individual's behavior. Kinch (1963:482-83) relates the following story (maybe fictitious) about the importance of self-judgment and self-identity for action. It also underlines the central importance of interaction and self.

> A group of graduate students in a seminar in social psychology became interested in the notions implied in the interactionist approach. One evening after the seminar five of the male members of the group were discussing some of the implications of the theory and came to the realization that it might be possible to invent a situation where the "others" systematically manipulated their responses to another person, thereby changing that person's self-concept and in turn his behavior. They thought of an experiment to test the notions they were dealing with. They chose as their subject (victim) the one girl in the seminar. The subject can be described as, at best, a very plain girl who seemed to fit the stereotype (usually erroneous) that many have of graduate student females. The boys' plan was to begin in concert to respond to the girl as if she were the best-looking girl on campus. They agreed to work into it naturally so that she would not be aware of what they were up to. They drew lots to see who would be the first to date her. The loser, under the pressure of the others, asked her to go out. Although he found the situation quite unpleasant, he was a good actor and by continually saying to himself "she's beautiful, she's beautiful . . ." he got through the evening. According to the agreement it was now the second man's turn and so it went. The dates were reinforced by the similar responses in all contacts the men had with the girl. In a matter of a few short weeks the results began to show. At first it was simply a matter of more care in her appearance; her hair was combed more often and her dresses were more neatly pressed, but before long she had been to the beauty parlor to have her hair styled, and was spending her hard-earned money on the latest fashions in women's campus wear. By the time the fourth man was taking his turn dating the young lady, the job that had once been undesirable was now quite a pleasant task. And when the last man in the conspiracy asked her out, he was informed that she was pretty well booked up for some time in the future. It seems there were more desirable males around than those "plain" graduate students.*

*John W. Kinch, "A Formalized Theory of the Self-concept." *American Journal of Sociology.* By permission of The University of Chicago Press. Copyright © 1963 by The University of Chicago. All rights reserved.

This story makes clear that identification and judgment of self is a complicated interacting process, one where other individuals influence self but also where the individual, in interaction with self, actively defines and judges self. Thus, although this woman may at first have been highly dependent on others for self-definition and self-judgment, she was able to break away and become increasingly independent in relation to self.

THE IMPORTANCE OF THE SELF: SELF-CONTROL, SELF-DIRECTION

The self is an object that is open to our manipulation. Objects are defined according to the line of action we take toward them, and the self in this sense is an object we are directing, influencing, and controlling. Objects out there are manipulated by us, and so it is with our own self. I direct Martha, I can control Daniel, and I influence Friska the freshman, but I can also do these things with *me*. That the individual has a self is important precisely because the individual has this ability to order self, control self, direct self. That is what we mean by "self-control," or "self-direction." The individual in this sense does not passively *respond* to commands but holds back action, considers options, hesitates, acts aggressively or quietly, guides acts according to a set of morals learned in other times and in other places, changes lines of action, and so on. To direct oneself is to point at oneself and give orders. Self-control and self-direction allow us to align our action with others and therefore to do our part in any cooperative venture. Also, self-direction and self-control mean we are able to say, *Stop*! don't you do that with those guys! You know better, *Me*! Thus, individuality, freedom, and nonconformity as well as cooperation depend on self-direction and self-control. Action is organized and planned for a purpose: It is "elicited and directed without the presence of immediate rewards, external agents of control, or controlling conditions" (Wells and Marwell, 1976:43). The alternative to self is a passive relationship with the environment, since without self-direction and self-control there is only direction and control by outside forces.

   Our self-direction and self-control like all else depend on other people. Our self is pointed out by others, and our self-control is in large part guided by others. We direct/control our action according to those whose perspectives we assume in the situation we encounter, those who are in the situation, and/or those outside of it. We are thus not "free" to direct and control self in any complete sense, but we are guided by the perspectives of others. The guides to our behavior, the guides we use to determine "right" action, appropriate action, rational action, depend on the perspectives of significant others, a generalized other, and reference groups. When Mead points out that the self and society are two sides of the same coin, he is referring to society's perspective becoming the individual's. The "generalized other" is the standard the individual uses to control his or her own action. According to Mead "the principal outcome of socialization that makes self-regulation possible is the development of the *self*" (Elkins and Handel, 1972:50). Human conscience in this sense is the assumption of a social world's perspective, and use of conscience is acceptance of this perspective as a guide for one's actions. The individual uses perspectives not to "determine response" but to converse with self, guide self, control self, and direct self. Each situation we enter is different, and each, to some extent, demands active participation by the individual in relation to self.

This quality of the self relates to the human's ability to solve problems. We can relate to problems we encounter through directing and redirecting our self. We work toward goals through directing our self toward achieving those goals. We work according to values we believe in (freedom, beauty, or the accumulation of friends or money) precisely because we are able to organize our action through direction of the self.

It is through this self-direction and self-control that the *active* human begins to be a reality. In a very basic sense, to possess a self that the actor can direct in situations is a prerequisite for freedom. This is Mead's real point in emphasizing the importance of self. As Tom Goff describes it:

> Man's relationship to nature is a *self*-conscious, reflexive relationship. . . . Other animals react to stimuli: men can, in addition, react to themselves as stimuli. . . . [This fact] is understood as the basis of the ability to inhibit overt and immediate reaction to stimuli, to think or act implicitly, or in mind, before responding overtly and intentionally to the environment. In his view, men thereby acquire a control over their own activity and their environment which is denied to other species. (1980:56–57)

And Herbert Blumer emphasizes exactly the same point:

> With the mechanism of self-interaction the human being ceases to be a responding organism whose behavior is a product of what plays upon him from the outside, the inside, or both. Instead, he acts toward his world, interpreting what confronts him and organizing his action on the basis of the interpretation. (1966:536)

It seems truly paradoxical that the origin of the free actor—selfhood—should be a *social* creation.

SUMMARY OF THE SOCIAL SELF

Let me try to bring together the central ideas about the self:

1. The self is social. It arises in interaction, and it changes or remains stable due to interaction.
2. The self arises in childhood through symbolic interaction with significant others (play stage). The child develops a mature self with the development of a generalized other (game stage). With adulthood come reference groups, each influencing a different view of the self, and making the self somewhat different in each situation.

3. The meaning of the self is that the person is able to see himself or herself as object. The person imaginatively gets outside of his or her person and looks back at self as others do. This process depends to a high degree on taking the role of others, both significant others and reference groups, to see self from their perspective.

4. So much of our action with other people is symbolic interaction, and that can also be said about the self. The essence of selfhood is that we can communicate with our self, and this fact makes possible our ability to perceive the self (including observing, judging, and giving identity to the self), and to direct and control self.

5. The self is one person in all situations the individual encounters, and the analysis of self as we interact with others is central to understanding social situations.

6. The self means that the individual can be "active" in relation to the world, for it allows for self-control, self-direction, and self-manipulation. The ability of the individual to influence the direction of his or her own action makes possible both individuality and cooperative behavior. It makes possible goals, values, morals, and ideas that the individual may use to guide interaction with others: to agree to fit in or to refuse to conform.

7. To have a self also gives the individual the opportunity to judge self, to feel good or bad about self.

8. Others label self, and we come to label self, so our identities are names we give our selves, and these names are the central definitions of "who we are" in relation to others we interact with.

THE SELF AND THE SYMBOLIC
INTERACTIONIST PERSPECTIVE

Throughout this chapter the self has been shown to be tied, like everything else we discussed earlier, to interaction as diagrammed in Figure 6-1.

We have also emphasized that one's action toward self, like all other social objects, depends on one's perspective, and that this perspective comes from significant others, a generalized other, and reference groups. Figure 6-2 illustrates the *emergence* of selfhood.

As the child continues to interact, the generalized other is supplemented by various reference groups, so that for the adult the model shown in Figure 6-3 seems more accurate.

The self as defined in this chapter is something that the individual *acts toward:* We communicate with, analyze, direct, judge, and label the self. *To say that the self*

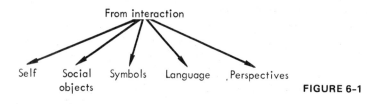

FIGURE 6-1

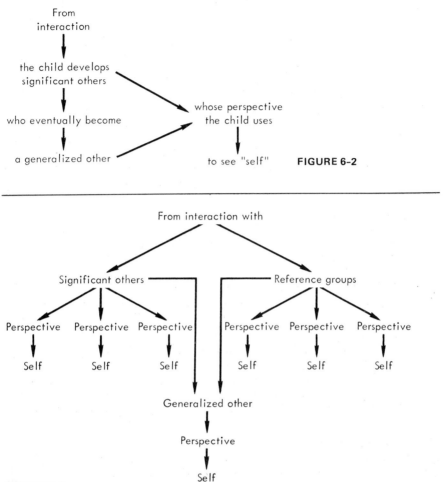

FIGURE 6-2

FIGURE 6-3

changes in interaction with others is to say that these acts change (see Figure 6-4). The point is that the self, as well as the symbol, is central to the development of both complex social life and human individuality. Chapters 9 and 10 will focus on human social action and interaction and will more fully develop the importance of the self described in this chapter.

THE "I" AND THE "ME"

We began this chapter with a warning that the "self" is defined a number of ways in the academic world and in everyday usage. Indeed, it is so complex that even symbolic interactionists are far from perfect agreement on its definition.

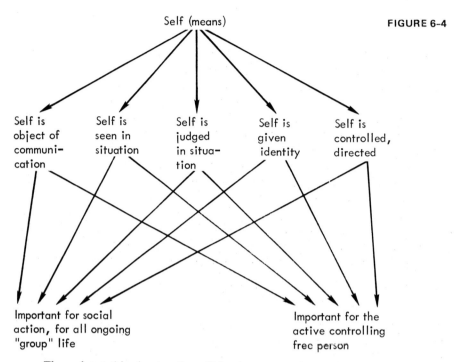

FIGURE 6-4

Throughout this chapter the self has been treated as *object*. On this symbolic interactionists agree, and generally they agree on the various ways actors act toward self. Self as object is usually referred to as the "me." However, Mead and other symbolic interactionists also describe another aspect of the self called the "I." This part of the self is not nearly as important as the "me" (self as object), and symbolic interactionists are far more ambiguous and inconsistent in how they define and use the "I."

Mead makes the distinction between the "I" and the "me" in several places, including the following:

> The "I" is the response of the organism to the attitudes of the others; the "me" is the organized set of attitudes of others which one himself assumes. The attitudes of the others constitute the organized "me," and then one reacts toward that as an "I." (1934:175)

Here Mead is giving probably the most commonly used description of the "I." The "I" is the individual *as subject*, the "me" constitutes the person *as object*. It is the "me" that has been described in this chapter up to now. The "me" is the *social self*, the object that arises in interaction, and that one communicates with, directs, judges, identifies, and analyzes in interaction with others. "The 'I,'" says Mead, "is something that is, so to speak, responding to a social situation that is within the experience of the individual" (1934:177). In this sense, the individual's "I" is his or her active nature, that aspect of the individual, as Meltzer (1972:17) points out, that gives propulsion to acts.

It would seem that this use of the "I" part of the self is almost synonymous with the term "actor." It has always been confusing to me, and I find it much better to reserve the term "actor" to the person, and the term "me" to the social self, or the self as object.

Mead, however, suggests that the "I" has another meaning. This meaning is much easier to grasp and is more consistent with the description of the self in this chapter. The "I" is simply that part of the individual that is impulsive, *spontaneous,* or in other words never fully socialized by society nor controlled by the actor. "It is because of the 'I,' " Mead states, "that we say that we are never fully aware of what we are, that we surprise ourselves by our own action" (1934:174). "The 'I' gives the sense of freedom, of initiative. The situation is there for us to act. . . . but exactly how we will act never gets into experience until after the action takes place" (1934:177–78). Yes, we do direct our acts, and yes, others influence our acts. But there is a part of us, the "I," which makes full control impossible. We are, to some extent, untouched by control for we are also spontaneous, creative, and impulsive. Ames gives a very interesting description of the interrelationship between the "I" and the "me":

> The "I" is spontaneous, impulsive, ceaselessly venturing, not only out into the world, but confronting the "me" in dialogue. The "me" is the result of dealing with other people. It is an internalization of the community, with its institutions, whereas the "I" remains more isolated, more untamed, though cautioned and controlled by the "me." On the other hand, the "me" is constantly prodded by the "I" which breaks away to say and do more or less unexpected things in society; while society in turn is constantly being stirred up and tested by fresh impetus from the "I" of each of its members. The plunging and daring "I" is civilized and guided, also given opportunities, incentives and support, by society. But there is always an unstable equilibrium between society, representing what has been achieved or bungled in the past, and the exploring, reforming, revolutionary "I." This sets the problem and promise of education confronting parents, teachers, and statesmen. (1973:51–52)

The "I" in some ways is that part of the actor that does not act because of symbolic interaction with the self, but that acts spontaneously or on impulse. We are creative in what we do not only because we think, but also because we are driven to try a new way of dealing with something in our world. No matter how much we are socialized, a part of us is always "untouched by human hands." This is the best meaning of the "I" aspect of the self. It may sometimes be important, but by far the emphasis in the symbolic interactionist perspective is that humans act toward self as object, and it is such action that is the primary source of what we do in situations. Indeed, unless I note otherwise, I will use the term "self" to mean the "me," the self as object. This is consistent with most symbolic interactionists.

THE SELF AND THE MIND

The mind, to Mead (1934), is the "twin emergent of the self." They arise in interaction together. Although Mead's book begins with "mind," it is probably best to "culminate rather than begin with his (Mead's) understanding of mind" (Troyer,

1946:198). The mind is, in a sense, made easy to understand since Mead's concept of the mind is an integration of the concepts of symbol and self. Mind is the person in *symbolic interaction* with the self. Its nature and importance will be the subject of Chapter 7.

REFERENCES

AMES, VAN METER
   1973 "No Separate Self." In ed. Walter Robert Corti, *The Philosophy of George Herbert Mead,* pp. 43–58. Winterthur, Switzerland: Amriswiler Bucherei.

BERGER, PETER
   1963 *Invitation to Sociology.* Garden City, N.Y.: Doubleday. Copyright © 1963 by Peter L. Berger. Reprinted by permission of Doubleday & Company, Inc., New York, and Penguin Press, Harmondsworth, Middlesex, England.

BLUMER, HERBERT
   1962 "Society as Symbolic Interaction." In ed. Arnold Rose, *Human Behavior and Social Processes,* pp. 179–92. Boston: Houghton Mifflin Co. Copyright © 1962 by Houghton Mifflin Company. Used with permission.
   1966 "Sociological Implications of the Thought of George Herbert Mead." *American Journal of Sociology* 71:535–44. By permission of The University of Chicago Press. Copyright © 1966 by The University of Chicago.

BROOKS, RICHARD
   1969 "The Self and Political Role: A Symbolic Interactionist Approach to Political Ideology." *Sociological Quarterly* 10:22–31.

COOLEY, CHARLES HORTON
   1970 *Human Nature and the Social Order.* New York: Schocken Books.

DENZIN, NORMAN K.
   1972 "The Genesis of Self in Early Childhood." *Sociological Quarterly* 13: 291–314.

ELKINS, FREDERICK, and GERALD HANDEL
   1972 *The Child and Society.* New York: Random House.

GOFF, TOM W.
   1980 *Marx and Mead.* London: Routledge & Kegan Paul.

GOFFMAN, ERVING
   1959 *Asylums.* Chicago: Aldine Publishing Co.

HICKMAN, C. ADDISON, and MANFORD H. KUHN
   1956 *Individuals, Groups, and Economic Behavior.* New York: Dryden Press.

JAMES, WILLIAM
   1915 *Psychology.* New York: Henry Holt & Co.

KINCH, JOHN W.
   1963 "A Formalized Theory of the Self-concept." *American Journal of Sociology* 68:481–86. By permission of The University of Chicago Press. Copyright © 1963 by The University of Chicago.

KUHN, MANFORD H., and THOMAS S. McPARTLAND
1954 "An Empirical Investigation of Self Attitudes." *American Sociological Review* 19:68–76.
McCALL, GEORGE J., and J. L. SIMMONS
1966 *Identities and Interactions.* New York: Free Press. Reprinted with permission of Macmillan Publishing Co., Inc. Copyright © 1966 by The Free Press, a division of The Macmillan Company.
MEAD, GEORGE HERBERT
1925 "The Genesis of the Self and Social Control." *International Journal of Ethics* 35:251–77.
1934 *Mind, Self and Society.* Chicago: University of Chicago Press. Reprinted by permission of The University of Chicago Press. Copyright © 1934 by The University of Chicago. All rights reserved.
MELTZER, BERNARD N.
1972 *The Social Psychology of George Herbert Mead.* Kalamazoo: Center for Sociological Research, Western Michigan University. By permission of Bernard N. Meltzer.
ROSENBERG, MORRIS
1979 *Conceiving the Self.* New York: Basic Books.
SHIBUTANI, TAMOTSU
1955 "Reference Groups as Perspectives." *American Journal of Sociology* 60:562–69. By permission of The University of Chicago Press. Copyright © 1955 by The University of Chicago. All rights reserved.
1961 *Society and Personality: An Interactionist Approach to Social Psychology.* Englewood Cliffs, N.J.: Prentice-Hall. Copyright © 1961. Reprinted by permission of Prentice-Hall, Inc.
STONE, GREGORY P.
1962 "Appearance and the Self." In ed. Arnold Rose, *Human Behavior and Social Processes,* pp. 86–118. Boston: Houghton Mifflin. Copyright © 1962 by Houghton Mifflin Company.
STRYKER, SHELDON
1959 "Symbolic Interaction as an Approach to Family Research." *Marriage and Family Living* 21:111–19. Copyright © 1959 by the National Council on Family Relations, St. Paul, Minnesota. Reprinted by permission.
TROYER, WILLIAM LEWIS
1946 "Mead's Social and Functional Theory of Mind." *American Sociological Review* 11:198–202.
TURNER, RALPH H.
1968 "The Self-conception in Social Interaction." In eds. Chad Gordon and Kenneth J. Gergen, *The Self in Social Interaction,* pp. 93–106. New York: John Wiley.
WELLS, L. EDWARD and GERALD MARWELL
1976 *Self Esteem.* Beverly Hills, Calif.: Sage Publications, Inc.

7
THE HUMAN MIND

When social scientists emphasize that people are conditioned, caused, shaped, and driven by such things as past, social structures, and culture, they are referring to the fact that people lack the tools necessary to act back on their world, to determine their own action, to direct themselves through some kind of choice. They seem, like all else in nature, passive, moved by deterministic forces. In Chapters 4, 5, and 6 we have maintained that by the introduction of the symbol and the self to understanding the human organism, this picture is transformed, and the potential to *act* and not just react is introduced. An active picture of the human being is emerging in these chapters.

MIND, SYMBOL, AND SELF

The picture of a symbol user and an organism with self is, in a way, incomplete without adding another element: mind. Mind is *action,* action that uses *symbols* (Chapters 4 and 5) and directs these symbols toward the *self* (Chapter 6). Mead writes that mind is "activity, and the different phases of consciousness are parts of this activity." It is the individual's attempt "to do something," to act in his or her world (1982:27).

The mind is probably best defined as *symbolic interaction with the self,* the symbolic activity the organism directs toward its own self. It is active communication with the self through the manipulation of symbols. Mead describes it as that which arises and is interdependent with the self, "an inner flow of speech . . . that calls out intelligent response . . ." (1936:381). Active symbolic interaction means that the human *manipulates symbols* covertly; we *think*, we engage in minded behavior, we literally hold conversations with ourselves—yes, we constantly talk to ourselves, and we often answer ourselves. Stop and reflect a moment: Blumer's insight that we are acting in mind all the time seems so obviously true. The mind, he states, is "conscious covert activity," "anything the individual indicates to himself," "and the individual . . . from the time that he awakens until he falls asleep, is a continual flow of self indications—notations of the things with which he deals and takes into account" (1962:181-82). We do not, then, *sometimes* think; we are constantly thinking in every situation we encounter. As we hold conversation with others, we hold conversation with our self: That is mind activity. As we walk into situations, we determine what is important for us in those situations, we define the situations: That is mind activity. The manipulation of symbols is not the same as simple recall of pictures. We may be stimulated in a situation and recall a picture, and that picture may lead to a response by us, but the active manipulation of things in our minds demands symbols that are capable of being purposely combined and recombined in a number of different ways. A picture cannot be manipulated; words can be. "A mind cannot be located in the brain or nervous system or anywhere inside the body. Mind is not a thing, and certainly not a thing to be located. It is *conduct*. . . . Mind then, will subside and disappear when communication is not going on, and come back when communication is resumed" (Ames, 1973:50-51). It is important to regard mind as *activity*.

Mind then should not be confused with brain. The two are not the same. All animals may have brains, but that is not to say that they have minds. Brains with the capacity to store and manipulate large numbers of symbols are necessary for minds, but "brains, *per se*, do not make mind" (Troyer, 1946:200). It is the manipulation of symbols, made possible through the learning of those symbols and the development of self, that makes mind. And these tools, you will recall, are developed in interaction with others (see Figure 7-1). Troyer puts the case clearly and to the point: "It is society—social interaction—using brains, which makes mind." (p. 200) Give the human the self and the words to communicate with the self, and the active person emerges, manipulating words, thinking, and creating.

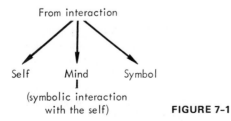

FIGURE 7-1

MIND ACTIVITY

Making Indications to Ourselves

Individuals make indications to themselves. This means that through mind activity, we point things out to ourselves in situations. We isolate, label, and develop lines of action toward things around us. We do not merely respond to these things but actively define them in the situation. Some things we pay special attention to; other things we ignore, at least for the moment. I may walk down the street and note the cold weather. I notice the wind on my thighs and realize I have not worn my long underwear today. I walk toward a snow-covered car I pray will start. On another occasion I may walk down this same street noticing the tickets on the cars and worrying about my car, which may have a ticket on it. Or I may take note of the different styles of clothing people are wearing this year. Or I might be walking down the same street noting the faces of everyone since I am looking for someone in particular: the no-good guy who stole my wallet, or the person who would make a good experimental subject, or someone who would make a good model, or the one who might protect me from a gang, or the one who might make a good date. The point is that people point things out to themselves as they walk down the street, or run, or talk, or play. Things that are out there are noticed and defined in our heads through minded activity. The world is transformed into a world of definitions because of mind; action is response not to objects but to the individual's active interpretation of these objects. Blumer emphasizes this throughout his work. We pull things out of our world, define them, and give them meaning according to the use they have for us at the time, and we act. We act, therefore, after manipulating these things in our heads.

> To indicate something is to stand over against it and to put oneself in the position of acting toward it instead of automatically responding to it. In the face of something which one indicates, one can withhold action toward it, inspect it, judge it, ascertain its meaning, determine its possibilities, and direct one's action with regard to it. With the mechanism of self-interaction the human being ceases to be a responding organism whose behavior is a product of what plays upon him from the outside, the inside, or both. Instead, he acts toward his world, interpreting what confronts him and organizing his action on the basis of the interpretation. (Blumer, 1966:536)*

Blumer argues that "by virtue of engaging in self-interaction the human being stands in a markedly different relation to his environment than is presupposed by the widespread conventional view" (1969:14–15).

Developing a line of action toward objects involves rehearsal of acts before they are performed. We think about what we are about to do before we do it, and this may very well include predicting the reactions of others to what we are about to do. Mind makes possible this rehearsal of acts. Mead uses the term "attitude" to mean a line of action that the individual decides to go with toward an object. Mead states:

> There is an organization of the various parts of the nervous system that are going to be responsible for acts, an organization which represents not only that which is immediately taking place, but also the later stages that are to take place. If one approaches a distant object he approaches it with reference to what he is going to do when he arrives there. If one is approaching a hammer, he is muscularly all ready to seize the handle of the hammer. The later stages of the act are present in the early stages—not simply in the sense that they are all ready to go off, but in the sense that they serve to control the process itself. They determine how we are going to approach the object, and the steps in our early manipulation of it. (1934:11)*

Without developing lines of action toward objects symbolically, and without rehearsing acts covertly before they overtly act, humans would indeed be limited to responding to objects that appear to them from out there. Delayed response, the consideration of strategies of action, and the active definition and redefinition of the world of objects are basic activities of the mind. Trial and error gives way to problem solving; response gives way to choice among alternatives.

Blumer (1981:115-16) shows us the importance of mind action, or what he calls "making indications to our self," by contrasting this with the response of organisms who lack it:

> The organism, by virtue of this indicatory facility that I'm assuming, is able to point this thing out to itself. The organism is not just there—in a relation of merely responding to the thing—it points it out to itself and consequently, it can do something. By indicating the thing to itself, the organism can stop and figure out what it will do before it acts toward the thing. To indicate something to oneself is to put oneself in the position of being able to talk with oneself about the thing. This cannot be done by the other organism which doesn't have the means of pointing out the thing to itself.

Mind and Interaction with Others

Of course, we talk to ourselves not only when we are alone but also when we are with others. *Social* situations must be defined, other people's words must be given meaning as they talk, and their acts and intentions must be interpreted. To understand others in a situation is to be engaging in minded activity. Their words, their actions, their intents, their motives, their "character," their past, their age, their talents are indicated to the self and considered by the actor in the situation. Sometimes we are concerned about what they think of us, or perhaps what we think of each other. We may wonder what they had for breakfast or how they look naked or on the toilet, or we may consider what their marriage is like or what their

*Reprinted from *Mind, Self and Society* by George Herbert Mead by permission of The University of Chicago Press. Copyright © 1934 by The University of Chicago. All rights reserved.

childhood consisted of. We may also consider how to escape the social situation, how to control it, how to appear to conform to others at least until we can get away, or how to disrupt the situation. We might escape the situation in our minds by thinking about last night's party, tonight's book that we're definitely going to get to, tomorrow's Super Bowl, or next year's job. But whenever we are with others, just as whenever we are alone with our own self, we are engaging in a constant conversation with self—not always a conversation that we are fully aware of, but a conversation nevertheless.

It is important not only to consider what others are saying to us but also what we are saying to others. To give off symbols to others is to give them off to our selves simultaneously. Our communication is an attempt to share something with others. What we share therefore has meaning to us. We are able to "know" the meaning that our words will have to others, only because the words have meaning to us. Ames points out that

> Mead's tremendous discovery is that the mind begins to appear at the point when certain gestures tend to call out in the individual making them the response which they simultaneously arouse in another form. Mead noted that the vocal gesture is especially apt to have this double effect, because it can be heard by the form which makes it in practically the same way and at the same moment as by another form. This is the main basis of communication among men: that the same utterance or other gesture should affect the organism initiating it as it does another. (1973:50)

Minded activity, therefore, includes the conversation with the self that necessarily must accompany the conversation with others.

Mind is involved in all social situations because other people are objects that must be defined like everything else. People pose greater problems for us, however, than other objects since we must understand what they are doing, we must make ourselves understood by them, and we must actively interpret their acts in situations in order to revise our own acts. We develop lines of action toward other people, but these lines of action are constantly being revised in the situation since each actor is also acting back and we must adjust accordingly. Rehearsing our acts before we act overtly is especially important in social situations since what we do overtly is seen and defined by others.

Games provide especially good examples of individuals engaging in mind action, rehearsing overt action, redefining the other person, and altering overt action. In a sense, games are slow-motion human action. In chess, for example, a move by Ivan may be preceded by something like: "I think that the capturing of his queen will be accomplished in three moves if I now move my castle to this position. The American might interpret this as meaning I am after his knight, and if he does, I have him. If he figures out my move, then I will have to alter my plans." Then as he moves, Ivan reexamines the situation, looking especially at John, his opposition. Noting that John moves the pawn, Ivan realizes that John has not fallen for the trap, and Ivan must now revise his line of action. Self-communication, making indications, rehearsing acts, developing and altering lines of action, understanding the meaning of the other—all of these activities characterize both Ivan and John playing chess, but they also characterize all of us in every social situation we encounter. Or the game of football: "I think the action will be right through the center of the line, since they won't be expecting it. Their backs are expecting a pass, and the center is weak. However, if they line up as if they were expecting it, I will change the play by calling a number 88." After the play is run: "We did that well, but they were somewhat ready for us. I wonder now if the time is right to try the same thing again." That is the quarterback, but all the actors on the field, including the opposition, the referees, the coaches, and the fans, are making indications to self, rehearsing acts, and doing all the other activities called mind.

These formal games are replayed throughout our lives in all social situations: the classroom, the party, the bull session, the meeting, through traffic, while shopping at the store, and while getting ready to meet someone for dinner. But mind is like all else—we become most conscious of it when it is pointed out to us by others and when we, in turn, point it out to our self. In a sense, what the perspective of symbolic interactionism does is to make us more aware of the mind activity that characterizes much of our lives.

Mind and Self

Mind is the activity made possible by the self. It is all the communication toward the self about the world out there and about the object within each person: the self. Figure 7–2 summarizes mind activity.

Mind is symbolic action taken toward the self. It arises from interaction with others, since it depends on both self and symbols. It is activity, covert activity, which plays a role in all human overt activity. Humans are constantly engaging in symbolic action toward the self, alone and in interaction with others. Mind is necessary to understand others, to make one's self understood by others, and to determine lines of action toward objects and situations. All action we take toward the self is mind action.

It is also important to emphasize that because of mind, humans develop an active relationship to their environment. Stimuli are selected, thought about, and

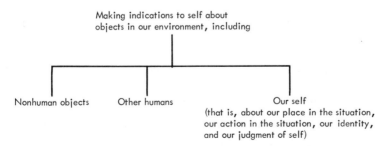

FIGURE 7–2

manipulated, and acts toward the objects are worked out, rehearsed, altered. Humans do not respond to just any physical stimuli out there, but in a real sense, they determine the nature of the stimuli acted toward. We have earlier discussed this active relationship in chapters on the symbol and the self. It is obvious now that it is through symbolic interaction with the self, minded activity, that humans actively participate in the world around them. Maurice Natanson points out the centrality of mind to the active nature of human behavior when he restates Mead's position: "The human animal has the unique capacity of isolating his responses to environmental stimuli and controlling those responses in the very act of isolation; he is able to pick out meanings in his responses and to indicate these both to himself and to other selves: this ability is the product of language" (1973:7). To Mead the introduction of minded activity is what is meant by "choice and conscious control" (Troyer, 1946:199). "Mind makes it possible," according to Meltzer, "to control and organize his response" (1972:20). To direct self, to hold back a response is a mind activity, an active relationship with one's social environment that makes possible cooperation with others or refusal to cooperate.

Mind and Problem Solving

The activity we call mind becomes most deliberate and conscious when the individual is faced with a problem situation. "Consciousness," says Mead, "is involved where there is a problem, where one is deliberately adjusting one's self to the world, trying to get out of difficulty or pain. One is aware of experience and is trying to readjust the situation so that conduct can go ahead. There is, therefore, no consciousness in a world that is just there" (1938:657). We may engage in mind action all day long, barely conscious of that activity, but when faced with a problem, we become more conscious. Things do not go smoothly anymore. When faced with a problem that interrupts the flow of action, we deliberate about how to resolve it. In a sense, we are like Robinson Crusoe, as described by Van Meter Ames. As a problem to be solved is forced on us by a situation, we come to redefine what we once took for granted, we begin to take note of things and to analyze our resources, and we come to take stock of the situation and our self in relation to that situation.

> Robinson Crusoe was in the act of sailing for Guinea when this act was interrupted by shipwreck. Other voyages and adventures of his had preceded, but the story associated with his name begins with his being wrecked off an unknown island. There the ongoing act of the voyage was halted when he was plunged into the sea. Now it was no longer a question of going to Guinea but of reaching a rock he could hold on to until a huge wave subsided. Then he made a dash for shore and clambered up a cliff. On the next page, as Defoe relates:

> After I had solaced my mind with the comfortable part of my condition, I began to look around me to see what kind of place I was in, and what was next to be done. . . . I was wet, had no clothes to shift me, nor anything either to eat or drink. . . . I had nothing about me but a knife, a tobacco-pipe, and a little tobacco in a box. . . . All the remedy that offered to my thoughts at that time was, to get up into a thick bushy tree. . . .

Things appear, with their limitation and promise, as he looks about. Taking in the surroundings, with himself as an organism in their midst, an object among objects, he sees things loom up on account of the antecedent act which had been thwarted. What Defoe tells is pure Mead. Mead is generalizing and analyzing what Defoe or any storyteller knows: that the appearance of things of interest must follow upon the blocking of activity. . . . Only then does the individual appear to himself as an object caught in the midst of things, scanning them for hints of how to get going again. Robinson Crusoe was previously too immersed in a smooth ongoing [act] to confront himself as something separate. He appears to himself, along with other objects, when he has to sort them out in search of cues for getting under way again. The situation takes on a structure momentarily lifted out of passage, by the fact that alternative options of different courses appear in the guise of different objects, before any one or one set of them is chosen for pursuit. Surveying land and sea, Robinson Crusoe brings distant points into his own breathing moment, suppressing the time it would take to get to them and touch them. The hills and trees, the rocks in the sea and the wreck beyond, are all magically present in his present, as if the completion and consummation of arriving at each of them were all achieved simultaneously. (Ames, 1973:46–47)

When our identity is threatened—"you are a stupid person," "you are a child," "you are boring"—we may find ourselves in a problem situation, which must be thought out and responded to appropriately. If we desire money or honor or love or sex and we are unable to get it in a situation, we will perceive that situation as a problem with which we must deal. When we see that someone is taking advantage of us, or when we are late for an important appointment, or when we have little time to study for an important test, or when we want someone to think well of us, or when we want to tell our roommate to cut out the chatter so we can get some sleep, we are faced with problems to be solved in order to continue our flow of action without hassle. We may carefully and deliberately look around for useful objects to help us in the problem situation. Meltzer emphasizes the importance of problem solving to Mead's view of minded action:

> Minded behavior (in Mead's sense) arises around problems. It represents, to repeat an important point, a temporary inhibition of action wherein the individual is attempting to prevision the future. It consists of presenting to oneself, tentatively and in advance of overt behavior, the different possibilities or alternatives of future action with reference to a given situation. The future is, thus, present in terms of images of prospective lines of action from which the individual can make a selection. The mental process is, then, one of delaying, organizing, and selecting a response to the stimuli of the environment. This implies that the individual *constructs* his act, rather than responding in predetermined ways. Mind makes it possible for the individual purposively to control and organize his responses. Needless to say, this view contradicts the stimulus-response conception of human behavior.
>
> When the act of an animal is checked, it may engage in overt trial and error or random activity. In the case of blocked human acts, the trial and error may be carried on covertly, implicitly. Consequences can be imaginatively "tried out" in advance. This is what is primarily meant by "mind," "reflective thinking," or "abstract thinking."

What this involves is the ability to indicate elements of the field or situation, abstract them from the situation, and recombine them so that procedures can be considered in advance of their execution. (Meltzer, 1972:20)

The human pursues interests, values, goals, and in these pursuits problems arise that must be resolved: Here lies the essence of minded activity, especially the most conscious and deliberate. "It is this process of talking over a problematic situation with one's self, just as one might talk with another, that is exactly what we term 'mental.' And it goes on within the organism" (Mead, 1936:385). McCall and Simmons also see problem solving as central to Mead's view of mind: Conversation with self is

> of utmost importance to intelligent behavior, for it makes possible elaborate vicarious trial-and-error activity. Mead claimed that intelligence arises when an act is blocked and ways must be found to circumvent the block. Instead of physically trying out impulses . . . the intelligent creature can react to his own verbal formulations of these impulses, and, because the symbols call out the same responses in him that they would call out in an audience of his fellows, he has a social check on his immediate impulses. (McCall and Simmons, 1966: 53–54)*

And so problems call forth from the individual the rehearsal of acts and control of self in relation to an interpreted environment. John Dewey, who focused on problem solving in most of his work and undoubtedly influenced Mead's thinking, also sees mind activity focused around problems:

> Deliberation is a dramatic rehearsal (in imagination) of various competing lines of action. It starts from the blocking of efficient overt action. . . . Deliberation is an experiment in finding out what the main lines of possible action are really like. . . . thought runs ahead and foresees outcomes, and thereby avoids having to await the instruction of actual failure and disaster. (1922:190)

TWO VIEWS OF MIND OR ONE?

This chapter has really developed two views of mind action, not one. The difference between these views is explained in part by the fact that Mead and his student Blumer take slightly different views. At first, we emphasized that mind action is a continuous process of the individual's making indications to self all day long. This is Blumer's point. Then we emphasized that mind action takes place whenever problems arise in situations, where our goals are not immediately met, where we must figure out strategies. Where our action is blocked, we must engage in mind action. This is Mead's emphasis.

Although different, both views are very important for understanding mind action. Mind action becomes most deliberate and conscious when we must stop and figure out how to solve a problem facing us in a situation. Yet, Blumer is also correct in suggesting that mind action—less deliberate and conscious—is necessary throughout our day, in every situation. Each situation is new for us, at least to some extent, and that means some problem solving is necessary. Each has objects we make into social objects around the goals we seek, each involves perceiving self in situation. Every situation we enter demands some adjustment on our part, presents itself as a "problem" to be resolved. Every situation takes some covert action, some self-indication, some rehearsal of various lines of action. When we speak to others, it may be a minimal problem to be understood, but it is still a problem, and we must pay some attention to organizing our presentation. To understand others is usually a minor problem, but it is a problem nevertheless, and we must pay some attention to meaning. Mind activity becomes more deliberate, and we become more conscious of it, when a major problem confronts us, and we must sit down and carefully analyze the situation, considering the consequences of what we are about to do. Mind covert activity should be conceptualized as present in all our situations, as a constant flow of activity, and this activity is organized around situations we encounter, where some definition and adjustment on our part must be accomplished.

We are, then, symbol users, we possess a self, and we engage in mind activity throughout everything we do. Is this the end of what we are? These qualities are interdependent with one other quality, one that is central to everything else, and one we have not even touched on up to now. This quality is called *taking the role of the other,* and it is important enough to spend all of Chapter 8 on.

REFERENCES

AMES, VAN METER
    1973 "No Separate Self." In ed. Walter Robert Corti, *The Philosophy of George Herbert Mead,* pp. 43–58. Winterthur, Switzerland: Amriswiler Bucherei.
BLUMER, HERBERT
    1962 "Society as Symbolic Interaction." In ed. Arnold Rose, *Human Behavior and Social Processes,* pp. 179–92. Boston: Houghton Mifflin Co. Copyright © 1962 by Houghton Mifflin Company. Used with permission.
    1966 "Sociological Implications of the Thought of George Herbert Mead." *American Journal of Sociology* 71:535–44. By permission of The University of Chicago Press. Copyright © 1966 by The University of Chicago.
    1969 *Symbolic Interactionism: Perspective and Method.* Englewood Cliffs, N.J.: Prentice-Hall, Inc. Copyright © 1969. Reprinted by permission of Prentice-Hall, Inc.

1981 "Conversation with Thomas J. Morrioni and Harvey A. Farberman." *Symbolic Interaction* 4:9–22.

DEWEY, JOHN
1922 *Human Nature and Conduct.* New York: Modern Library.

McCALL, GEORGE J., and J. L. SIMMONS
1966 *Identities and Interactions.* New York: Free Press. Reprinted with permission of Macmillan Publishing Co., Inc. Copyright © 1966 by The Free Press, a division of The Macmillan Company.

MEAD, GEORGE HERBERT
1934 *Mind, Self and Society.* Chicago: University of Chicago Press. Reprinted by permission of The University of Chicago Press. Copyright © 1934 by The University of Chicago. All rights reserved.

1936 *Movements of Thought in the 19th Century.* Ed. Merritt H. Moore. Chicago: University of Chicago Press. Reprinted by permission of The University of Chicago Press. Copyright © 1936 by The University of Chicago. All rights reserved.

1938 *The Philosophy of the Act.* Ed. Merritt H. Moore. Chicago: University of Chicago Press.

1982 "1914 Class Lectures in Social Psychology." In ed. David L. Miller, *The Individual and the Social Self,* pp. 27–105. Chicago: University of Chicago Press.

MELTZER, BERNARD N.
1972 *The Social Psychology of George Herbert Mead.* Kalamazoo: Center for Sociological Research, Western Michigan University. By permission of Bernard N. Meltzer.

NATANSON, MAURICE
1973 *The Social Dynamics of George Herbert Mead.* The Hague: Martinus Nijoff.

TROYER, WILLIAM LEWIS
1946 "Mead's Social and Functional Theory of Mind." *American Sociological Review* 11:198–202.

8
TAKING THE ROLE OF THE OTHER

It has been very difficult up to now to refrain from introducing one of the central concepts in the symbolic interactionist perspective: taking the role of the other. This concept is intimately associated with every other concept discussed so far in this book. Taking the role of the other is central to the development of selfhood, it is probably the most important mind activity, and it is necessary for both the acquisition and the use of symbols.

DESCRIPTION OF THE CONCEPT

Taking the role of the other is the activity that children perform when they play mommy's role, or daddy's, or the fireman's, or Wonder Woman's. Children leave their own bodies behind, so to speak, and imagine themselves in the shoes of others, playing at the roles of others, perceiving themselves and the world from the perspectives of others. As they imagine, so they act, and they act toward self and others as though they were someone else. When Mead discusses the importance of significant others and the generalized other in the development of self, he points out that these others who are so important to the child constitute those whose role the child takes in viewing self. It is this ability to get outside himself or herself, and to see the world imaginatively in the roles of others, that allows the child to see self objectively, from out there. In a real sense, taking the role of the other (or "role taking") is taking the *perspective* of the other, seeing the world from the other's perspective and directing self accordingly. Selfhood is dependent on this process. The four stages in the development of the self, discussed in Chapter 6, can be related to the role-taking process:

1. *The preparatory stage:* The child *imitates the acts of significant others;* the act of symbolically imagining self from the perspective of others is not yet possible. Role taking here is a matter of imitating other individuals' acts rather than understanding their perspective. In a way, we come to be aware of the "other" by imitating the other before we become aware of self. We then also come to imitate acts toward *self,* and thus develop self as object.

2. *The play stage:* The child *takes the role of significant others,* seeing self, directing self, controlling self, judging self, identifying self, analyzing self from the perspectives of important individuals. No organized perspective on the self has yet formed. The child takes the role of one individual at a time.

3. *The game stage;* The child's selfhood has matured into an organized whole. Here the child *takes "their role,"* the perspective of the generalized other, assuming the role of "the Community, the Law, the rules of the game, and so on. Such role taking involves generalizing the attitudes of constituent members of the whole and reacting to one's self from the standpoint of those generalized attitudes" (Natanson, 1973:14).

4. *The reference group stage:* The individual's self is not a single whole so much as it is divided between various social worlds. Here the self to which we communicate changes depending in part on which group's perspective is being assumed in a given situation. We are here able to assume the perspective (*take the role*) *of a number of groups.*

Taking the role of the other is an important *mind activity.* We imagine the other's perspective, we communicate that perspective to self on the basis of what we see and hear the other do. We take the other's role through inferring perspectives from the other's action. It is through mind (symbolic interaction with the self) that individuals tell themselves how others see things and how other people's perspectives operate, and it is through mind that individuals understand the meaning other people's words and acts have. As others act, we imagine ourselves symbolically as they, and we come to share part of their meaning. That is the essence of taking the role of the other, and it is obviously dependent on the development of mind in the individual. It is, however, so central to human activity that we are treating it as a *special mind activity* rather than including it in the chapter on the mind.

ROLE TAKING'S RELATIONSHIP TO MIND, SYMBOLS, AND SELF

Taking the role of the other is usually mind activity, but in the very initial stage, it seems to precede mind, symbols, and self in the child's development. Mead argues that role taking is first, that we come to know the *other* first, before we come to

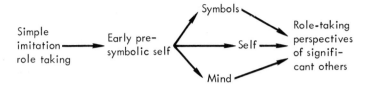

FIGURE 8-1

distinguish self, that the child first imitates the acts of others, and in an early pre-symbolic stage, assumes the action, but not yet the perspective, of the other. From this simple beginning in imitation, we might argue, comes the earliest glimmerings of that object we call self, as the child directs imitative acts toward his or her self, then with self, develops mind and symbols, followed by more complex symbolic role taking, or taking the *perspective* of the other (see Figure 8-1).

The importance of the *order* of these human qualities should *not* be overly emphasized since, in the long run, it makes little difference. A good case might be made for a different order, but doing so can be like splitting hairs or counting the number of angels dancing on the tip of a needle. It matters little. The important point is that the four qualities are linked together and are interdependent in their development. It is most accurate, perhaps, to see self, symbols, mind, and role taking *emerging together* as we interact with others. Something like the diagram in Figure 8-2 would be in order:

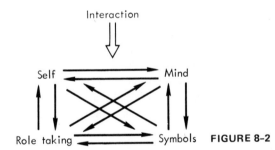

FIGURE 8-2

Another way of stating the interdependence is to point out that each one of these qualities is the result of the other three, and each one of the qualities is a necessary condition for the emergence of the other three. Let us briefly take each of these four qualities and show how the other three are necessary conditions.

SYMBOLS
MIND   } ARE NECESSARY FOR THE DEVELOPMENT OF THE
ROLE TAKING   SELF

1. *Symbols* are used to define social objects; the self, as a social object, is pointed out, named, created through symbols used by others, and understood by an individual.

2. *Mind* is activity that points things out and must therefore point out the self.
3. *Role taking* is said to be the origin of the self. It is through others that we come to see and define self, and it is our ability to role take that allows us to see ourselves through others.

SELF
SYMBOLS } ARE NECESSARY FOR THE DEVELOPMENT OF *MIND*
ROLE TAKING

1. *Self* is one ingredient of mind, since mind is symbolic interaction with the *self*.
2. *Symbols* constitute the other ingredient of mind.
3. *Role taking* is necessary for both self and symbols, and these in turn, are necessary for mind (which is *symbolic* interaction with the *self*).

SELF
MIND } ARE NECESSARY FOR THE DEVELOPMENT OF *SYMBOLS*
ROLE TAKING

1. *Self* makes meaning possible, since a symbol, in order to be a symbol, must have meaning to *self* as well as to the *other*. Self makes sharing and understanding meaning possible.
2. *Mind* makes symbols possible, since mind is the communication of meaning to the self.
3. *Role taking* is basic to understanding the symbolic acts and words the other gives off, and it is necessary for our ability to use symbols to communicate effectively with others.

SELF
MIND } ARE NECESSARY FOR ROLE TAKING
SYMBOLS

1. *Self* is the object toward which we communicate the perspective of others.
2. *Mind* gives us the ability to leave our own perspectives and assume the perspectives of others.
3. *Symbols* are the tools we use to see the world from the perspective of others.

IMPORTANCE OF ROLE TAKING

More than Child's Play

Obviously, taking the role of the other is much more than the child playing at the roles of others. Play is a good example of role taking, but role taking is done by both children and adults in more serious moments, indeed in all interaction with others. The child takes some cookies, then looks at the parent's stern face and searches that face in order to determine the meaning that the face is giving off, the action that is symbolized. The child tries to see himself or herself at that moment from the parent's perspective in order to know if it is best to laugh or cry or run away or look sorry. Understanding others' meaning demands that we role take so that we understand the meaning of the other from the other's perspective. So role taking is more important than play and more important than figuring out Mom's view of our cookie stealing; it becomes an integral part of all interaction, *necessary for understanding the other and being understood by the other.*

If we pause a second and analyze our everyday interaction, it will become more and more obvious how important role taking is. The child figures out what adults are thinking in order to manipulate them, to get the most from them, to escape bad things, and sometimes just to be left alone. The child takes the role of other children and figures out how to stay away from fights, how to win in a game, how to make and keep friends. The conscientious mother takes the role of her child in order to know what the child needs at any moment in time. The teacher figures out what students need through taking their role, and the students figure out what the teacher wants through taking his or her role. A good salesperson knows what customers want by taking their roles and saying the right things. The employee who is totally dependent on the employer must know the employer through role taking and must be careful to conform or know how far he or she can go without bringing forth negative sanctions. The employer who is all-powerful need not always take the employee's role, but if it is totally ignored, the employer too may go too far and end up losing wealth or power or both. We take the role of the other when we love or when we feel sorry for another, and we take the role of the other when we want to exploit or use the other. Taking the role of the other can lead us to see things from the perspective of someone different from us, can cause us to understand that perspective and respect the person, and can make us more tolerant and loving. On the other hand, taking the role of the other can cause us to see other people's perspectives, and we can use that to manipulate them and gain our own interests without concern for them. Taking the role of the other may help us understand the problems of the poor and cause us to take action to work for the poor, or it can help us take advantage of the poor, exploit them, and become rich at their expense.

General Importance of Role Taking to the Human Actor

Taking the role of the other, or taking the perspective of the other, is a basic part of all interaction. Its importance must not be missed. In the following pages we analyze systematically its contribution to all interaction, to the individual, and to all group life.

1. *Taking the role of the other is important to the emergence of the self.* Mead makes this point clearly:

> The individual experiences himself as such, not directly, but only indirectly, from the particular standpoints of other individual members of the same social group, or from the generalized standpoint of the social group as a whole to which he belongs. For he enters his own experience as a self or individual, not directly or immediately, not by becoming a subject to himself, but only in so far as he first becomes an object to himself just as other individuals are objects to him or in his experience; and he becomes an object to himself only by taking the attitudes of other individuals toward himself within a social environment or context of experience and behavior in which both he and they are involved. (1934:138)*

The child takes the role of significant others, then develops a generalized other, whose perspective becomes important in the judgment of self, direction of self, and all the other self processes discussed earlier.

> So the self reaches its full development by organizing these individual attitudes of others into the organized social or group attitudes, and by thus becoming an individual reflection of the general systematic pattern of social or group behavior in which it and the others are all involved. . . . (Mead, 1934: 158)

2. *Taking the role of the other is important for self in all situations.* We take the role of the other in all situations and converse with our self and direct our action accordingly. We direct ourselves, at least in part, according to what we think others will think of our acts (if not others in the situation we are in, then perhaps significant others or reference groups outside the situation). Direction of the self according to the controls of society is what we mean by social control, and this becomes possible through role taking. Each situation calls for self-communication, including self-control and self-direction, and this involves role taking in the situation. Mead describes the important link between role taking and social control.

> This of course, is what gives the principle of social control, not simply the social control that results from blind habit, but a social control that comes

---

from the individual assuming the same attitude toward himself that the community assumes toward him . . . he will be acting toward himself as others act toward him. He will admonish himself as others would. That is, he will recognize what are his duties as well as what are his rights. He takes the attitude of the community toward himself. This gives the principal method of organization which . . . belongs to human society and distinguishes it from social organization which one finds among ants and bees and termites. (1936:377)*

We exercise self-control and self-direction by understanding "the other," and that is done through the process of taking the role of the other in each situation. We must also, in the same way, identify our self, judge our self, and analyze our self in situations; to do so demands role taking. Indeed, as was pointed out in the chapter on self, what we think of self—our self-judgment—is in large part a looking-glass image, gained through the eyes of others whose roles we take.

3. *Taking the role of the other is important for learning our perspectives on all things.* We learn how to view reality through interacting and learning the perspectives of others, not through memorizing them by rote but through understanding the others' view by taking their role. Learning the perspectives of others, from Socrates to Jesus, from the KKK to the Republican party, from our father to our tenth-grade world history teacher, from ancient Greece to American society in the 1970s, is to actively take the role of the other and to see from another perspective. Indeed, if this book is to be a learning experience for anyone, then reading it demands role taking: What is Charon trying to say anyway? Where's he coming from? To gain a perspective is to understand the other through taking his or her role and to come to share that perspective.

4. *Taking the role of the other is necessary for working through all social situations.* We enter a social situation and know what to do in part by taking the role of others in the situation and acting in ways expected of us, or by doing things contrary to what is expected but still within the bounds of acceptability of others in the situation, or by purposely upsetting the expectations and the situation. When we take the role of the others in the situation, according to Anselm Strauss (1959: 59), we must assess the others in terms of (1) their general intent, (2) their response toward themselves, and (3) their responses and feelings toward us. This ongoing assessment causes us to look at our own acts, which leads, in turn, to further action. The point is that others do indeed make a difference most of the time in what we do, and to figure out what to do in a situation, we must take the role of the other. Indeed, that is crucial if we act and then want feedback from others concerning our action. We must see our selves from the perspective of others in the situation to know what to do next.

5. *Taking the role of the other helps the individual control the interaction situation through knowing how to manipulate, direct, or control others.* The good salesperson, the good con artist, the good lover, the good politician, or the good advertising person knows the perspectives of those interacted with because he or she must "give them what they want," must persuade others to do or think a certain way: This is done through effective role taking. The effective teacher takes the role of the students, the successful student knows how to take the role of the teacher, and the good parent knows how his or her children think and may use that to influence them to go to bed. In a real sense, to know how to take the role of the other brings power in interpersonal relationships.

6. *Taking the role of the other is necessary for love.* Love implies respect for the other's ways, the other's ideas, the other's goals and values, and to have this respect demands understanding at least minimally the other from his or her perspective. Some of us may empathize with the other—see the other person's feelings, ideas, perspective, and problems and understand objectively what he or she is feeling. Some of us may come to sympathize with the other—not only understanding objectively but also sharing the concerns, the problems, and the perspective and feeling as the other does. Sympathy and empathy both demand understanding the other. Real concern for others, being able to give to others, to respond to their needs, demands first and foremost that we understand the other. This means understanding from the other's perspective; this means taking the role of the other.

7. *Taking the role of the other is basic to human cooperation.* To cooperate means to know where the others are at, what they are doing, and often, what they are thinking.

> By taking the attitude of the others in the group in their co-operative, highly complex activity, the individual is able to enter into their experiences. The engineer is able to direct vast groups of individuals in a highly complex process. But in every direction he gives, he takes the attitude of the person whom he is directing. It has the same meaning to him that it has to others. We enter in this way into the attitudes of others, and in that way we make our very complex societies possible. (Mead, 1963:375)

Complex group behavior demands not only a division of labor but also an understanding of how one's own behavior fits into a whole process; knowledge of others' tasks is essential for this. To coordinate one's acts with others demands a certain amount of understanding where others are going. Cooperation at any level demands the simultaneous understanding of one's own acts and the meaning of others' acts.

> Coordination requires that each participant be able to anticipate the movements of the others, and it is for this purpose that men who are cooperating watch one another. . . . anticipating what another human being is likely to do requires getting "inside" of him. (Shibutani, 1961:141)

The football team, the marriage partners, the committee that makes the decisions for the annual dance, the General Motors Corporation—in each there must be people role taking—understanding and anticipating each other's actions—if any kind of cooperative action is to take place toward a goal. If we do not role take we are doomed to keep bumping into each other, duplicating tasks, unable to adjust our own acts to the other's acts—all of which, of course, makes cooperation impossible.

8. *Taking the role of the other is the basis for human symbolic communication.* To understand the other demands taking the other's role in order to understand where the other is "coming from," to see the meaning of the other's words and acts. Meaning is obtained through determining what a word or act represents— to the other. This suggests that the individual must "complete imaginatively the total act which a gesture stands for," and to do that "must put himself in the position of the other person, must identify with him" (Meltzer, 1972:14). That is also true when we try to communicate with the other: We must understand where the other is at in order to get him or her to understand our words or acts.

> To indicate to another what he is to do, one has to make the indication from the standpoint of that other; to order the victim to put up his hands the robber has to see this response in terms of the victim making it. Correspondingly, the victim has to see the command from the standpoint of the robber who gives the command; he has to grasp the intention and forthcoming action of the robber. Such mutual role taking is the *sine qua non* of communication and effective symbolic interaction. (Blumer, 1969:10)

Indeed, Mead's whole definition of the symbol, which is the basis of human communication, is dependent on role taking. Miller (1973:91) summarizes Mead's position: In making a significant gesture, "there is a triadic relation: O_1 by taking the role of the other, stimulates himself in turn to respond as O_2 will respond to O_1's gesture." I am stimulated by my own words as I speak to you. That stimulation comes from my imagining the effects my words will have on you, and these effects are known by me only through taking your role in the situation. "The significant gesture involves two fundamental elements: first, the individual making the significant gesture places himself in the position of the individual to whom his gesture is addressed; second, from the point of view of the other, the individual then regards the content of his own gesture" (Natanson, 1973:8). We do that all day long as we interact with countless others. It is impossible to be fully *aware* of our own role taking, for that would demand too much from the human being. However, continuous attempts at taking the role of others as we communicate are evident if we take the time to notice. There are times, of course, when we must very deliberately take the other's role, such as when we want to make certain that others understand us, and then we may become very aware of the others' cues as to whether or not we are being understood. A question by the other about what we are saying tells us, in a sense, if we are indeed being understood, and when we respond to ourselves that "that's a stupid question!" we are usually recognizing that the other is not understanding us. A good public speaker, a good teacher, a good politician, or a good comedian makes sure that he or she is understood exactly, and that necessitates consciously taking the role of the other.

"It becomes communication when the individual indicating the object takes also the attitude of the individual to whom he is indicating it plus that of his response, while the individual to whom the object is indicated takes the attitude of him who is indicating it" (Mead, 1938:51). Mead more clearly states this same idea in this more extensive passage:

> The common expression of this is that a man knows what he is saying when the meaning of what he is saying comes to him as readily as it goes to another. He is affected just as the other is. If the meaning of what he says affects the other, it affects himself in the same way. The result of this is that the individual who speaks, in some sense takes the attitude of the other whom he addresses. We are familiar with this in giving directions to another person to do something. We find ourselves affected by the same direction. We are ready to do the thing and perhaps become irritated by the awkwardness of the other and insist on doing it ourselves. We have called out in ourselves the same response we have asked for in another person. We are taking his attitude. It is through this sort of participation, this taking the attitudes of other individuals, that the peculiar character of human intelligence is constituted. (1936: 379)

9. *Finally, taking the role of the other allows us to see the present both from our own past and from future perspectives.* We are able to imagine how the perspective that we held ten years ago would view what we do now. Or, we may imagine how we would view what we do now ten years hence. This ability to take the role of our self outside the present means that whatever we do in the present can be tempered not only by other people in our past, present, and future but also by our own perspectives from our past and future. "Two years ago I would never have done such a thing." "If I marry this person now, what will I think of this decision five years from now?" "If I sign this agreement today, will I be sorry for it tomorrow?" "How can I live with myself if I do this?"

AND IF WE DON'T ROLE TAKE—SO WHAT?

In a very basic sense, the ability to take the role of the other amounts to what we might term "social intelligence." It is basic to all we do as we interact with others. If we are highly capable role takers, and if we actually make use of this ability, then we will be more able to understand others, to meet the expectations of others if we choose, to bend the rules and not get into trouble with the authorities unnecessarily, to rebel successfully in light of unjust demands, to direct others rather than to be directed, to love, to cooperate, and to communicate effectively with others.

Role-taking skills are probably not the only important skills for success in interaction situations, but they are probably the most important ones. Their importance might become even clearer if we try to understand what happens when individuals do not effectively take the role of the other while acting in situations. Here are a few examples; I am sure that each reader can add another fifty.

1. The "cool" guy who is trying to talk it up with a young woman, treating her the way he treats all the women he has met before, not being sensitive to her perspective, her definition of him, her definition of herself, her reference groups. She happens to be head of Dakota National Organization for Women. He talks. She listens. She talks. He leaves.
2. The teacher who runs the class without taking the role of the students. He is also doomed to fail. Mr. Mumble-to-himself is busy playing with words but does not attempt to see himself or what he is saying from his students' perspective. He just keeps rollin' on; then he can never really understand why those kids don't know what he is trying to teach them.
3. Then there are many misunderstandings and conflicts that accompany the woman who decides to shift her priorities toward the world of the professional: Husband, children, friends, and even employers may fail to take her role and to understand that it is important for her self-worth, that it is not necessarily rebellion but an attempt to develop her abilities, that it is not that "she wants to be like men" but that she regards herself as more than a wife and mother. Conflict may also result from the woman's failure to take the roles of those who feel threatened by her attempts to improve her life.

Family life, possibly the most intimate interaction we participate in, is filled with role taking and problems that result from inaccurate role taking. The list seems endless. We are role taking whenever we are with others. Failure to role take or inaccurate role taking will inevitably have implications for the continuation of interaction. A friend of mine in economics, thinking that he had discovered a profound truth one day, confessed to me: "You know, Joel," he said, "there is no way that I can ever really know what's going on in your head. No matter how well we know each other, we cannot penetrate what's going on in the other person's head." Of course he is right, and we all know it. However, role taking is part of what we all do: (1) We take the role of the other continuously in interaction; (2) we *must* do this in order to understand the other, in order to communicate effectively and to cooperate; and (3) the fact that we cannot role take perfectly makes the individual's life both exciting and highly complex, makes group life continuously tenuous, and demands that we always attempt to open up communication with those with whom we wish to interact. Most important, if we have difficulty taking the role of the other through observing action, then it is incumbent on us to ask the other, "What *is* going on in your head?" Otherwise, our goals, whatever they are, will not be achieved. McCall and Simmons realistically describe the difficulty inherent in role taking:

> Our images of people will always contain some admixture of truth and error but . . . this must be a *workable* admixture. That is to say, it must contain just enough of the relevant truth about our alter to allow us to take minimally

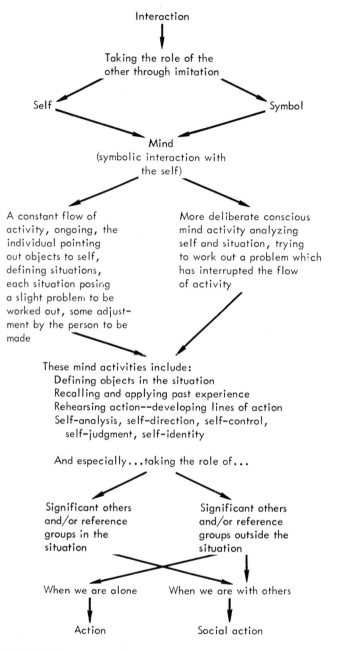

Interaction

↓

Taking the role of the
other through imitation

Self   Symbol

Mind
(symbolic interaction with
the self)

A constant flow of
activity, ongoing, the
individual pointing
out objects to self,
defining situations,
each situation posing
a slight problem to be
worked out, some adjust-
ment by the person to be
made

More deliberate conscious
mind activity analyzing
self and situation, trying
to work out a problem which
has interrupted the flow
of activity

These mind activities include:
  Defining objects in the situation
  Recalling and applying past experience
  Rehearsing action--developing lines of action
  Self-analysis, self-direction, self-control,
    self-judgment, self-identity

And especially...taking the role of...

Significant others
and/or reference
groups in the
situation

Significant others
and/or reference
groups outside the
situation

When we are alone   When we are with others

Action   Social action

FIGURE 8-3

successful action toward him. Seldom are we truly *en rapport* with him, for we do not truly know him. Ordinarily, we understand him just well enough to work out a sort of fumbling, on-again, off-again accommodation in which we manage to get along with, and past, one another without serious conflict. Only rarely, and then most often in quite intimate relationships, do we truly communicate and interact in harmony. (1966:123–24)*

Not a great deal has been done in examining the qualities necessary for accurate role taking, but McCall and Simmons (1966:135–36) list two that they feel are important:

1. "Amount and breadth of our experiences." Our ability arises in part from a wide range of experiences with various individuals and various roles. Further, we also come to understand "from observing the counterrole performances of those who have interacted with us."
2. Our ability also depends on the nature of the other person's identity, whether or not what he or she is doing is known to us, and whether or not it is a recognized line of action.

A SUMMARY OF MIND AND ROLE TAKING

Self, mind, and taking the role of the other, which have been the topics of the last three chapters, are concerned with human *covert activity,* activity that is not directly seen by others but must be inferred. It is maintained throughout this book that this kind of activity is central to human life, that individuals and groups can be understood only by taking account of covert activity, and that covert activity is basic to all that we do overtly toward things and toward other people. Figure 8-3 summarizes the points made in the chapters on mind and role taking. We must always start with *interaction.*

Mind activity, of course, is only part of the activity that humans engage in. We have not yet examined overt activity, that activity that is open to the senses of others. Covert activity is basic, and that is why we have spent so long on symbols, self, mind, and role taking. But overt activity is, in the end, what has consequences for other people, and it is overt activity that is used by all of us to understand each other's covert activity. It is time, therefore, to turn our attention to overt action, social action, and social interaction.

REFERENCES

BLUMER, HERBERT
    1969 *Symbolic Interactionism: Perspective and Method.* Englewood Cliffs, N.J.: Prentice-Hall. Copyright © 1969. Reprinted by permission of Prentice-Hall, Inc.

McCALL, GEORGE J., and J. L. SIMMONS
    1966 *Identities and Interactions.* New York: Free Press. Reprinted with permission of Macmillan Publishing Co., Inc. Copyright © 1966 by The Free Press, a division of The Macmillan Company.

MEAD, GEORGE HERBERT
    1934 *Mind, Self and Society.* Chicago: University of Chicago Press. Reprinted by permission of The University of Chicago Press. Copyright © 1934 by The University of Chicago. All rights reserved.

    1936 *Movements of Thought in the 19th Century.* Ed. Merritt H. Moore. Chicago: University of Chicago Press. Reprinted by permission of The University of Chicago Press. Copyright © 1936 by The University of Chicago. All rights reserved.

    1938 *The Philosophy of the Act.* Ed. Merritt H. Moore. Chicago: University of Chicago Press.

MELTZER, BERNARD N.
    1972 *The Social Psychology of George Herbert Mead.* Kalamazoo: Center for Sociological Research, Western Michigan University. By permission of Bernard N. Meltzer.

MILLER, DAVID L.
    1973 "Mead's Theory of Universals." In ed. Walter Robert Corti, *The Philosophy of George Herbert Mead,* pp. 89–106. Winterthur, Switzerland: Amriswiler Bucherei.

NATANSON, MAURICE
    1973 *The Social Dynamics of George Herbert Mead.* The Hague: Martinus Nijoff.

SHIBUTANI, TAMOTSU
    1961 *Society and Personality: An Interactionist Approach to Social Psychology.* Englewood Cliffs, N.J.: Prentice-Hall. Copyright © 1961. Reprinted by permission of Prentice-Hall, Inc.

STRAUSS, ANSELM
    1959 *Mirrors and Masks.* New York: Free Press.

9
ACTION
AND SOCIAL ACTION

In Chapter 3 we looked at the philosophical foundations of symbolic interactionism and, in particular, at pragmatism as an important foundation of the symbolic interactionist perspective. We pointed out that pragmatists concentrate on action, on what humans *do,* rather than on what they *are* as individuals or as part of groups. Social scientists, according to Charles Warriner (1970:6-7), should emphasize *"action* as the ultimate referent for our ideas of man, as the source of all of our basic data about man, and as the focus of our questions about man." Humans *act,* and from this action we can come to understand both the individual and the group. It is from a consistency in *action* over time, for example, that social scientists are able to infer "personality," and it is from a consistency in *action* between actors that a group or society is inferred. We also infer change in the individual or in the group from action. "The action orientation says that persons and societies are to be known through what they *do,* are to be postulated from continuities in action and conduct and that both [persons and societies] are equivalent inferences from these observations" (Warriner, 1970:8). This chapter will concern itself with human action and social action from a symbolic interactionist perspective. Humans perform "acts," they engage in a "stream of action," as Warriner calls it, and much of the time their acts are "social acts." These three concepts—acts, stream of action, and social acts—are the important ones to focus on for understanding human action.

"ACTS" AND THE "STREAM OF ACTION"

It is difficult to define exactly what is meant by an *act*. On the one hand, we are tempted to view an act in an isolated fashion with a beginning, a middle, and an end. From that point of view, the human is said to take part in a number of separate acts in a single day—we get up, wash ourselves, get dressed, make breakfast, eat breakfast, leave the house, start the car, drive the car, park it, arrive at the office, and collapse in our office chair for a morning nap. Although it may sometimes be difficult, we can locate a beginning and an end to each of these acts and can call everything else "in-between." Each act, it should be noted, is not just a single, isolated, muscular movement but a highly complex and organized pattern of be-havior, and each has been assigned a *name*. The name we give an act is, of course, a symbol, which has been designated by people through shared agreement. By assign-ing a name these people have isolated the act and given it importance. What consti-tutes an act, then, is convention, agreement. Acts are designated objects; indeed, acts are good examples of *social objects*. The acts that we point out to each other are like the people, the objects, and the symbols that we also point out.

Here is Warriner's description of "social acts." In a way, it is unfortunate that he uses that label since the term *social act* is used by most sociologists to describe something else. But if we keep in mind that Warriner calls acts "social" because they are *defined by people and given a name,* then his description is well worth reading.

> A segment of the stream of action is a *social act* because . . . it is recognized by the members of the society as a unit act with a particular meaning. . . . The "sawing of a board" by a carpenter has primary significance for sociological purposes, not because it involves certain muscles and nerves, not because the carpenter has particular motivations, not even because the board gets sawed, but because the act is given a name, conceptually separated from the other parts or aspects of the stream of action and from other social acts. . . . the naming of an action is the primary identification of its existence as social act.
>
> "Thumbing one's nose," "punishing the child," "giving a speech," "going to church," "riding a bus," "going to class" . . . are all social acts because they are named and are identified by the conventional understandings of the mem-bers of the society. (1970:17–18)

Anything that humans do, therefore, and which is also given a name, is an "act." Consistent with the chapter on mind, action includes covert action, so "thinking about a good meal," or "thinking about how to get away from an em-barrassing situation," and "telling oneself not to be afraid" are all acts. "Eating a meal," "excusing oneself from a conversation," and "telling a big bully to get lost" are also acts, overt acts.

The reality of action, however, is that it is continuous, a constant process that is never-ending except when we die. It is a *"stream of action."* "This stream of ac-tion is complex, manifold, multiplex. It is the full reality with many aspects, charac-teristics, features, dimensions, and interconnections. No one and no science can know it completely, but each science focuses on different aspects and different interrelationships . . ." (Warriner, 1970:15-16). No perspective can hope to take apart and analyze this stream of action in any complete sense, but each perspective pulls out certain things and labels them as important, i.e., designates them as social objects, calls them *acts*.

This description of human action as a stream of action, focusing on innumerable social objects, changing from goal to goal, is not all that obvious to a casual observer. The tendency is to focus attention on single, isolated acts. He stole a pig, she took a bus to the store, he robbed a bank, she got an A on her exam, he became a lawyer, he did the dishes, she put the kids to bed—this kind of description seems to most of us to be accurate and certainly simpler than conceptualizing the human as engaging in a never-ending stream of action that shifts from object to object, where acts are not clearly delineated from one another, where the beginning of one act and the end of another are not clear.

The way the stream of action is divided up depends on the perspective one uses. Some perspectives, for example, emphasize large units of action (driving a car to California), others emphasize much smaller units (turning the key in the ignition). Indeed, it is undoubtedly best to see that any isolated "act" is a *social object* designated within the stream of action for a purpose or use (as are all social objects). It is therefore useful to the psychiatrist that you "got angry last night," to your friend that you "called him," to your instructor that you "arrived on time to make up the test." All or any of these may be important to you and therefore isolated as social objects, but only if they in some way relate to your goals in a situation.

Even though it is most correct to regard human action as a stream of action rather than as divided into distinct acts that have a beginning and a definite end, it is useful for all of us to divide action into separate acts. It helps us understand what is taking place, it gives us a handle on what others are doing as well as what we ourselves are doing. Like everything else: We must divide up the world out there in a manner that makes sense to us. Any way we divide it is somewhat artificial, but it must be done to live. We must always remember, however, that whatever way we divide reality—including the stream of action—is limited, incomplete, and changes as our purposes change.

HUMAN ACTION, GOALS, AND SOCIAL OBJECTS

The symbolic interactionist, like everyone else, also divides up the stream of action so that action is manageable for understanding. Acts are sometimes even said to have a "beginning" and an "end," but such designations are usually used for analytical purposes.

Acts are viewed as performed in situations, beginning with the individual's defining goals, immediate or distant, then defining objects in the situation around those goals. Humans are goal-directed; we establish and work for goals in every situation we enter. Each act, in a sense, can be said to begin with a goal that we establish for ourselves in the situation. We are planners; we plan our acts around these goals.

McCall and Simmons point out the importance of goals and planning for us: *Man is a planning animal. . . . things take on meaning in relation to plans. . . .*

> Man is a thinker, a planner, a schemer. He continuously constructs plans of action . . . out of bits and pieces of plans left lying around by his culture, fitting them together in endless permutations of the larger patterns and motifs that the culture presents as models. This ubiquitous planning is carried on at all levels of awareness, not always verbally but always conceptually. (1966: 60)*

Our acts begin with situations and defined goals, and they end with goals achieved, altered, or forgotten. Objects in any situation become tied to our goals in the situation, and they are defined according to our use for them; objects become part of our plan. Objects, of course, include other people. We act in a stream of action that does not stop for us during the day but focuses on first one goal and set of objects in a situation, then another goal and set of objects in another situation. My goal is to get to George's house as soon as possible. I see Marsha down the street. I decide to talk briefly to Marsha, or evade her, or kiss her and run along, or shake her hand, or treat her with cool respect, or reject her completely—and then I act overtly. Action toward the object may change during the course of action—for example, Marsha might tell me she is about to quit her job, and my goal may immediately change to trying to convince Marsha that that is not wise. Thus my definition of Marsha as "someone to greet and get away from as soon as possible" is replaced by a definition of Marsha as "someone to take the time to help." I may eventually achieve my goal in getting to George's house—after helping Marsha solve her problem, giving Mark the brush, running across a beautiful lawn with "Please Do Not Walk on the Grass" signs, and waiting "forever" for a train to pass. However, once at George's house my goals will change, my social objects are transformed, and, for example, Mark may now become someone that I had better call to explain why I was in so great a hurry. Indeed, now that I am at George's and I see who else is there, my action may be organized around getting out of George's house as soon as possible.

"The object and the lines of action in which the individual is engaging, are worked out by the actor in terms of what he is trying to do in the given situation in which he is lodged," Herbert Blumer emphasizes. Definition of objects arises around the goal, and this is continuous:

> In carrying out that line of action, he has to take note of various things in the situation as that situation appears to him. The line of action, accordingly, may take new directions, new twists, in terms of what the individual points out to himself in that situation. Objects that the individual notes act back upon the line of action being executed. The line of action in which the individual is engaged is of great significance in determining what kinds of objects he's going to select out of what confronts him. (1981:114)

*Reprinted with permission of Macmillan Publishing Co., Inc., from *Identities and Interactions* by George J. McCall and J. L. Simmons. Copyright ©1966 by The Free Press, a division of The Macmillan Company.

The human, from the moment of waking in the morning to the moment of falling asleep at night, is engaged in a continuous stream of action toward an innumerable list of social objects that are defined around a great number of goals, changing lines of action as he or she acts, altering directions, redefining goals, and redirecting action as objects in the environment act back. The person we make love to is someone we feel affection for, try to give happiness to and gain happiness from. Making love is an act, and once it has been completed, our goals change immediately, objects take on new meaning, and our action changes direction. The beautiful, wonderful person whom we desired to make love to is redefined as one to speak softly to, to share a meal with, to joke with, perhaps to quietly say good-bye to until later in the day or week. As we leave that person's presence, he or she becomes someone to remember with affection, perhaps someone to talk about to parents or friends. But as we leave, we walk toward an elevator, and we act toward the button in order to get downstairs, in order to leave the building, in order to make our appointment at two o'clock. Other social objects have begun to replace our loved one ever so slowly, and our stream of action continues, centered on new goals and objects. As we prepare for bed at night, our thoughts may be directed toward the morning hours, so our action includes setting the alarm, picking out our clothes, perhaps preparing a lunch that we will take to work the next day. When we wake, the stream of action continues, guiding us from one social object to another. Blumer points out: "In this process, given lines of action may be started or stopped, they may be abandoned or postponed, they may be confined to mere planning or to an inner life of reverie, or if initiated, they may be transformed" (1969:16). But the action continues throughout our waking day, directions always changing, sometimes slightly, sometimes greatly.

LOCATING THE "CAUSE" OF AN ACT

By dividing up our stream of action into isolated acts, it is also easier for us to locate the "*cause*" of our acts. Why did he do that (isolated act)? Three answers to this question seem most logical: (1) He did it because he wanted to do it, he did it intentionally, he chose to do it, or (2) he did it because some personal characteristics—attitudes, needs, self-image—forced him to do it, or (3) something in his environment made him do it. We can handle these causes: We can punish or reward the individual who purposely did *it,* we can try to rehabilitate the man whose action was caused by his personal traits, or we can build up or alter a person's environment that caused *it.*

To regard the acts as part of a *stream* of unfolding action is much more complex, too complex for most of us to try to handle. To see action as developing over time, as part of a larger stream of action, is to become aware that although a certain intention that one had at one point may have initiated a direction of activity, other intentions and goals entered in at other points—that a multitude of factors, some in the environment (including other people), some in the individual's definition of the situation, altered the direction of the action several times over. What might appear to us (the casual observer) as a clear-cut, motivated, planned act might well have been started long ago with a very different end in mind, and the end act that we designate as important was a result of several factors that entered the stream of action.

And to regard the act as part of a stream of unfolding action is to regard the relationship between the organism and the environment as one of a dynamic and interdependent character. The environment constantly changes, and the individual engaging in activity in relation to it is constantly redefining it and self in relation to it. Both personal traits and environment may be factors influencing what we do in any stream of action, but the unfolding stream of action itself that leads up to a given designated "act" is more properly the "cause" of that act. To understand any given act, therefore, it is necessary to analyze the major factors that enter into and lead a stream of action in one direction rather than in others. Individual traits and environmental factors must be understood, but these must not assume a static character, and many other factors must be considered, especially significant others, reference groups, perspectives, mind activity, role taking, self-analysis, self-judgment, identity, self-communication—all of those covert activities that are going on as we act overtly.

A better way to understand the stream of action is to see it as a *series of decisions* made by the actor, each decision (involving definition, interpretation, choice) influenced by two factors: (1) interaction with others, and (2) interaction with self. Along our stream of action each decision directs our action along one branch of the stream rather than another. Each definition is important: all the decisions together are responsible for the directions we go in life. When we say that our decisions result from interaction with self we mean that the act is

> self-caused, self-sustaining, ongoing behavior of the organism, initiated by want or problem, and directed to the end of satisfying the want or solving the problem by means of available elements in the environment . . . [the mind] is an "instrument" in the service of the organism's better adjustment to its environment. (Pfuetze, 1961:40–41)

When we say that our decisions arise from interaction with others, we mean that perspectives are shared and objects are continuously defined in new ways. We also mean that our acts, whatever they may be, become important to others around us, and their acts in turn become elements in the situation we have to define. This adjustment *to each other* that interaction brings means that action *unfolds*, and that it is impossible to know exactly which direction the individual will go in his or her stream of action because the adjustments we make to each other are impossible to predict perfectly.

An exciting, classic, and clear illustration of the centrality of interaction to decision making and directing the stream of action, is this description by a college student (from *The Gang*, by Frederic M. Thrasher):

> We three college students—Mac, Art, and Tom—were rooming together while attending V____ University, one of the oldest colleges in the South. On the

day of our crime all three of us spent over three hours in the library—really working. That was on Sunday and our crime was committed at 1:30 that night (or rather Monday morning).

The conversation began with a remark about the numerous recent bank failures in the state, probably stimulated by one of us glancing at a map of the state. It then shifted to discussion of a local bank that had closed its doors the day before. Tom, who worked at the post-office occasionally as special mail clerk, happened to mention that a sack containing a large amount of money had been received at the post-office that afternoon, consigned to a local bank that feared a run.

The conversation then turned to the careless way in which the money was handled at the office—a plain canvas sack thrown into an open safe. We discussed the ease with which a thief could get into the building and steal the money. Tom drew a plan showing the desk at which the only clerk worked and the location of the only gun in the office. At first the conversation was entirely confined to how easily criminals might manage to steal the money. Somehow it shifted to a personal basis: as to how easily we might get the money. This shift came so naturally that even the next morning we were unable to decide when and by whom the first vital remark had been made.

A possible plan was discussed as to how we might steal the package. Tom could go to the office and gain admittance on the pretense of looking for an important letter. Then Art and I, masked and armed, could rush in, tie Tom and the clerk, and make off with the package. We had lost sight of the fact that the package contained money. We were simply discussing the possibility of playing an exciting prank with no thought of actually committing it. We had played many harmless pranks and had discussed them in much the same way before; but the knowledge that there was danger in this prank made it a subject to linger over.

After about an hour and a half of talk, I started to take off my shoes. As I unlaced them, I thought of how it looked as if I were the one to kill our interesting project. I foolishly said something to the effect that if Tom was going down town, I thought I would write a letter that was already overdue. Tom was anxiously awaiting a letter that should be in that night. He suggested that I go down also as it was a very decent night. I consented and Art decided to join us. I sat down and wrote the letter—meanwhile we continued our talk about the money package. My letter finished, something seemed to change. We found further inaction impossible: we had either to rob the post-office or go to bed. Tom brought out his two guns; I hunted up a couple of regular plain handkerchiefs, and Art added some rope to the assortment. At the time we were still individually and collectively playing a game with ourselves. Each of us expected one of the other two to give the thing the horse laugh and suggest going to bed and letting the letters wait till morning. But it seemed that we forgot everything—our position in school, our families and friends, the danger to us and to our folks. Our only thought was to carry out that prank. We all made our preparations more or less mechanically. Our minds were in a daze.

Putting on our regular overcoats and caps, we left the rooms quietly. On the way down town we passed the night patrolman without any really serious qualms. Tom entered the post-office as was his usual custom, being a sub-clerk, and Art and I crept up to the rear door. Tom appeared at a window with his hat, a signal that there were no reasons why our plan would not be effective. At the door, in full illumination of a light, we arranged our handkerchiefs over our faces and took our guns out of our pockets. We were ready.

"Have you enough guts to go through with this thing?" I asked, turning to Art, who was behind me.

"If you have," he answered.

Frankly I felt that I had gone far enough, but for some unknown reason I did not throw out a remark that would have ended it all then and there. And Art didn't. He later said that he was just too scared to suggest anything. We were both, it seems, in a sort of daze.

Tom opened the door and we followed our plan out to the end. There was no active resistance by the regular night man.

Then after we left the office with thousands of dollars in our hands we did not realize all that it meant. Our first words were not about getting the money. They were about the fact that our prank (and it was still that to us) had been successful. When we reached our rooms, having hidden the money in an abandoned dredger, the seriousness of the thing began to penetrate our minds. For an hour or so we lay quietly and finally settled on a plan that seemed safe in returning the money without making our identity known. Then I went to sleep. (1936:300–303)*

Here is an illustration, perhaps dramatic but nevertheless important for understanding, of action unfolding as individuals interact with themselves and each other, redefining the situation as they go along, acting in ways "unintended" at first, but acting in ways that outside observers might assume were intended right from the start. The final act must be understood in terms of the history of the unfolding action between the actors. Why did *you* do that? Are you immoral? Are you stupid? Are you evil? Are you a criminal at heart? Did your poverty or your riches lead you to that? We ask this kind of question continuously about ourselves and others. We look for easy answers—that was *his* choice, the environment caused it, his personality is just that way—but the history of action, the many factors that enter one's stream of action, must be the proper study of cause. And no factor is more important than *interaction:* with others and with self.

MEAD'S FOUR STAGES OF THE ACT

George Herbert Mead was aware of the difficulties in describing the nature of human action and attempted to dissect the human act analytically to break it down into its components, although he realized that beginnings and ends are difficult to delineate clearly. Mead (1936) divided the act into four stages.

Stage 1: Impulse

Mead suggests that the act begins with the organism in a "state of disequilibrium." There is "discomfort leading to behavior" and an "activation through disruption." *Impulse* is a "generalized disposition to act." It does not tell the organ-

---

*Reprinted from *The Gang* by Frederic M. Thrasher by permission of The University of Chicago Press and William E. Girton. Copyright © 1972 by The University of Chicago. All rights reserved.

ism what to do nor even what goal to achieve. It does not determine the direction of the act but only that there will be action of some sort. The organism is constantly undergoing at least slight disequilibrium, discomfort, and disruption and must take care of those disturbances by dealing with various aspects of the environment. That is, humans act from a state of slight or great disturbance that does not come only once in a while but characterizes their entire life (description borrowed from Shibutani, 1961:65-66). Other symbolic interactionists do not go so far as to give a reason for action: we act, and that's all there is to it. John Dewey (1922:119) states that the human being "is an active being and that is all to be said on that score." Gregory Stone and Harvey Farberman (1970:467) announce proudly: "Man simply acts, period!" In essence, Mead, Dewey, and most symbolic interactionists *assume* action on the part of the organism and pay little attention to why we act but focus instead on understanding the direction that action takes. Mead's "impulse" is not developed extensively in the literature, is still somewhat vague, yet imbalance or disequilibrium seems as good a reason as any for the beginning of an act.

Stage 2: Perception

In this stage individuals first define their situation. The acting organism seeks out stimuli and notices and defines aspects of the environment that can be used in order to attain goals in that situation. We seek something in all situations, objects are seen by us as useful to what we seek, and we act toward them accordingly. "Stimuli, therefore, do not initiate activity; they are pivots for redirection..." (Shibutani, 1961:68). The individual acts in a world of meaning, a world of objects, social objects, that become defined according to their *use* for defined goals in a situation. Perception and definition are by individuals who have goals; it is selective, and it is ongoing. This part of the act is central to Mead's conceptualization of human action: "... for an intelligent human being his thinking is the most important part of what he does and the larger part of that thinking is a process of the analysis of situations, finding out just what it is that ought to be attacked, what has to be avoided" (1936:403). Mead explains how this second stage is related to the first: Our goals in a situation are formed in order to restore our equilibrium, i.e., we decide to go to lunch (goal) in order to satisfy our hunger (impulse), or we decide to sing loud (goal) in order to satisfy our uneasiness (impulse) in the social situation. That is, individuals define goals, and they perceive and define objects in situations in order to maintain an equilibrium that has been upset. Or we might more simply state that in every situation the individual defines goals for himself or herself, selects and defines objects to meet those goals, and acts overtly. We need not try to relate this second stage to the impulse, as Mead found necessary. We are active naturally! And part of that activity—a very important part—is defining goals for ourselves and perceiving objects in our environment in relation to these goals.

Stage 3: Manipulation

In the third stage humans manipulate their environment, act in it, handle it, and come "into contact with the relevant aspects" (Shibutani, 1961:68), using objects according to goals they have defined for themselves. Humans manipulate the things and persons by physically handling them, talking to them, breaking them, writing letters to them, or caressing them. We act toward objects overtly, after the foundations have been laid in stages one and two, both covert phases.

Mead emphasizes the importance of human hands, the ability to take physical objects, dissect them, put them together with other objects, change them, use them in a creative way. We become aware of the object, we plan a use for it, we then alter its use. We handle objects in situation as tools, as means to an end, as objects whose purpose lies in the future. We thus manipulate objects physically in the present to achieve future goals.

Stage 4: Consummation

This stage, consummation, is the end of the act—the goal achieved and the "restoration of equilibrium" (Shibutani, 1961:68-69) even though only for a moment. Acts are not always consummated, since we may start another act before ending an act, focusing our attention on something else, shifting our stream of action. After consummation, if it takes place, another sequence of impulse, perception and definition, manipulation, and consummation takes place, and the stream of action continues.

The importance of Mead's description is the fact that humans *actively* perceive, define, and manipulate their environment to achieve goals. This point was emphasized when we discussed the mind in Chapter 7. Activity is not only overt manipulation, but much of it—indeed, most of it, some would say—is covert, minded activity (found especially in Mead's second stage). Covert activity is action a person takes toward the self, primarily pointing things out to it about the situation but also analyzing it (the self), judging it, identifying it, controlling it, and directing it. The overt action (the third stage) is action toward objects that have been perceived, defined, and manipulated covertly, objects toward which a line of action has been developed. Blumer beautifully summarizes this whole process of definition and action:

> Action is built up in coping with the world instead of merely being released from a pre-existing psychological structure by factors playing on that structure. By making indications to himself and by interpreting what he indicates, the human being has to forge or piece together a line of action. In order to act the individual has to identify what he wants, establish an objective or goal, map out a prospective line of behavior, note and interpret the actions of others, size up his situation, check himself at this or that point, figure out what to do at other points, and frequently spur himself on in the face of dragging dispositions or discouraging settings. The fact that the human act is self-directed or built-up means in no sense that the actor necessarily exercises excellence in its construction. Indeed, he may do a very poor job in constructing his act. . . . What he takes into account are the things that he indicates to himself. They cover such matters as his wants, his feelings, his goals, the actions of others, the expectations and demands of others, the rules of his

group, his situation, his conceptions of himself, his recollections, and his images of prospective lines of conduct. (1966:536-37)*

We do not "release" action, but we construct it, we define self and situation, we establish goals and determine lines of action toward objects, then overt action takes place: this, in essence, is the importance of Mead's stages of the act.

COVERT AND OVERT ACTION

Covert and overt activity are not always easy to distinguish. We talk to ourselves, for example, and we sometimes end up talking out loud. We think of a tune, then hum it, only to be embarrassed on finding out that we have an audience. We give things to others, clearly overt action, then we suddenly realize that we gave too much, then we fumble all over the place with words and hands, and we try to recover part of what we gave. Our action is a constant interplay between overt and covert activity, each affecting the other. Mead brilliantly describes the intimate connection between the two, and that is Mead's importance. The act, he says, begins with covert activity, then flows into overt activity. But the process is never-ending since what we do overtly is, in turn, analyzed covertly.

Mead describes the usual <u>covert activity as *slow deliberate rehearsal*</u> of an <u>overt act</u>. We all catch ourselves carefully deliberating now and then in the way that Mead describes, but Mead does not mean that covert activity is limited only to slow, conscious deliberation. Indeed it is applicable to all situations we encounter:

> There is a field, a sort of an inner forum, in which we are the only spectators and the only actors. In that field each one of us confers with himself. We carry on something of a drama. If a person retires to a secluded spot and sits down to think, he talks to himself. He asks and answers questions. He develops his ideas and arranges and organizes those ideas as he might do in conversation with somebody else. He may prefer talking to himself to talking to somebody else. He is a more appreciative audience, perhaps. . . . He takes different roles. He asks questions and meets them; presents arguments and refutes them. . . . We will say he is thinking out what he is going to say in an important situation, an argument which he is going to present in court, a speech in the legislature. That process which goes on inside of him is only the beginning of the process which is finally carried on in an assembly. It is just a part of the whole thing, and the fact that he talks to himself rather than to the assembly is simply an indication of the beginning of a process which is carried on outside. (Mead, 1936:401-2)†

*Reprinted from "Sociological Implications of the Thought of George Herbert Mead," by Herbert Blumer in *The American Journal of Sociology,* by permission of The University of Chicago Press. Copyright © 1966 by The University of Chicago.

†Reprinted from *Movements of Thought in the 19th Century* by George Herbert Mead, ed. Merritt H. Moore, by permission of The University of Chicago Press. Copyright © 1936 by The University of Chicago.

I think of my question before I raise my hand. I rehearse my lectures before I give them. I tell myself you are a fool and that I must tell you that—then I actually do tell you. Sometimes my "inner forum" takes place long before I do my act for an audience, more usually it is very close to the overt action. And it continues to go on while my action is aimed at the audience out there. John Dewey presents the same picture:

> We begin with a summary assertion that deliberation is a dramatic rehearsal (in imagination) of various competing possible lines of action. ... Deliberation is an experiment in finding out what the various lines of possible action are really like. It is an experiment making various combinations of selected elements of habits and impulses, to see what the resultant action would be like if it were entered upon. But the trial is in imagination, not in overt fact. The experiment is carried on by tentative rehearsals in thought which do not affect physical facts outside the body. Thought runs ahead and foresees outcomes, and thereby avoids having to await the instruction of actual failure and disaster. An act overtly tried out is irrevocable, the consequences cannot be blotted out. An act tried out in imagination is not final or fatal. It is retrievable. (1922:190)

Human action in the symbolic interactionist perspective, because it involves forming definitions, establishing goals, designating social objects, problem solving, and understanding and communicating symbols, is thought to arise principally from a continuous stream of covert action. Mind action is forever with us.

HABITUAL ACTION

Of course, our activity is not always a matter of careful deliberation, of contrasting competing lines of action. As we emphasized in the chapter on mind, it is when we are confronted by interruptions in our flow of activity, where we are faced with serious "problems," that we become more aware and deliberate. However, every situation poses problems to be worked out, goals to be achieved, and objects to be defined, so we are really talking here of *degree* of awareness and deliberation. Habitual action is overt action that does not involve covert activity. Habitual action may take us through some situations. We may be able to "respond" without thinking, based entirely on past learning, but usually some covert activity enters in, some definition of the situation is established by the individual, some analysis of past and future is made, and some definition of objects in that situation is done. Habitual action is functional, allowing the individual to act without waiting; it is good where immediate response is necessary. On the other hand, action that is purely habitual is dysfunctional for most situations, since each situation is unique to some degree and, to be handled appropriately, demands some definition and self-direction, some alteration of previous action. Walking to work in the morning may become highly habitual to us, but often we must tell ourselves to speed up or slow down or watch out for a car at this intersection, or we must adjust to an increase in traffic, perhaps by taking a slightly different route. Driving a car may also be a highly habitual act, but that too is loaded with covert action—giving ourselves direction and acting toward lights, other cars, pedestrians, and detours. Indeed, the more habitual we are, the less prepared we become for alterations in situations that demand some adjustment on our part. Perhaps we can afford habitual action for *small, simple acts* (putting the key in the ignition, putting on the seat belt, putting the car in gear), but when the acts are conceptualized as larger than these simple motor movements (driving a car or driving a car to work or driving a car to California), we must rely less on habitual response and more and more on covert definition and interpretation. Purely habitual action would be especially inappropriate to activities where other people are involved, since the individual must constantly make adjustments to an ever-changing interaction situation. Definition and analysis of self and others are absolutely essential to working out social situations.

Purely habitual action is probably extremely rare, except for some small, simple acts we perform; covert activity, in which humans must define situations and determine lines of action, becomes the rule. In some cases careful deliberation is necessary. In others covert activity moves right along at a fast pace, accompanying overt action, not noticed by us unless someone points it out to us. But it is there if we only stop and analyze what we do.

THE PAST, THE PRESENT, AND THE FUTURE IN ACTION

Needless to say, action always takes place in the present. We act *now,* and when we are through our act becomes part of our past. Past is massive, the present is a split second. Although we act *now,* past and future are part of our action. It is not so much that the past and future *cause* what we do now; it is not that our action is a result of our past actions or a result of forces from our past but that past and future are *considered* by us as we act. Both are part of our definition of the situation. The future, for example, is part of our action in that we plan our acts. The present is influenced by our conception of the future. Mead calls an "attitude" the "internal organization of the act," (Troyer, 1946:199), the plan of action we develop for an object, the future we have in store for it. In this sense, the "later stages of the act are present in the early stages" (Mead, 1934:11), what we do now is affected by what we imagine in the future.

> If one approaches a distant object he approaches it with reference to what he is going to do when he arrives there. If one is approaching a hammer he is muscularly all ready to seize the handle of the hammer. The later stages of the act are present in the early stages—not simply in the sense that they are all ready to go off, but in the sense that they serve to control the process itself. They determine how we are going to approach the object, and the steps in our early manipulation of it. (1934:11)*

Humans are planners. We reflect on the future when we act. When faced with a problem, we consider various lines of action, considering consequences of each line, and then we go with a strategy which seems best for us. The importance of the future for understanding human intelligence is underlined by Mead:

> When . . . we speak of reflective conduct we very definitely refer to the presence of the future in terms of ideas. The intelligent man as distinguished from the intelligent animal presents to himself what is going to happen. The animal may act in such a way as to insure its food tomorrow. A squirrel hides nuts, but we do not hold that the squirrel has a picture of what is going to happen. The young squirrel is born in the summer time and has no directions from other forms, but it will start hiding nuts as well as the older ones. Such action shows that experience could not direct the activity of the specific form. The provident man, however, does definitely pursue a certain course, pictures a certain situation, and directs his own conduct with reference to it. The squirrel follows certain blind impulses, and the carrying-out of its impulses leads to the same result that the storing of grain does for the provident man. It is this picture, however, of what the future is to be as determining our present conduct that is the characteristic of human intelligence—the future as present in terms of ideas. (1934:119)

Not only do we act out of consideration for the future, but the past also plays an important role in what we do. The symbolic interactionist means not that what we do now is *caused* by the past but that the past experiences of the individual are used to help determine the kind of action to take in a situation. "Intelligence is essentially the ability to solve the problems of *present* behavior in terms of its possible *future* consequences as implicated on the basis of *past* experience. . . . it involves both memory and foresight" (Mead, 1934:100). The past is the remembered experience we use to make sense out of the present and the future.

> The ability to keep this past conveniently present for what Mead liked to call the "area of manipulation" is the measure of whatever presence-of-mind one may have to anticipate the still undetermined future. In this way a present becomes eventful and meaningful, and of indefinite extent in space-time. (Schneider, 1973:87)

We draw freely from our past. It contains our experiences, our significant others, our reference groups, our perspectives. Any of these are available to us to apply to the present, to analyze self and situation, and to look into the future in order to analyze consequences of what we do. The past is rich for us, and it provides us with the tools to define the present. The past changes every second, since the present is always moving forward, with new experiences being added to it. Further, our past is always changing because our new experiences, the new situations we encounter, and the new perspectives we come to believe in reinterpret the past and cause us to see it altered. As a society we are increasingly rewriting our past: blacks, women, and American Indians, to name a few groups, are clearly restructuring our past for us, causing us to see it anew, and that is affecting what we do *now.* It is also true of our personal biographies: The man who becomes a parent sees his own parents in a new light and understands their anxieties, hopes, and feelings when he was a child. He is redefining his past, as is the adult who looks back twenty years at his high school days fully remembering some beautiful moments, conveniently forgetting the horrors of adolescence experienced at the time.

The future and the past are therefore "social objects" to the actor. A memory is applied to the present; a future consequence is considered in the present. Like all else, the past and future change as we change our uses for them.

The focus is always on present action. "The past and the future do not exist in themselves, but are the past and the future of a particular present. The past is a different past for every particular present; a new present means a new past and a new future." (Tillman, 1970:537) Memory brings "the past into the present," and imagination brings "the future into the present" (Tillman, 1970:541).

ACTION AND MOTIVES

According to the symbolic interactionist, individuals are goal-directed. We are constantly determining lines of action toward objects in keeping with our goals. Goals are not static, and therefore lines of action are constantly shifting. Whatever is done at a given moment must be understood as having developed over a period of time, with a number of factors contributing to the direction of action at different points, with goals in mind shifting, objects being redefined, and other people's acts affecting direction. Action is to be explained not by deep-seated stable motives but by shifting goals and definitions of the situation.

The distinction between motives and goals is a subtle but very important one. If we imagine human action as being the result of individual *motives,* there is a tendency to see action determined by an internal state, stable over time, having little to do with individual definition of situations encountered. Motives are conceptualized as internal states, preceding situations and action, and motives are thought to stay relatively stable in situations guiding the actor, despite the interaction that takes place there. If goals are emphasized in our analysis of human action, a rational process is seen as taking place, the human is conceptualized as defining and redefining situations and action according to a number of factors in the *situation,* and the situation, including the action of others, becomes an important variable in what is done by the individual. The point is that human action is now conceptualized as a stream of action.

Yet motives are important in a sense. Humans *impute motives*—we explain each other's behavior through assigning motives. Motives are the *stated* reasons for an act, the *verbalized* cause of human action, which assumes intentions on the part of the actor. You kept my money because you "cheated me," because you wanted to take advantage of my weakness in order to get rich; or you treated me to lunch because you need me for your friend; or you saved that man from drowning because you are a loving person and were doing a decent thing in light of the danger facing you. Whatever the many complex reasons for our action going in a certain direction, the explanation we usually give is filled with motives. Motives, however, are *oversimplified* explanations of human action, which we all make as we interact with each other. They are important in the sense that what we *say* is the reason for our act or the acts of others makes a difference in what we do. Motives are attempts by people to summarize and make some sense out of complex acts. They are labels, summary statements, of reasons we give that some act occurs. Brissett and Edgeley (1975:6) define motives as communications used "to justify or rationalize the conduct of the actors . . . [and] enable certain interactions to persist." Both Max Weber and C. Wright Mills describe motives in this same vein: motives are verbalized explanations of behavior, and as such serve to explain, rationalize, or condemn one's own acts or the acts of others.

One reason, then, that we impute motives is that we are better able to separate the good guys from the bad guys. There are, to all of us, acceptable and unacceptable motives. When we observe others and impute unacceptable motives to them, we may withdraw from interaction. Or, if we examine our own acts and find our motives questionable, we may change what we do. We may act toward others in order to give the impression that our motives are good ones, and they, we may assume, do the same in their acts. Motives are important, therefore, for understanding how people come to explain and rationalize each other's acts and their own acts in a relatively simple way. In symbolic interactionism it is this *definition* of self and other that are important variables in each situation. Our labels of each other, although oversimplified perhaps, lead us to smile at the other, put the other in prison, go out on a date with the other, marry the other, vote for the other, or make fun of the other.

In sum, humans act to achieve goals in situations, to solve problems that confront them. In effect they engage in a stream of complex action, the direction of which shifts because of decisions made, influenced by interaction with others and with self. That action is interpreted by the actors as springing from some motivational state for purposes of understanding, or justifying, or condemning the action. Whether or not a single motive—stated or unstated—is indeed the cause of the action is an empirical question. It may or it may not be, but alone it usually is not. To emphasize motive, however, is to divert attention away from action as a stream of action with a history, directed by actors defining goals and objects as the action unfolds over time.

ACTION AND CHOICE

Action in the end means *choice* in the symbolic interactionist perspective, at least to some degree. Humans *act* and do not just *react* to their world. Humans determine their lines of action toward objects, they redefine situations, and they revise their lines of action. They consider past experience and balance future consequences of their acts. Their action is a combination of both overt and covert activity, a result of interpreting and controlling direction of the stream of action. Mead states that ideas are "possibilities of overt responses which we test out implicitly in the central nervous system and then reject in favor of those which we do in fact act upon or carry into effect. The process of intelligent conduct is essentially a process of selection from among various alternatives; intelligence is largely a matter of selectivity" (1934:99). All this implies active thinking, choice, self-direction. It is, to Mead, "delayed response," holding back action, that makes possible deliberation and choice:

> The central nervous system, in short, enables the individual to exercise conscious control over his behavior. It is the possibility of delayed response which principally differentiates reflective conduct from non-reflective conduct in which the response is always immediate. (1934:117)

Action is conscious control, selection, deliberation, holding back, self-direction, self-controlled, reflective—action is here described as individuals *actively* determining their own direction. The human is regarded here as one of the most important causes of his or her own action through interaction with self. Freedom is indeed one of the key elements in Mead's thought. According to Desmonde, who is here interpreting Mead,

> Through man's capacity to readjust his developing acts to his anticipations of the future, he achieves freedom. The knowledge of what is necessary enables us to make an appropriate adjustment to that reality when it eventuates. We are not bound by the past, but can utilize the past to prepare for the future. (1957:39)

And Meltzer (1972:20) casually points out: "Needless to say, this view contradicts the stimulus-response conception of human behavior."

SOCIAL ACTION

Thus far we have discussed the meaning of action, but we have not considered *social action* to any extent. Warriner, as we said earlier, defines social action as action that is labeled by people and thus pulled out from the stream of action. However, although Warriner describes an important idea, we pointed out then that "social action" is usually used to refer to something else.

The most commonly used definition of social action, and the one that makes good sense in the symbolic interactionist perspective, is this: that action is social action when the individual orients his or her acts to others besides self. Action is social in the sense that we act, to a great extent, for others as well as for ourselves. Others make a difference to us when we act. They are important "social objects" to us. We take others into account. We are influenced by other people's presence. For example, we try to influence other people's acts, or we try to influence their view of us, we share something with others, we help others, we hurt them, we love, we reject, we aid, we destroy, but almost everything we do, we do in part, because of other people's presence. In each case, others are social objects used in a situation. That makes action social action. Max Weber held this view of social action. It is, he said, action oriented to others, action meant to have some influence on others as well as on one's self. Herbert Blumer calls this process *taking the other into account:*

> In my judgment, the most important feature of human association is that the participants *take each other into account.* . . . Taking another person into account means being aware of him, identifying him in some way, making some judgment or appraisal of him, identifying the meaning of his action, trying to find out what he has on his mind or trying to figure out what he intends to do. Such awareness of another person in this sense of taking him and his acts into consideration becomes the occasion for orienting oneself and for the direction of one's own conduct. (1953:194)

Thus social action is action influenced by the presence of another. If I dress for others as well as for myself, that is social action. If I throw a ball at others, that is social action. If I remain quiet in order not to disturb others in the library, this is social action. If I walk down the street with others "in mind," and if my action is affected in some way by their presence—if their presence makes a difference in how I act—then my walking is social action.

Social action is acting with others in mind. That means there is usually some attempt to *communicate something* to the other, even though that attempt may be quite subtle. If my action has others in mind, then I am trying to tell others something (or for that matter, I can purposely try not to communicate something, to be anonymous, and that is an attempt to communicate anonymity). Social action, therefore, is symbolic action: The actor does something *meant* to *stand for* something to others. Talking to others is obviously social action, but so is almost everything else we do. Social action tells them something about me, tells them I'm good, I'm kind, I'm in a hurry, I'm strong, or I'm about to hit someone. Social action tells other people what we are, what we were, and what we are about to do. It tells others our ideas, our perspectives, our wants, our motives, our intentions, our morals, our background, our strengths, our identity. If we think about it, almost all of our action is around other people, and if we think about it further, whenever we are around others we are intentionally communicating something to them. Other people are thus very important to what we do; they are important social objects moving in and out of our stream of action, and their presence (or even imagined presence) affects what we do. Human beings are social actors through and through:

> Inclinations, impulses, wishes and feelings may have to be restrained in the light of what one takes into account and in the light of how one judges or interprets what one takes into account. The presence of the other and his developing acts become occasions for the orientation of one's own act and thus provide the incidents of experience which lead one as he is guiding his own

action to check himself at this point or that point, to withhold expression of given feelings and to recognize that certain wishes must be held in abeyance. (Blumer, 1953:197)

Social action, then, is action that takes others into account. Taking others into account affects what we do both overtly and covertly. We act differently because of the presence of others. When we act socially (with others in mind) we are usually attempting to communicate something to them. And since others act back with us in mind, their action is also social and symbolic, and thus human action becomes *social symbolic interaction.* That will be our focus in Chapter 10.

REFERENCES

BLUMER, HERBERT
  1953 "Psychological Import of the Human Group." in eds. Muzafer Sherif and M. O. Wilson, *Group Relations at the Crossroads,* pp. 185–202. New York: Harper & Row.
  1966 "Sociological Implications of the Thought of George Herbert Mead." *American Journal of Sociology* 71:535–44. By permission of The University of Chicago Press. Copyright © 1966 by The University of Chicago.
  1969 *Symbolic Interactionism: Perspective and Method.* Englewood Cliffs, N.J.: Prentice-Hall, Inc. Copyright © 1969. Reprinted by permission of Prentice-Hall, Inc.
  1981 "Conversation with Thomas J. Morrioni and Harvey A. Farberman." *Symbolic Interaction* 4:9–22.
BRISSETT, DENNIS, and CHARLES EDGLEY
  1975 *Life as Theater.* Chicago: Aldine.
DESMONDE, WILLIAM H.
  1957 "George Herbert Mead and Freud: American Social Psychology and Psychoanalysis." In ed. Benjamin Nelson *Psychoanalysis and the Future,* pp. 31–50. New York: Psychological Association for Psychoanalysis.
DEWEY, JOHN
  1922 *Human Nature and Conduct.* New York: Modern Library.
McCALL, GEORGE J., and J. L. SIMMONS
  1966 *Identities and Interactions.* New York: Free Press. Reprinted with permission of Macmillan Publishing Co., Inc. Copyright © 1966 by The Free Press, a division of The Macmillan Company.
MEAD, GEORGE HERBERT
  1934 *Mind, Self and Society.* Chicago: The University of Chicago Press. Reprinted by permission of The University of Chicago. Copyright © 1934 by The University of Chicago. All rights reserved.
  1936 *Movements of Thought in the 19th Century.* Ed. Merritt H. Moore. Chicago: University of Chicago Press. Reprinted by permission of The University of Chicago Press. Copyright © 1936 by The University of Chicago. All rights reserved.

MELTZER, BERNARD N.
> 1972 *The Social Psychology of George Herbert Mead.* Kalamazoo: Center for Sociological Research, Western Michigan University. By permission of Bernard N. Meltzer.

PFUETZ, PAUL
> 1961 *Self, Society, Existence.* New York: Harper & Row.

SCHNEIDER, HERBERT W.
> 1973 "Presence-Dasein." In ed. Walter Robert Corti, *The Philosophy of George Herbert Mead,* pp. 83–106. Winterthur, Switzerland: Amriswiler Bucherei.

SHIBUTANI, TAMOTSU
> 1961 *Society and Personality: An Interactionist Approach to Social Psychology.* Englewood Cliffs, N.J.: Prentice-Hall, Inc. Copyright © 1961. Reprinted by permission of Prentice-Hall, Inc.

STONE, GREGORY P., and HARVEY A. FARBERMAN
> 1970 *Social Psychology through Symbolic Interaction.* Waltham, Mass.: Ginn-Blaisdell.

THRASHER, FREDERIC M.
> 1936 *The Gang.* Chicago: University of Chicago Press. By permission of The University of Chicago Press and William E. Girton. Copyright © 1927 by The University of Chicago. All rights reserved.

TILLMAN, MARY KATHERINE
> 1970 "Temporality and Role-taking in G. H. Mead." *Social Research* 37 533–46.

TROYER, WILLIAM LEWIS
> 1946 "Mead's Social and Functional Theory of Mind." *American Sociological Review* 11:198–202.

WARRINER, CHARLES K.
> 1970 *The Emergence of Society.* Homewood, Ill.: Dorsey Press. By permission of the Dorsey Press.

10
INTERACTION

Interaction means *mutual social action,* individuals communicating *to each other* in what they do, orienting their acts to each other.

> What are some examples of social interaction? A conversation, a knife fight, a chess game, love-making. None of these things can be done by one. It takes two to tango, just as it takes two bodies to produce gravitational attraction or two electrons to produce electrostatic repulsion. None of these things can be viewed simply as a result of two independent units simultaneously unwinding their self-determined lines of action. The action of one unit is dependent upon the action of the other, *and vice versa.* . . . There must be mutual influence. . . . (McCall and Simmons, 1966:48–49)*

SYMBOLIC INTERACTION

Thus we arrive at the significance of *symbolic interaction:* humans are constantly acting in relation to each other, communicating symbolically in almost everything they do. This interaction has meaning to both the giver and the receiver of the ac-

*Reprinted with permission of Macmillan Publishing Co., Inc., from *Identities and Interactions* by George J. McCall and J. L. Simmons. Copyright © 1966 by the Free Press, a division of the Macmillan Company.

tion, thus requiring both persons to interact symbolically with themselves as they interact with each other. That is obvious when we talk to each other, but it is also true, when we sing a song or dance, frown, run, walk, jump up in the air, shake our fists, or do all the other things that we do in relation to others. Most human action is social and it is symbolic, and further, most social action is really interaction. Individuals, according to Blumer, "are caught up in a vast process of interaction in which they have to fit their developing actions to one another. This process of interaction consists of making indications to others of what to do and in interpreting the indications as made by others" (1969:20).

"We modify our own lines of action," McCall and Simmons point out, "on the basis of what we perceive alter's implications to be with respect to our manifest and latent plans of action" (1966:136). I determine a line of action, act overtly. The other (alter) acts overtly toward me, and I interpret what that act means (represents) in light of my own act. I alter my line of action slightly or to a great extent. The other must do the same in acting toward me. The conceptualization of actors constantly shifting what they do in relation to what others do is a highly complex view of the human being. We must interpret the other, and we must communicate to the other, and the other, in turn, must alter his or her direction accordingly. This is a constant, never-ending process.

> Symbolic interaction involves *interpretation,* or ascertaining the meaning of the actions or remarks of the other person, and *definition,* or conveying indications to another person as to how he is to act. Human association consists of a process of such interpretation and definition. Through this process the participants fit their own acts to the ongoing acts of one another and guide others in doing so. (Blumer, 1966:537–38)

Human interaction is symbolic through and through. It is not the interaction of billiard balls, or ants, or baseballs and bats, or teeth, or birds, or bees. When you push me out of line, I interpret your act, and then I act toward you. When I push you back, you, in turn, interpret my act. We may end up in a fist fight or in a conversation about the movie we are about to see or in an argument with several people around us who don't care for our playing. In fact, we may very well end up very differently from the way we meant to end up: a shove that was meant as a joke could end up being interpreted as too strong for a joke. That was the point we made in the chapters on symbols: our acts in relation to each other are symbolic—we intend to communicate, and we interpret others' acts as intending to communicate. Mead emphasizes acts as symbolic in his description of "significant gestures," the human act that has meaning both to the actor and to the other toward whom the actor gestures. Other animals gesture, and the act does indeed lead to a response in the other, but the "conversation of gestures" between other animals is not "significant," that is, it is without symbolic meaning, and thinking is not part of the interaction:

The act of each dog becomes the stimulus to the other dog for his response. There is then a relationship between these two; and as the act is responded to by the other dog, it, in turn, undergoes change. The very fact that the dog is ready to attack another becomes a stimulus to the other dog to change his own position or his own attitude. He has no sooner done this than the change of attitude in the second dog in turn causes the first dog to change his attitude. We have here a conversation of gestures. They are not, however, gestures in the sense that they are significant. We do not assume that the dog says to himself, "If the animal comes from this direction, he is going to spring at my throat and I will turn in such a way." What does take place is an actual change in his own position due to the direction of the approach of the other dog. (Mead, 1934:42–43)*

"The term 'gesture,'" Mead continues, "may be identified with these beginnings of social acts which are stimuli for the responses of other forms" (1934:43). Animals act and other animals respond to that act. It is when the act represents something to both the actor and the other that it becomes a *significant* gesture, a symbol: "If somebody shakes his fist in your face you assume . . . not only a hostile attitude but . . . some idea behind it. You assume that it means not only a possible attack, but that the individual has an idea in his experience." (Mead, 1934:45) Mead is emphasizing that your fist represents to *you* what you're about to do to me. Human words, many human objects, and most human acts represent and communicate, and meaning is assigned by the one who *acts* as well as by the other. Human interaction is a series of significant gestures, vocal and nonvocal.

The dogs are not talking to each other; there are no ideas in the minds of the dogs; nor do we assume that the dog is trying to convey an idea to the other dog. But if the gesture, in the case of the human individual, has parallel to it a certain psychical state which is the idea of what the person is going to do, and if this gesture calls out a like gesture in the other individual and calls out a similar idea, then it becomes a significant gesture. It stands for the ideas in the minds of both of them. (Mead, 1934:48)

Symbolic Interaction as Cause

What happens between actors at any single moment is not determined simply by an attitude, a motive, an opinion, or the memory of a previous experience that each brings to the situation from other places. These predispositions to act in a given direction may or may not play some role in the interaction. Significant others, reference groups, and perspectives also should not be seen as the *cause* of our action. It is important to regard the interaction itself between the actors as well as the interaction within each actor as central factors influencing the direction of the action. Factors outside the situation may exert some influence, but that influence is tempered, altered, and reinterpreted by the actors, who are defining and redefining themselves and each other as the interaction continues. Blumer emphasizes that the individual's behavior, accordingly:

> is not a result of such things as environmental pressures, stimuli, motives, attitudes, and ideas but arises instead from how he interprets and handles these things in the action which he is constructing. The process of self-indication by means of which human action is formed cannot be accounted for by factors which precede the act. The process of self-indication exists in its own right and must be accepted and studied as such. It is through this process that the human being constructs his conscious action. (1962:183)

Outside factors such as past experiences, significant others, reference groups, and perspectives are indeed important, especially in the initial stages of the interaction, since they play key roles in defining the situation. As the interaction takes place, however, they are always altered to deal with the specific situation. Interaction is *mutual* social action: action where individuals take each other into account when they act and are thus at least partially affected by each other.

> Put simply, human beings in interacting with one another have to take account of what each . . . is doing or is about to do; they are forced to direct their own conduct or handle their situations in terms of what they take into account. Thus, the activities of others enter as positive factors in the formation of their own conduct; in the face of the actions of others one may abandon an intention or purpose, revise it, check or suspend it, intensify it, or replace it. . . . One has to *fit* one's own line of activity in some manner to the actions of others. The actions of others have to be taken into account and cannot be regarded as merely an arena for the expression of what one is disposed to do or sets out to do. (Blumer, 1969:8)

Our acts have histories, and much of the history concerns interaction with others. It is not that I commit murder because something happened to me fifteen years ago, or that I got a college degree because I became interested in school at the age of six, or that I have a job teaching school because that is what my father did. To understand isolated acts it is important to understand the interaction between others and myself that led up to these acts, to see that my decisions at one point are a result of a whole series of interacting situations as well as my definition of these situations. It is important for us to step out of the perspectives that see actions as caused by single predispositional factors within the individual and to focus instead on the interaction with others and with self.

> The central point [is] that human interaction is a positive shaping process in its own right. The participants in it have to build up their respective lines of conduct by constant interpretation of each other's ongoing lines of action. (Blumer, 1966:538)

Shibutani states this even more directly:

> *The direction taken by a person's conduct is seen as something that is constructed in the reciprocal give and take of interdependent men who are adjusting to one another.* Furthermore, a man's personality—those distinctive behavior patterns that characterize a given individual—*is regarded as developing and being reaffirmed from day to day in his interaction with his associates.* (1961:23)

It is important to emphasize: To understand the individual's action there must be a full consideration of interaction with others and with self. Humans act with others in mind—they communicate and they interpret others. Their acts unfold in relation both to each other and to the definitions of each other's actions.

Symbolic Interaction: A Summary

To describe what happens in interaction, we might try to dissect the situation carefully (albeit artificially, since situations and interaction must first of all be described as *dynamic*). The symbolic interactionist sees actors coming to situations with significant others and reference groups, with symbols, perspectives, selfhood, and mind, and with role-taking ability. Each actor has a past to draw on to help define the situation, and each has a view of the future. The actors give meaning to situations using these tools, sometimes paying particular attention to those with whom they interact in the situation, often using those outside the situation as guides. The manner in which *living actors* analyze the situation is diagrammed in Figure 10-1.

INTERACTION AND DEFINITION

The dynamic nature of interaction and definition is somehow lost on the printed page. But we can capture the very basics. Definitions and interpretations are rapidly developed and transformed in interaction. Where there is time for deliberation, such as in games or in dealing with "serious problems," all of the steps are evident. However, any individual faced with any problem involving others must also carefully but quickly go through these steps, and as has been emphasized throughout this book, every situation poses some problem to be worked out. Familiar situations are easily defined and do not take extensive deliberation. As others act back, however, we must redefine and alter our definition accordingly, and usually that means going from the "familiar" to the less familiar, from the usual definitions to the idiosyncrasies of the social situation. We apply to the situation a perspective learned in interaction elsewhere, and because it seems appropriate, we begin to put things in place according to that perspective. Since we are active in the situation, we continue to analyze ourselves and others, we determine a line of action, we alter that

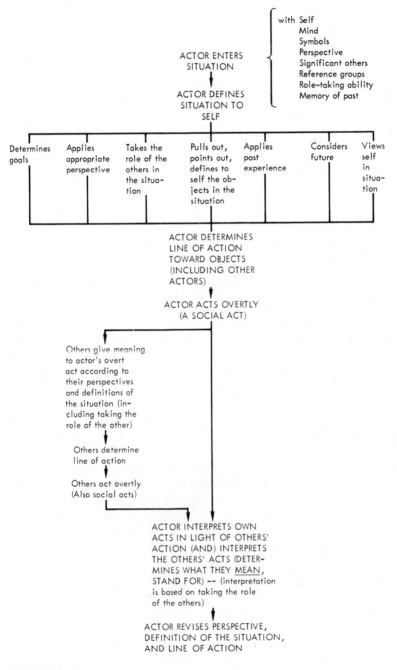

ACTOR ENTERS
SITUATION

with Self
Mind
Symbols
Perspective
Significant others
Reference groups
Role-taking ability
Memory of past

ACTOR DEFINES
SITUATION TO
SELF

| Determines goals | Applies appropriate perspective | Takes the role of the others in the situation | Pulls out, points out, defines to self the objects in the situation | Applies past experience | Considers future | Views self in situation |

ACTOR DETERMINES
LINE OF ACTION
TOWARD OBJECTS
(INCLUDING OTHER
ACTORS)

ACTOR ACTS OVERTLY
(A SOCIAL ACT)

Others give meaning
to actor's overt
act according to
their perspectives
and definitions of
the situation (in-
cluding taking the
role of the other)

Others determine
line of action

Others act overtly
(Also social acts)

ACTOR INTERPRETS OWN
ACTS IN LIGHT OF OTHERS'
ACTION (AND) INTERPRETS
THE OTHERS' ACTS (DETER-
MINES WHAT THEY MEAN,
STAND FOR) -- (interpretation
is based on taking the role
of the others)

ACTOR REVISES PERSPECTIVE,
DEFINITION OF THE SITUATION,
AND LINE OF ACTION

FIGURE 10-1

line of action, and our action changes as others act in relation to us after going through the same kind of analysis. It becomes impossible to predict with a high degree of accuracy the action of individuals in giving meaning, taking the role of the other, using and altering perspectives, and so forth. That is why analysis of interaction is so difficult: so much is going on between and within actors. If we add to this the fact that as we interact we may come to share a perspective with those in the situation, putting aside perspectives we brought to the situation, the complexity increases greatly. Indeed, one of the most important principles describing interaction is that as people interact over time, they come to *share,* and sharing inevitably brings a greater opportunity for cooperation, accurate role taking, and predictable action on the part of each actor. Continuous interaction and the sharing that results comes to replace the outside perspective for defining the world. Those who excel at "brainwashing" know this principle well.

Definition of the Situation

Throughout this book, and especially in these two chapters on action, it has been emphasized that humans act in a world that they define. We enter a host of situations, most of them social, define those situations according to a perspective, pull out the objects in those situations that are important for our goals, and then act. It is a continuous process of defining and acting overtly. The central importance of this process is captured in a phrase that has become central to the symbolic interactionist perspective: definition of the situation. William and Dorothy Thomas capture the importance of this concept in their brilliant and simple pronouncement: "If men define situations as real, they are real in their consequences" (1928:572). Humans, this implies, do not respond to a world out there, but to a reality actively defined by them. In the end, it does not matter if you are a scoundrel or not; what matters is that I see you as a scoundrel and I act toward you as if you were one. And you, in turn, may not be a scoundrel, but you may accept my definition of you as one and then proceed to act that way. If I see a situation as threatening, then I will act accordingly, even if people in that situation did not mean to appear threatening. If I define school as hard or good or silly, then I will act toward school in that manner, no matter if others feel as I do and no matter if it is in reality harder, better, sillier than other schools. Our realities are our definitions of situations. Definitions of the situation may be influenced by others (indeed they usually are), but in the end, each individual must define the situation through engaging in mind activity. We each act in a world that we create through interaction with others and through interaction with our self.

Donald Ball (1972:63) describes the definition of the situation as "*sum total of all recognized information, from the point-of-view of the actor, which is relevant to his locating himself and others, so that he can engage in self-determined lines of action and interaction.*" It is, as we have described throughout this book, the social objects the actor regards as relevant for action. It is a "social construction of reality," and its consequences are real in terms of the overt action that takes place. Most important for interaction, other people and their acts become an important part of our definition of the situation.

This concept should not be lightly put aside. "Definition of the situation" is especially relevant to interaction. When we interact we must define others, we label them, based perhaps on what they do or how they are dressed or what we have heard or based on the identity that they declare to us. Our label defines who they are for us and we act accordingly. We sometimes stereotype others; that is, we apply a negative label to them based on a single piece of information and refuse to change the label as we interact. More often, we label those we interact with very tentatively and during interaction come to revise our definition of them many times over. The label we apply may be easy for us in some situations, difficult in others.

> For example, if we walk into a theater and find a man in nonmilitary uniform standing expectantly at the door, we know automatically that he is a ticket-taker and that we must present to him valid tickets if we wish to continue into the theater. The ticket-taker is not so labeled, nor is his uniform particularly distinctive, yet we do not have to ask why he is blocking our entrance, because the situation itself is so standardized in our culture that it provides sufficient clues as to the mutual implications of the persons involved. (McCall and Simmons, 1966:128)

Men are usually easy to distinguish from women, it is usually easy to label someone as very elderly or very young, we may label some people black and some white, and often we can even spot strangers in our city. Situations are often standardized and easy to define: a lecture class is a lecture class is a lecture class; a football game is a football game is a football game. But very often labeling other people and situations where we interact is more complicated, based on subtle, not clearly delineated, clues, and usually subject to a great deal of alteration as we interact.

> This clarity of circumstance does not obtain in every human encounter or even in the majority of them. In fact, it is most likely to occur in precisely such routine and superficial interactions as the exchange of a ticket for entrance to the theater. And even then, the interaction may "spill over" from the specified into other exchanges and responses if the ticket-taker has a curious haircut, is an attractive girl, or is the son of one's insurance man. (McCall and Simmons, 1966:128)

Through labeling others we draw on past experiences and guide ourselves through situations we encounter. Berger and Luckmann refer to labeling as applying "typifications":

> The reality of everyday life contains typificatory schemes in terms of which others are apprehended and "dealt with" in face-to-face encounters. Thus I apprehend the other as "a man," "a European," "a buyer," "a jovial type," and so on. All these typifications ongoingly affect my interaction with him as, say, I decide to show him a good time on the town before trying to sell him my product. Our face-to-face interaction will be patterned by these typi-

fications as long as they do not become problematic through interference on his part. Thus he may come up with evidence that, although "a man," "a European," and "a buyer," he is also a self-righteous moralist, and that what appeared first as joviality is actually an expression of contempt for Americans in general and American salesmen in particular. At this point, of course, my typificatory scheme will have to be modified, and the evening planned differently in accordance with this modification. Unless thus challenged, though, the typifications will hold until further notice and will determine my actions in the situation.

The typificatory schemes entering into face-to-face situations are, of course, reciprocal. The other also apprehends me in a typified way—as "a man," "an American," "a salesman," "an ingratiating fellow," and so on. The other's typifications are as susceptible to my interference as mine are to his. In other words, the two typificatory schemes enter into an ongoing "negotiation" in the face-to-face situation. In everyday life such "negotiation" is itself likely to be prearranged in a typical manner—as in the typical bargaining process between buyers and salesmen. Thus, most of the time, my encounters with others in everyday life are typical in a double sense—I apprehend the other *as* a type and I interact with him in a situation that is itself typical. (1966:30–31)*

Who people are and what situations are, are determined through interaction and redefinition, what Berger and Luckmann here refer to as a negotiation process. Defining others in situations will be based on the interpretation we give to their acts and words. Those are symbols we give meaning to, almost always a mixture of what the other intends to communicate and what he or she does not. We may jump to a conclusion before it is warranted, or we may be careful before we identify the other, but always definition of the other as an object, a social object, is part of interaction.

Our definition of the other person may even cause him or her to define self differently—the label we give may cause the other to think of self in this way. Robert Merton (1957:421) calls this the "self-fulfilling prophecy," which has now become a popular term describing this process. We act as though something were true of the other, and even though it may not be, the other, in turn, thinks of self in these terms and acts that way. We call students "dumb," children "bad," little girls "cute," women "emotional," men "aggressive," teachers "wise," homosexuals "sick." The labels define things as real, we act toward the objects as though the label were true, and the others, in turn, may think of themselves in this manner and act in such a way as to fulfill our definition. This process, of course, is not inevitable, since definitions can be made, labels applied, but the other's action can fail to conform to the definition and help create a new definition.

Definition of the Situation for Others

The "definition of the situation" is also an extremely important concept in another sense, one that is also central to *interaction*. Since we do define the world

*Excerpt from *The Social Construction of Reality,* copyright © 1966 by Peter L. Berger and Thomas Luckmann. Reprinted by permission of Doubleday & Company, Inc., New York, and Penguin Press, Harmondsworth, Middlesex, England.

we act in, and since most of us seem to know that, then we may well attempt to take steps to define situations *for others.* We may announce our identity, dress to kill, turn down the lights, put on that old phoney smile, paint our office white, or put spoiled milk in a sterile-looking tin container. The point is that the individual not only defines the situation for his or her own action, but also makes an effort to define each situation for others. Gregory Stone deals with appearance and dress in this context, as important for telling others who we are, announcing our identities. He points out that "Appearance *substitutes* for past and present action and, at the same time, conveys an *incipience* permitting others to anticipate what is about to occur. Specifically, clothing represents our action, past, present, and future, as it is established by the proposals and anticipations that occur in every social transaction" (1962:100).

Advertising is another good example. The purpose of advertising is to define the situation for the consumer, giving out the message that "you need this product," "we're in business because we like you," "you are an evil father if you do not buy our insurance," "America needs Bob Octopus for president," and "dress makes the man." This is the nature of all interpersonal influence: Somehow an attempt is made to define the situation, including one's self, for others. One of the very best descriptions of how we try to influence others' views of us is Erving Goffman's description at the beginning of *Presentation of Self in Everyday Life.* Here Goffman makes the point that each of us attempts to present that part of us to others that we choose to present in order to make public what we want, knowing full well that what we do will influence other people's definition of us. We try to impress others.

> When an individual enters the presence of others, they commonly seek to acquire information about him or to bring into play information already possessed. They will be interested in his general socio-economic status, his conception of self, his attitude toward them, his competence, his trustworthiness, etc. Although some of this information seems to be sought almost as an end in itself, there are usually quite practical reasons for acquiring it. Information about the individual helps to define the situation, enabling others to know in advance what he will expect of them and what they may expect of him. Informed in these ways, the others will know how best to act in order to call forth a desired response from him . . . If unacquainted with the individual, observers can glean clues from his conduct and appearance which allow them to apply their previous experience with individuals roughly similar to the one before them or, more important, to apply untested stereotypes to him. . . .
>
> Let us now turn from the others to the point of view of the individual who presents himself before them. He may wish them to think highly of him, or to think that he thinks highly of them, or to perceive how in fact he feels toward them, or to obtain no clear-cut impression; he may wish to ensure sufficient harmony so that the interaction can be sustained, or to defraud, get rid of, confuse, mislead, antagonize, or insult them. Regardless of the particular objective which the individual has in mind and of his motive for having this objective, it will be in his interests to control the conduct of the others, especially their responsive treatment of him. This control is achieved largely by influencing the definition of the situation which the others come to formulate, and he can influence this definition by expressing himself in such a way

as to give them the kind of impression that will lead them to act voluntarily in accordance with his own plan. Thus, when an individual appears in the presence of others, there will usually be some reason for him to mobilize his activity so that it will convey an impression to others which it is in his interests to convey. (Goffman, 1959: 1-4)*

We not only present *self* in a certain manner in order to define the situation for others, but we also alter the physical environment. We turn down the lights, we choose the right records, put out the wine, and even burn the right incense. The realtor turns on all the lights, gets rid of the occupants of the house, and shuts the right doors. The teacher who must meet parents on PTA night puts a globe on the desk, puts students' "typical" work on the bulletin board, and makes sure that the desks are neat. One of the most interesting descriptions of this process of altering the physical environment for purposes of defining the situation for others is Ball's description of an abortion clinic in Mexico during the days when abortion was illegal in the United States, and when for most women the abortion experience was filled with the added burden of an "illegitimate" and perhaps even a "dangerous" act. The highlights of Ball's description follow:

A paramount feature of the clinic's rhetoric is its physical and spatial characteristics. Especially important for patrons generally is the stereotype-contradicting waiting room, the first impression of the clinic itself—and the dominant one for supportive others. The waiting room is likely to be the only room in which the supportive others will be present during their entire visit to the clinic, save the possibility of a short interval in the office if they happen to be holding the fee, a frequent occurrence, especially if the other is also a client.

Spatially, the waiting room is L-shaped and extremely large; approximately 75 feet long and 50 feet wide at the base leg. Its size is accentuated by the fact that most of the room is sunken about three feet below other floor levels. Fully and deeply carpeted, well furnished with several couches, arm chairs, large lamps, and tables, the room speaks of luxury and patron consideration, also implied by the presence of a television set, a small bar, and a phonograph, in addition to the usual magazines present in waiting room situations.

Both the size of the room and the placement of the furniture function to provide private islands which need not be shared; space is structured so as to create withdrawal niches for each set of patrons. Couches and chairs are arranged along the walls of the room, maximizing distance between groupings and minimizing the possibilities of direct, intergroup eye-contact between the various patron-sets who, despite their shared problem and the recently experienced forced propinquity of the ride to the clinic, tend to keep their anxieties private. Thus, interaction among patrons in the waiting room is closed, confined to patients and their own accompanying supportive others only. . . .

Turning to the medical wing: The picture is a far cry from the shabby and sordid image of "kitchen table abortion" drawn in the popular press; it is one of modern scientific medicine, and with it comes assurance to the patient. Once the patient has donned a gown, her next stop is the operating room, a designation used without exception by the staff. In addition to a gynecological table, the room contains familiar (to the lay patient) medical paraphernalia: surgical tools, hypodermic syringes, stainless steel pans and trays, bottles and vials enclosing various colored liquids, capsules, pills, etc.—props effectively neutralizing the negative stereotypes associated with abortion as portrayed in the mass media.

After the procedure has been completed, the patient is moved from the scientific arena of the operating room and back again into luxury. As is the waiting room, the rooms in which the patients spend their short period of post-operative rest are expensively furnished.

Ultimately, after resting, the patient returns to the waiting room and, for most, to supportive others, and receives a final post-operative briefing before being returned to the rendezvous site. Parenthetically it may be noted that throughout the entire episode piped-in music has pervaded every room in which patrons are present. . . .

Appearance and Manner. A widespread device for visibly differentiating various social categories or types is clothing. Items of dress may function as insignia or uniforms to label the persons so garbed as members of particular social groups, occupations, etc. Such institutionalized symbols act as both identifiers and identities; to be attired in certain ways is to be a certain kind of person, not only in the eyes of the audience, but also in terms of the actor's perception of himself. Dress is an integral aspect of social identity.

So it is with the staff of the clinic: practitioners, patient, nurse—all wear the appropriate symbols, from the layman's point of view, of dress for surgically centered roles. White tunics are worn by the practitioners; the patient is surgically gowned; the nurse and even the janitress wear white uniform dresses. This element of the rhetoric is highlighted at the beginning of the procedure when both practitioners ostentatiously don surgical gloves, visibly emphasizing their, and the clinic's, concern with the necessities of asepsis. This ritualistic activity also serves to forcefully identify these actors in their roles as defined by the rhetoric. . . .

As with appearance, the manner of the staff is essentially directed toward the medical elements of the clinic's rhetoric; their demeanor is professional at all times, with one exception. This exception is the receptionist-bookkeeper, whose role is, by definition, outside the strictly medical aspects of the clinic. As a result, freed of the obligations of professional men, the receptionist is able to interact with patrons in a reassuring and supportive manner; in effect, her presentation of the rhetoric is through expressive strategies, while the manner of other staff members is more instrumentally oriented. (Ball, 1967: 293-301, *footnotes omitted*)

The first example (Goffman), illustrates how we try to define the situation for others through presenting a favorable picture of our *self* to others, or at least portraying ourselves in a way we choose. The second example (Ball) is meant to show how we may manipulate the physical *situation* in order to direct interaction. Another possibility, of course, is to attempt to define the *other people* in the situation so that they might come to agree with our definition and act accordingly. Weinstein and Deutschberger (1963) refer to this as "altercasting," casting the other in the role we choose for him or her in order to manipulate the interaction. "You are a good Christian person. Christian people don't do those kinds of things. Please don't do them." Casting others into identities that make sense to us and aid our plans in interaction is controlling the situation. I cast you into an inferior status (based on socioeconomic class, occupation, looks, or intelligence), and then I am able to control you and the interaction between us. Or, I shame you in front of others, I embarrass you, I purposely degrade you—this is defining you, casting you in a position that aids me in the situation. Or, I may cast you positively, telling you how sweet you are, how smart you are, what a fine person you have been all these years—again, in order to define the situation for you and to help control the direction of the interaction.

   I may define you, and even though you refuse to believe my definition, others in the situation may, and that is what may be the important thing. In a court of law I define you as a liar, to a friend I call you a cheat, to a business associate I define you as a bright rising star. The process of degradation is perhaps an extreme example, but it is an excellent one and highly appropriate here. Harold Garfinkel describes how one can be effective in degrading someone in public. Degradation he defines as a situation "whereby the public identity of an actor is transformed into something looked on as lower in the local scheme of social types" (1956:402). Garfinkel is specifically referring to "alteration of total identities." He carefully and cleverly lists the important ingredients of successful denunciation of the other. His description is fascinating reading, and I think we can all learn something about how skillful actors are able to define the *other* for the group as well as for the other being defined:

> How can one make a good denunciation?
>   To be successful, the denunciation must redefine the situations of those that are witnesses to the denunciation work. The denouncer, the party to be denounced (let us call him the "perpetrator"), and the thing that is being blamed on the perpetrator (let us call it the "event") must be transformed as follows:
>
>   1. Both event and perpetrator must be removed from the realm of their everyday character and be made to stand "out of the ordinary."
>   2. Both event and perpetrator must be placed within a scheme of preferences that shows the following properties:
>   A. The preferences must not be for event A over event B, but for event of *type A* over event of *type B*. The same typing must be accomplished for the perpetrator. Event and perpetrator must be defined as instances of a uniformity and must be treated as a uniformity throughout the work of the denunciation. The unique, never recurring character of the event or perpetrator should be lost. . . .
>   B. The witnesses must appreciate the characteristics of the typed person and event by referring the type to a dialectical counterpart. Ideally, the witnesses should not be able to contemplate the features of the denounced person without reference to the counterconception. . . .
>   3. The denouncer must so identify himself to the witnesses that during the denunciation they regard him not as a private but as a publicly known person. He must not portray himself as acting according to his personal, unique experiences. He must rather be regarded as acting in his capacity as a public figure, drawing upon communally entertained and verified experience. He must act as a bona fide participant in the tribal relationships to which the wit-

nesses subscribe. What he says must not be regarded as true for him alone, not even in the sense that it can be regarded by denouncer and witnesses as matters upon which they can become agreed. In no case, except in a most ironical sense, can the convention of true-for-reasonable-men be invoked. What the denouncer says must be regarded by the witnesses as true on the grounds of a socially employed metaphysics whereby witnesses assume that witnesses and denouncer are alike in essence.

4. The denouncer must make the dignity of the suprapersonal values of the tribe salient and accessible to view, and his denunciation must be delivered in their name.

5. The denouncer must arrange to be invested with the right to speak in the name of these ultimate values. The success of the denunciation will be undermined if, for his authority to denounce, the denouncer invokes the personal interests that he may have acquired by virtue of the wrong done to him or someone else. He must rather use the wrong he has suffered as a tribal member to invoke the authority to speak in the name of these ultimate values.

6. The denouncer must get himself so defined by the witnesses that they locate him as a supporter of these values.

7. Not only must the denouncer fix his distance from the person being denounced, but the witnesses must be made to experience their distance from him also.

8. Finally, the denounced person must be ritually separated from a place in the legitimate order, i.e., he must be defined as standing at a place opposed to it. He must be placed "outside," he must be made "strange."

These are the conditions that must be fulfilled for a successful denunciation. If they are absent, the denunciation will fail. Regardless of the situation when the denouncer enters, if he is to succeed in degrading the other man, it is necessary to introduce these features. (Garfinkel, 1956:422–23)*

Symbolic interactionism is a perspective that sees humans actively defining their situations and acting according to their definitions. Further, humans also attempt to define situations for others in interaction. To do so is to help determine the direction the interaction takes. The presentation of self, the manipulation of the environment, and the definition of others are all attempts to define the situation for others and are therefore attempts to exert power in relation to others. To lack the ability, the resources, or the willingness to define the situation is to put oneself in a situation where others are trying to do the defining and where one's dependence on others' definitions is increased.

INTERACTION AS TIED TO THE OTHER CONCEPTS IN SYMBOLIC INTERACTIONISM

Throughout this book we have pointed out how interaction is part of our basic nature. It is tied to each of the concepts discussed: social objects, symbols, language, perspectives, self, mind, and role taking. In each case a two-way reciprocal relationship is established: Interaction leads to each one of these concepts, and in turn, each one is a necessary ingredient in human interaction.

1. *Social objects* are defined in interaction.

   Interaction ⟶ Social objects

   People talk to each other and point things out in their environment. Things take on meaning, stand for a line of action, as a result of this interaction process. We come to share the objects around us; they become social objects. "Symbolic interactionism sees meanings as social products, as creations that are formed in and through the defining activities of people as they interact" (Blumer, 1969:5).
   On the other hand, we interact with each other according to how we define objects in the situation. Inanimate objects as well as other people and their acts are social objects for us, and as such, influence the direction of our social action and interaction.

   Social objects ⟶ Interaction

2. *Symbols* and *language* are also defined in interaction.

   Interaction ⟶ Symbols
              ⟶ Language

   By definition, symbols and language represent something else and are assigned this representation by individuals who act toward each other. The meaning of any object, symbol, or word is determined by the responses the actors together make toward it. It is an interactive process, the meaning of any given thing coming about through people's defining and redefining something as they interact.
   We have also emphasized, however, that interaction *is* symbolic; our acts in relation to each other are meant to communicate something; our acts are used to represent something to the other; and our acts have meaning assigned by both communicator and the other. The meaning that acts have to people in interaction makes a difference in the direction of that interaction.

   Symbols ⟶ Interaction

3. *Perspectives* also arise in interaction.

   Interaction ⟶ Perspectives

   Our view of reality—our angle of vision, our guide to reality—comes through sharing with others in interaction. Our approach to reality is social; it changes as our interaction changes, and it is stable because our interaction is stable.
   Furthermore, perspectives are basic to all interaction. We define others and self in the situation according to perspectives we bring to the situation and ac-

cording to the perspective that develops in interaction. Perspectives define the situation within which we interact.

Perspectives ⟶ Interaction

4. *Self* arises in interaction. The activities toward the self also depend on interaction.

Interaction ⟶ Self

We come to see ourselves as objects, owing to our interaction with others. We interact with significant others and reference groups, develop selfhood, and with selfhood are able to do a number of things in relation to our self, including directing, controlling, communicating, analyzing, naming, and judging. Further, this process of directing action toward self depends in large part on the kinds of action being directed toward us in interaction. Thus what we say to ourselves, including the judgments we make of ourselves, depends in large part on interaction.

Conversely, self-interaction influences our acts with others. Judgment of self, identity of self, analysis of self are all important in determining the direction of our social action.

Self ⟶ Interaction

5. *Mind* also arises in interaction, since we have defined mind as *symbolic* interaction with the *self*.

Interaction ⟶ Mind

Furthermore, mind covert action makes up a great deal of our action and interaction. Both slow, careful deliberation and very rapid symbolic manipulation of the situation are essential for each of us in working out the interaction "problems" that face us in each situation.

Mind ⟶ Interaction

6. *Role taking* first develops because of interaction with significant others. In all situations, we take the role of those with whom we are interacting.

Interaction ⟶ Role taking

Children role take first without symbols, through imitation. Then they use symbols to look at the world from someone else's perspective. That involves first of all interacting with others.

Role taking is also an integral part of all interaction situations. In order to understand the meaning of the other, in order to communicate, in order to help direct the interaction, in order to cooperate with others in interaction, role taking is central.

Role taking ⟶ Interaction

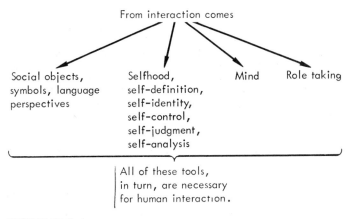

From interaction comes

| Social objects, symbols, language perspectives | Selfhood, self-definition, self-identity, self-control, self-judgment, self-analysis | Mind | Role taking |

All of these tools, in turn, are necessary for human interaction.

FIGURE 10-2

It is hoped that this chapter has communicated the importance of interaction. Interaction makes possible a host of human qualities, and all of these qualities, in turn, are basic to all interaction, as illustrated in Figure 10-2.

"But which comes first?" the skeptic must ask. "Does interaction precede these individual qualities or do they precede interaction?" It is not completely clear, nor is it very important. It is the *interdependence* between the individual's qualities and interaction that should not be lost. An order in the child's development can be established tentatively, as was pointed out in Chapter 9. However, the child's qualities arise very early, and with them the two-way, reciprocal relationship with interaction is established. Based on the discussion in Chapter 9, Figure 10-3 shows the order of events that seems most plausible in the individual's development.

INTERACTION AND SOCIETY

Interestingly, interaction not only gives rise to these *individual* human qualities, which have been emphasized up to now, but also is the basis for all *group* life, from the dyad to the society. It is through interaction that people are able to share with each other whatever is necessary for social organization (see Figure 10-4).

Thus far this book has focused on the relationship between interaction and the individual. All that we are as individuals is tied to interaction, and human interaction, in turn, is dependent on certain human individual qualities. It is time to look at the nature of the group, the nature of society from a symbolic interactionist perspective. Most symbolic interactionists would probably say to me: "At last! You should have done society first, since the individual is built on society." The order of the chapters in this book was determined by what I felt was the clearest approach. Furthermore, it is extremely important to realize that society is built on individuals in symbolic interaction with each other and with themselves, so that has been the emphasis throughout the chapters on symbol, self, mind, action, and interaction. Never has it been my intention to imply that human qualities are possible

Child is born
into a society
where other
people act
toward him
or her

↓

Child imitates
the acts of
others

↓

Beginning of
selfhood

↓

Beginning of symbols,   Symbolic
mind, perspectives,   interaction
social objects,   →   with
perspectives, role taking   others

↓

More symbols,
mind activity,
perspectives,
social objects,
role taking

↓

Symbolic
interaction
with
others

↓

etc.   **FIGURE 10–3**

From interaction comes

The individual with   Shared reality
social objects, symbols,   between individuals
language, perspectives,
self, mind, role taking

↓

makes possible the   Shared perspective   Accurate
active person, defining   consensus, culture   role
situations, problem   taking
solving, directing and
controlling self

Complex cooperative
group life is possible   **FIGURE 10–4**

without society. The opposite has been emphasized: Human qualities arise only because society exists. The human is social through and through. Human qualities arise in interaction with others, and others together make up society. It is to the important topic of *society* that we now turn.

REFERENCES

BALL, DONALD
   1967 "An Abortion Clinic Ethnography." *Social Problems* 14:293–301. Reprinted by permission of The Society for the Study of Social Problems.
   1972 "The Definition of Situation." *Journal for the Theory of Social Behavior* 2:24–36.
BERGER, PETER L. and THOMAS LUCKMANN
   1967 *The Social Construction of Reality.* New York: Doubleday. Copyright © 1966 by Peter L. Berger and Thomas Luckmann. Reprinted by permission of Doubleday & Company, Inc., and Penguin Press, Harmondsworth, Middlesex, England.
BLUMER, HERBERT
   1962 "Society as Symbolic Interaction." In ed. Arnold Rose, *Human Behavior and Social Processes,* pp. 179–92. Boston: Houghton Mifflin Co. Copyright © 1962 by Houghton Mifflin Company. Used with permission.
   1966 "Sociological Implications of the Thought of George Herbert Mead." *American Journal of Sociology* 71:535–44. By permission of The University of Chicago Press. Copyright © 1966 by The University of Chicago.
   1969 *Symbolic Interactionism: Perspective and Method.* Englewood Cliffs, N.J.: Prentice-Hall. Copyright © 1969. Reprinted by permission of Prentice-Hall, Inc.
GARFINKEL, HAROLD
   1956 "Conditions of Successful Degradation Ceremonies." *American Journal of Sociology* 61:420–24.
GOFFMAN, ERVING
   1959 *The Presentation of Self in Everyday Life.* New York: Doubleday. Copyright © 1959 by Erving Goffman. Reprinted by permission of Doubleday & Company, Inc., and Penguin Press, Harmondsworth, Middlesex, England.
McCALL, GEORGE J., and J. L. SIMMONS
   1966 *Identities and Interactions.* New York: Free Press. Reprinted with permission of Macmillan Publishing Co., Inc. Copyright © 1966 by The Free Press, a division of the Macmillan Company.
MEAD, GEORGE HERBERT
   1934 *Mind, Self and Society.* Chicago: University of Chicago Press. Reprinted by permission of The University of Chicago Press. Copyright © 1934 by The University of Chicago. All rights reserved.
MERTON, ROBERT K.
   1957 *Social Theory and Social Structure.* New York: Free Press.
SHIBUTANI, TAMOTSU
   1961 *Society and Personality: An Interactionist Approach to Social Psycholo-*

gy. Englewood Cliffs, N.J.: Prentice-Hall. Copyright © 1961. Reprinted by permission of Prentice-Hall, Inc.

STONE, GREGORY P.
1962 "Appearance and the Self." In ed. Arnold Rose, *Human Behavior and Social Processes,* pp. 86–118. Boston: Houghton Mifflin Company. Copyright © 1962 by Houghton Mifflin Company.

THOMAS, WILLIAM I., and DOROTHY THOMAS
1928 *The Child in America.* New York: Alfred A. Knopf.

WEINSTEIN, E. A., and P. DEUTSCHBERGER
1963 "Some Dimensions of Altercasting." *Sociometry* 26:454–66.

11
SOCIETY

Sociology was defined as the "science of society" by the French philosopher Auguste Comte in the early nineteenth century. Although sociologists may differ on what exactly should be the emphasis in what they study, all seem to agree that society must enter into the analysis somewhere, that one goal must be to understand the nature of society as well as the interrelationship between the individual and society. Therefore, it is imperative for a social psychology that has relevance to sociology to consider these matters.

Comte divided the study of society into statics (structure) and dynamics (change). Throughout the history of sociology, thinkers have clustered around two poles, some emphasizing structure, others dynamics; some describing the permanence of society's controls, some emphasizing the ever-changing nature of society and even shying away from the terms *structure,* and *society.* Those who have emphasized structure have tended to examine the historical reality of society—society as a set of institutions, stratification systems, and cultural patterns into which individuals are born and are socialized, playing roles according to scripts laid down by others, living and dead. The criticism by some sociologists of this view is that it tends to be too deterministic, that there is little room for the active person who defines society and directs self. A second criticism, and it is related to the first, is that social change is usually not adequately explained.

The second view of society is one that emphasizes a dynamic, changing nature, deemphasizes structure and the historical development of institutions, stratification systems, and cultural patterns. It focuses instead on change, on individuals interacting—influenced by the past, but also defining that past—developing new definitions of the present, and shaping society. Society is described as a process, society is individuals who interact. The criticism of this view is that it tends to overlook the power of society, the deterministic nature of institutions, of structure, and of cultural patterns. And a second important criticism is that it focuses too much on interacting individuals constantly redefining society, changing society: it becomes a wonder that society is able to exist at all and maintain its structure with the constant self-direction that takes place.

Both perspectives of society are useful, and although some theorists attempt to integrate them, few are able to do so successfully, and most emphasize one or the other view. Most sociologists tend to be more on the side of society as structure, society as historical, society as permanent, society as determining, although most will also attempt to look at the dynamics of human relations, and many will describe society as interacting individuals. The symbolic interactionists, probably more than any other school in sociology, conceptualize society in the dynamic sense: as individuals in symbolic interaction with each other, defining and altering the direction of each other's acts. Certain qualities are necessarily emphasized, while others are ignored. "Human society might best be regarded as an on-going process, a *becoming* rather than a *being*. Society might be viewed most fruitfully as a succession of events, a flow of gestural interchanges among people" (Shibutani, 1961: 174).

The purpose of this chapter will be to look at the symbolic interactionists' view of *society*, to emphasize its dynamic nature, and to relate every concept discussed in this book to an understanding of it.

COLLECTIVES, GROUPS, ORGANIZATIONS, AND SOCIETY

There is, in symbolic interactionism, no reason for a distinction between kinds of organization. Each dyad, each group, each organization, each interaction situation, even the most temporary, is a society, or at least a society in an early stage of development. Even the crowd, where interaction is considered "primitive," is the beginning of society. Through studying even the crowd we can come to understand the nature of society, for some of the same dynamics that characterize the crowd characterize all organization.

Crowds, groups, organizations, communities, and societies are all made up of individuals who interact. Society—all group life—is defined here as *individuals in interaction,* doing the kinds of things discussed in earlier chapters: role taking, communicating, interpreting each other, adjusting their acts to one another, directing and controlling self, sharing perspectives. Individuals *act,* and it is through the processes listed here that group life from dyads to large complex organization (e.g., society) are said to exist. In this chapter, and throughout the rest of this book, the terms *group, society, organization,* and *collective* will be used interchangeably— we will regard all groups as societies. In other contexts, it may be useful to distinguish them, but for purposes of understanding the nature of organization from a symbolic interactionist perspective, it is not necessary.

SOCIETY IS INDIVIDUALS IN SYMBOLIC INTERACTION

In Chapter 3 the ideas of Shibutani were introduced, and his article, "Reference Groups as Perspectives," was analyzed extensively. Shibutani emphasizes that societies, or what he also refers to as "social worlds," are made up of individuals communicating with symbols, coming to share a perspective in interaction. He points out that in this sense, the readers of a professional journal make up a society, as does a family unit, as do the Boy Scouts of America. The critical qualification for society is interaction, communication, *symbolic interaction.*

Symbolic Interaction Involves Individuals Taking Each Other Into Account

In a sense, there is no chapter needed here on society, since the chapter on interaction (Chapter 10) is also a chapter on society. Interaction, as we have emphasized, refers to the fact that individuals interpret each other's acts and then come to align their acts in relation to each other. Groups are made up of individuals who take each other into account as they act. As Blumer points out:

> Taking each other into account in this mutual way not only relates the action of each to that of the other but intertwines the actions of both into what I would call, for lack of a better word, a transaction—a fitting of the developing action of each into that of the other to form a joint overbridging action. (1969:109)

The patterns in *action* that we might observe between individuals we label "group" or "society." This does not mean that groups are individuals who imitate one another, or even that they agree on the direction in which the interaction should go. Instead, groups are individuals communicating and engaging in mutual social action. Society is made up of individuals working things out in relation to each other. Blumer (1966:540) labels interaction in which people "are fitting together their acts" as *joint action.* Any example of joint action—a marriage ceremony, two strangers helping one another in a rainstorm, a classroom learning situation, or a committee meeting—is an example of individuals in symbolic interaction. Each is also an example of a society, and each is part of a larger society of interacting individuals. Blumer states:

> I use the term "joint action" in place of Mead's term "social act." It refers to the larger collective form of action that is constituted by the fitting together of the lines of behavior of the separate participants. . . . Joint actions range

from a simple collaboration of two individuals to a complex alignment of the acts of huge organizations or institutions. Everywhere we look in a human society we see people engaging in forms of joint action. (1966:540)*

A joint action can be individuals doing the same things together or doing complementary things—things that satisfy each other. Individuals do not necessarily have the same goals or values when they interact. The employer and the employee each has his or her own goals in the interaction, and both have different things at stake, but they are involved in joint action, interaction, in that together they are able to meet each other's goals.

> Such alignment may take place for any number of reasons, depending on the situations calling for joint action, and need not involve, or spring from, the sharing of common values. The participants may fit their acts to one another in orderly joint actions on the basis of compromise, out of duress, because they may use one another in achieving their respective ends, because it is the sensible thing to do, or out of sheer necessity. . . . In very large measure, society becomes the formation of workable relations. To seek to encompass, analyze, and understand the life of a society on the assumption that the existence of a society necessarily depends on the sharing of values can lead to strained treatment, gross misrepresentation, and faulty lines of interpretation. I believe that the Meadian Perspective, in posing the question of how people are led to align their acts in different situations in place of presuming that this necessarily requires and stems from a sharing of common values is a more salutary and realistic approach. (Blumer, 1966:544)

Society, then, is defined first of all as individuals *acting* in relation to each other, taking each other into account. A family unit, the First Baptist Church, the crowd at a football game, two people who meet at Sam's bar—to the extent that each one of these examples is characterized by individuals who act with each other in mind, by individuals who take account of each other as they act, we call it a society. Each "joint action," each "transaction," to use Blumer's terms, is an example of society, sometimes a society that has only a momentary existence, often a much longer life. The United States is a society with large numbers of people engaged in innumerable and overlapping joint action—a very large and complex "society."

Symbolic Interaction Involves Individuals Communicating

Society is symbolic interaction in which individuals (1) take each other into account, *and* (2) communicate as they act. *Society is people communicating.* Mead describes communication and society best. The human being, in contrast to other animals:

> can be interwoven into a community activity through its ability to respond to the gestures of other forms that indicate to it the stimuli to which it is to

*Reprinted from "Sociological Implications of the Thought of George Herbert Mead," by Herbert Blumer in *The American Journal of Sociology,* by permission of The University of Chicago Press. Copyright © 1966 by The University of Chicago. All rights reserved.

respond. We point things out. This pointing-out process may be with the finger, by an attitude of body, by direction of head and eyes; but as a rule it is by means of the vocal gesture, that is, a certain vocal symbol that indicates something to another individual and to which he responds. Such indication as this sets up a certain definite process of pointing out to other individuals in the group what is of importance in this cooperative activity. (1936:378-79)*

It is through understanding each other's meaning, through taking the role of the other, through pointing out to self what one points out to others, and what they, in turn, are pointing out to us, that people are able to come together, form a collective, and continue to act toward one another meaningfully for any length of time. Warriner also emphasizes communication as the central ingredient of society:

It is only as men use their capacity to symbol as a tool of communication that they create the essential ingredient of society. When they treat their acts as signs of meaning men are able to gain access to the mind of the other. And when they use succeeding acts to confirm (or deny) these inferences the knowledge becomes reciprocal for each can know that the other knows what is in his mind. It is at this point that society comes into being for they then can agree upon what their acts, themselves as actors, and other events shall mean to them *together*.

Communication is thus more than mere message sending. Communication involves a totally new phenomenon, that of a *collective* meaning. Although this collective meaning exists in the separate minds of the individual actors its content is defined by their communication and by the implicit and explicit agreements that this is the meaning that things shall have for them *in their interaction*. It is in this sense that it is collective and social, and not individual, for each participates in collective meaning that may differ from the individual meanings which he may use at other times. (1970:133)

Blumer in his description of communication, points out most clearly how communication and aligning acts between people are intimately related:

Fundamentally, group action takes the form of a fitting together of individual lines of action. Each individual aligns his action to the action of others by ascertaining what they are doing or what they intend to do—that is, by getting the meaning of their acts. For Mead, this is done by the individual "taking the role" of others—either the role of a specific person or the role of a group (Mead's "generalized other"). In taking such roles the individual seeks to ascertain the intention or direction of the acts of others. He forms and aligns his own action on the basis of such interpretation of the acts of others. This is the fundamental way in which group action takes place in human society. (1962:184)

It is, then, essential to understand that when we define society as individuals in symbolic interaction, we are saying that society is (1) individuals acting with each other in mind, aligning their acts to each other, and (2) individuals communicating to and interpreting each other's acts.

SOCIETY IS INDIVIDUALS COOPERATING

Society is also defined as *individuals engaging in cooperative action.* Almost all cases of interaction are also cases of cooperative problem solving, but a few are not. Enemies who are eternally hostile to each other may take each other into account and may communicate, may even understand each other very clearly, may even act alike, but will not constitute a society, since their action is not characterized by a cooperative effort to deal with a situation. When two enemies are threatened, they may join forces, and they begin to be a society. America is a society to the extent that people cooperate in dealing with situations. Cooperation does not necessarily mean that we have common goals, although shared goals and shared problems might be commonplace. It is not, however, the fact that people have the same goals that makes society but rather that their action is such that they are able to use each other's resources to act effectively in situations encountered, to deal with problems, major or minor. Differences in goals and in problems deemed important may still be part of the interaction, but as long as people work together in spite of their personal differences, a society exists. Society is more a matter of interdependence, with individuals acting together and helping each other resolve problems each faces, than it is a matter of everyone acting alike or having the same ideas or goals. People may have different things at stake—for example, a student may want to graduate, a teacher may want to teach something vital—yet the interaction can be cooperative problem solving and the people qualify as a group or society.

This sounds very much like the chapter on *action.* People act in situations, they must work out problems in situations, they must establish goals, they must define objects. *Society* is people *acting* in situations *cooperatively,* either through working together for common goals, or through helping one another achieve individual goals, or both.

Usually, however, groups or societies are characterized by individuals who symbolically interact, align acts, and *come to share goals.* Groups come to confront situations and problems that individuals in the group must work out together. Lines of action are determined, objects are defined, overt action is taken, and interpretations are made by individuals in symbolic interaction, working together in situations. Designated leaders of the group may act in the name of the group, or the members may all act together, each playing a part in the whole action.

> The same sort of picture exists in the case of the social action of a collectivity, such as a business corporation, a labor union, an army, a church, a boy's gang, or a nation. The difference is that the collectivity has a directing group or individual who is empowered to assess the operating situation, to note different things that have to be dealt with, and to map out a line of action. The self-interaction of a collectivity is in the form of discussion, counseling,

and debate. The collectivity is in the same position as the individual in having to cope with a situation, in having to interpret and analyze the situation, and in having to construct a line of action. (Blumer, 1969:55-56)

To understand the action of any collective—from a dyad to a society—one must understand how individuals in various positions in the collective interpret the situation encountered as well as how the interaction between individuals in positions defines the problem, the goals, and the objects in the situation. "The point of view of symbolic interactionism is that large-scale organization has to be seen, studied, and explained in terms of the process of interpretation engaged in by the acting participants as they handle the situations at their respective positions in the organization." (Blumer, 1969:58)

Individuals act: when they act *cooperatively* they make up a society. Individuals act in situations, and their action is aimed at working out problems, major or minor, in the situation; when individuals act *cooperatively* to solve problems in situations, they are said to form a society. Communication and cooperation are the basic qualities of all human group life.

Whether the collectivity be an army engaged in a campaign, a corporation seeking to expand its operations, or a nation trying to correct an unfavorable balance of trade, it needs to construct its action through an interpretation of what is happening in its area of operation. The interpretative process takes place by participants making indications to one another, not merely each to himself. Joint or collective action is an outcome of such a process of interpretive interaction. (Blumer, 1969:16)

Human society (i.e., symbolic interaction, cooperation) demands certain qualities from the individual if it is to exist. If individuals are to solve problems cooperatively and if individuals must interpret each other's acts and then align their acts in relation to that interpretation, then the individual qualities discussed throughout this book are absolutely essential. Human society demands individuals who are able to *take the role of the other,* who possess *selves,* and who use *minds.*

HUMAN SOCIETY IS MADE UP OF INDIVIDUALS TAKING THE ROLE OF THE OTHER

Cooperation in groups, problem solving, goal-directed action between actors, demands an understanding of each other as action unfolds. Thus, society is made up of actors who are able to take the role of the other, to understand the acts—both overt and covert—of the others in order to align their own acts with the acts of the others. To act cooperatively is to be able to know what to do so that it does not conflict with others and so that it does not do the same work that the other does. Football, baseball, basketball, and hockey teams must excel in cooperative action as must army units, businesses, and mountain climbing expeditions. It is essential to know how the other sees you, what the other expects of you, how the other sees self, past and future, as well as how the other defines the situation at hand. To co-operate is to take the role of the others effectively in a situation. The chapter on role taking emphasized that point.

> Coordination requires that each participant be able to anticipate the move-ments of the others, and it is for this purpose that men who are cooperating watch one another. . . . A knowledge of the external circumstances is not enough; anticipating what another human being is likely to do requires getting "inside" of him—to his subjective experiences, his particular definition of the situation and his conception of his own place within it. . . . the behavior of another person can be anticipated only through effective role-taking. (Shi-butani, 1961:141)

HUMAN SOCIETY IS MADE UP OF INDIVIDUALS WITH SELVES

Herbert Blumer emphasizes that the important insight of the symbolic interactionist perspective is that society is made up of individuals with *selves*. It is a critical insight and should not be given mere lip service. In relation to society, Blumer's point is important for two basic reasons.

Humans Determine the Direction of Their Acts

The first reason is that humans are therefore actively involved in determining the direction of their own acts—they do not passively respond to a society out there. They direct themselves, and they participate in the definition of society. This view of society sharply contrasts with the usual description of society as a structure out there to be reckoned with, shaping or stamping out its members. Blumer points out that the symbolic interactionist conception, emphasizing individuals with selves:

> sees human society not as an established structure but as people meeting their conditions of life; it sees social action not as an emanation of societal struc-ture but as a formation made by human actors; it sees this formation of ac-tion not as societal factors coming to expression through the medium of human organisms but as constructions made by actors out of what they take into account; it sees group life not as a release or expression of established structure but as a process of building up joint actions; . . . accordingly, it sees society not as a system, whether in the form of a static, moving, or whatever kind of equilibrium, but as a vast number of occurring joint actions, many closely linked, many not linked at all, many prefigured and repetitious, others being carved out in new directions, and all being pursued to serve the purposes of the participants and not the requirements of a system. (1966:543)

We may, of course, still be tempted to describe society as the repetitive and habitual acts of individuals conditioned by the agencies of socialization. And it may be true that people do indeed do things in relation to each other that appear automatic and do not appear to demand a self. Yet, as was emphasized in previous chapters, situations need definition by the individual, even situations we have encountered before must be defined as we act. Our definitions may be exactly the same between two situations, and we might act exactly alike in both, but almost always they are at least slightly different—the reference group/perspective we use is slightly different, or our goals in the situation have changed. The history or career of interaction "is generally orderly, fixed and repetitious by virtue of a common identification or definition of the joint action that is made by its participants" (Blumer, 1966:541). Each situation is defined, our past is recalled and applied, and for us to act the same in many situations means that our definitions, as well as the perceived definitions of other people, remain the same. Humans and situations are highly dynamic and definitions are ever changing between actors. It is a wonder, in a sense, how it is that humans could possibly act identically in two situations, or that two individuals could act exactly the same way in a situation. Blumer emphasizes this point:

> We have to recognize that even in the case of pre-established and repetitive joint action each instance of such joint action has to be formed anew. The participants still have to build up their lines of action and fit them to one another through the dual process of designation and interpretation. . . . the meanings that underlie established and recurrent joint action are themselves subject to pressure as well as to reinforcement, to incipient dissatisfaction as well as to indifference. . . . Behind the facade of the objectively perceived joint action the set of meanings that sustains that joint action has a life that the social scientists can ill afford to ignore. (1969:18)

Here then, the symbolic interactionist conceives of society as a process, with both stability and change inherent in the meanings that individuals develop in interaction with each other and with themselves. "The reliance on symbolic interaction makes human group life a developing process instead of a mere issue or product of psychological or social structure" (Blumer, 1966:538), and "human association is a moving process in which the participants note and gauge each other's actions, each organizing his action with regard to the other and, in doing so, inhibiting himself, encouraging himself, and guiding himself as he builds up his action" (Blumer, 1953: 197). The point to be emphasized is that *self is central here:* participants point things out to *self,* inhibit *self,* encourage *self,* guide *self,* as they align their acts with each other. Individuals are active in society.

Humans Cooperate Actively

The second reason why it is important to regard society as made up of individuals with selves is that cooperation is seen in a different light: It is accomplished by individuals who are *working together,* coordinating their activities, each doing his or her "own thing," keeping in mind others, directing and controlling self to go first in one direction, then another, dealing rationally in situations by sharing with others what to do and what not to do about the situation at hand. With self, individuals can engage in cooperative problem solving, rather than relying on imitation, instinct, or simple response to situations. Shibutani makes this point:

> It has been contended that flexible coordination is achieved as each participant acts independently, taking the contributions and expectations of his associates into account, but making his own decisions as he goes along. (1961: 64)

> . . . social control rests largely upon self-control. Human society is an on-going process in which each participant is continually checking his own behavior in response to real or anticipated reactions of other people. Coordination is possible because each person controls himself from within, and it is self-consciousness that makes such voluntary conduct possible. Concerted action depends upon the voluntary contributions of the individual participants, but since each person forms a self-image from the standpoint of the perspective shared in the group, such self-criticism serves to integrate the contributions of each into an organized social pattern. (1961:92–93)

This idea allows for tremendous flexibility in social action. Humans in their organized life need not be bound to any pattern but instead can constantly determine new directions depending on the situation at hand. Discussion, deliberation, communication, *and self-direction* allow individuals to adjust their action to each other and to the situation as they go along rather than responding habitually together to external stimuli. To direct and control self is to be constantly adjusting self according to the interaction that is going on with others.

HUMAN SOCIETY IS MADE UP OF INDIVIDUALS
WITH MINDS

There is no reason to belabor the point: Complex problem solving, where individuals must work out situations by analyzing both past experience and future consequences, demands mind. Furthermore, the activity described earlier in relation to self—self-direction, self-control, self-communication—is *mind activity* as it was described in Chapter 7.

But an important point must not be missed here. Both self and mind are central to understanding society precisely because that makes some sense (at last) out of the old, outworn sociological declaration: "Society makes 'man,' and 'man' makes society." Usually an author will state this on page one of an introductory text, then spend the next five hundred pages showing how society makes people, leaving the question of how people make society up to the imagination of the reader. Individuals define and act in society and may affect the direction of society. Mead, more than any other, clearly and simply points out how people make society with self and mind:

Human society, we have insisted, does not merely stamp the pattern of its organized social behavior upon any one of its individual members, so that this pattern becomes likewise the pattern of the individual's self; it also, at the same time, gives him a mind, as the means or ability of consciously conversing with himself in terms of the social attitudes which constitute the structure of his self and which embody the pattern of human society's organized behavior as reflected in that structure. And his mind enables him in turn to stamp the pattern of his further developing self (further developing through his mental activity) upon the structure or organization of human society, and thus in a degree, to reconstruct and modify in terms of his self the general pattern of social or group behavior in terms of which his self was originally constituted. (1934:263, footnote)*

This point is perhaps Blumer's greatest emphasis in all his work:

Established patterns of group life exist and persist only through the continued use of the same schemes of interpretation; and such schemes of interpretation are maintained only through their continued confirmation by the defining acts of others. It is highly important to recognize that the established patterns of group life just do not carry on by themselves but are dependent for their continuity on recurrent affirmative definition. Let the interpretations that sustain them be undermined or disrupted by changed definitions from others and the patterns can quickly collapse. . . . In the flow of group life there are innumerable points at which the participants are *re*defining each other's acts. Such redefinition is very common in adversary relations, it is frequent in group discussion, and it is essentially intrinsic to dealing with problems. (And I may remark here that no human group is free of problems.) Redefinition imparts a formative character to human interaction, giving rise at this or that point to new objects, new conceptions, new relations, and new types of behavior. (1966:538)

Because humans have selves, because they interact with those selves while they interact with others, each individual is in a position to redefine society, to redirect society, to be determining as well as determined. Anyone who demands that children obey, that employees toe the line, that students conform to the rules, that citizens believe and do what the authorities say, is naive to expect what is demanded: Humans with selves and minds think and define their own situations and may attempt to influence others' definitions. As long as humans symbolically interact with each other and with selves, there is no way to control what definitions and actions will emerge.

Human society, then, is defined here as individuals in symbolic interaction with each other, aligning their acts, and acting cooperatively to resolve problems in situations. It is made up of individuals who role-take, and who possess mind and self. Two further points should be made about human society:

*Reprinted from *Mind, Self and Society* by George Herbert Mead by permission of The University of Chicago Press. Copyright © 1934 by The University of Chicago. All rights reserved.

1. As a result of symbolic interaction, over time individuals come to share a perspective and a generalized other, and their shared understandings increase considerably.
2. Both a perspective and a shared generalized other become important ingredients in keeping the interaction going over time: They are important for the continuation of society.

SOCIETY PROVIDES THE INDIVIDUAL WITH A PERSPECTIVE AND A GENERALIZED OTHER

One of George Herbert Mead's major contributions to the study of human society is the concept of "the generalized other." The generalized other is the individual's "society," the society whose rules become his or her own.

Shibutani (1955) borrows from Mead, but he calls society a "reference group" or a "social world," and the generalized other that is taken on by the individual is referred to as a perspective. There is a great deal of overlap between the conceptualizations of Shibutani and Mead, but in my opinion, there are two important differences that should be kept in mind.

Differing Views of Shibutani and Mead

First, Shibutani emphasizes the fact that the individual uses several reference groups, has several perspectives, and interacts with a number of social worlds, and he claims, therefore, that the individual can no longer be said to have a single generalized other. Mead, on the other hand, sees the generalized other as a composite, as a society, *the* society for the individual, a totality of individuals who are important and who represent the wider society, developed historically with rules long established. Shibutani (1955:569) describes "mass society" especially as made up of many social worlds. He states that each individual may interact with several of those worlds and may therefore have many perspectives. Mead tends to view the generalized other as society, a single society for the individual, which each interaction serves to reinforce and build up. Yet this point is not altogether clear in Mead, for he sometimes describes the generalized other in the same terms as Shibutani, as emerging out of each group and somewhat different in each group in which one interacts. For example:

> The organized community or social group which gives to the individual his unity of self can be called "the generalized other." The attitude of the generalized other is the attitude of the whole community. Thus, for example, in the case of such a social group as a ball team, the team is the generalized other insofar as it enters—as an organized process or social activity—into the experience of any one of the individual members of it. (Mead, 1934:154)

The ball team as generalized other is really the same idea as Shibutani's reference group. In summary, whereas Shibutani emphasizes the different social worlds that become reference groups and perspectives for the individual, Mead emphasizes each interaction as establishing a single generalized other for the individual, creating for the individual a composite "society" that becomes important to the individual, which the individual carries to each interaction situation. Both views—Shibutani's and Mead's—are valuable for understanding: Individuals in interaction can be said to develop a perspective, and that perspective becomes a part of a broader overall perspective of the most general society he or she uses to define reality, which is referred to as a *generalized other* (see Figure 11-1).

The second important difference between Shibutani and Mead is that Shibutani emphasizes the *perspectives* of reference groups that the individual comes to use, whereas Mead focuses on the generalized other of society as a *set of rules,* the expectations that society has for the individual—what the individual is to *obey* to be a member in good standing in society. Perspectives lead to definition of self, others, and objects, the generalized other to self-control, self-direction, self-judgment. Perspectives are viewpoints, frameworks used for definition assumptions, and beliefs held. A generalized other is the law that must be obeyed, it is the system, it is "the conscience" of the individual more than the something used by the individual to define situations. Berger and Luckmann give an excellent description of the generalized other—how it is developed in the individual and how it comes to influence behavior.

> Primary socialization creates in the child's consciousness a progressive abstraction from the roles and attitudes of specific others to roles and attitudes *in general.* For example, in the internalization of norms there is a progression from "Mummy is angry with me *now*" to "Mummy is angry with me *whenever* I spill the soup." As additional significant others (father, grandmother, older sister, and so on) support the mother's negative attitude toward soup-spilling, the generality of the norm is subjectively extended. The decisive step comes when the child recognizes that *everybody* is against soup-spilling, and the norm is generalized to *"One* does not spill soup"—"one" being himself as part of a generality that includes, in principle, *all* of society insofar as it is

FIGURE 11-1

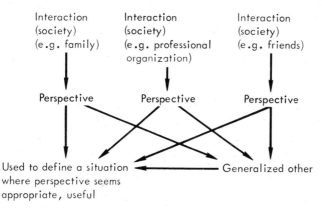

significant to the child. This abstraction from the roles and attitudes of concrete significant others is called the generalized other. Its formation within consciousness means that the individual now identifies not only with concrete others but with a generality of others, that is, with a society. Only by virtue of this generalized identification does his own self-identification attain stability and continuity. He now has not only an identity *vis-a-vis* this or that significant other, but an identity *in general,* which is subjectively apprehended as remaining the same no matter what others, significant or not, are encountered. This newly coherent identity incorporates within itself all the various internalized roles and attitudes—including, among many other things, the self-identification as a non-spiller of soups.

The formation within consciousness of the generalized other marks a decisive phase in socialization. It implies the internalization of society as such and of the objective reality established therein, and, at the same time, the subjective establishment of a coherent and continuous identity. Society, identity *and* reality are subjectively crystallized in the same process of internalization. This crystallization is concurrent with the internalization of language. Indeed, for reasons evident from the foregoing observations on language, language constitutes both the most important content and the most important instrument of socialization. (1967:132–33)*

Here too the distinction between Shibutani and Mead is not clear-cut. Indeed, it probably makes good sense to see both a perspective (with its emphasis on *definition* of situation) and a generalized other (with its emphasis on guides used by the individual for self-control) as emerging from symbolic interaction.

Shibutani does not distinguish between generalized other and perspectives, since, he argues, Mead was indeed referring to perspectives in his description. That makes good sense, although most writers who discuss the two terms do not equate them. Here is Shibutani's description: To take the role of the generalized other is to approach the world "from the standpoint of the culture of [the] group." Each person

perceives, thinks, forms judgments, and controls himself according to the frame of reference of the group in which he is participating. Since he defines objects, other people, the world, and himself from the perspective that he shares with others, he can visualize his proposed line of action from this generalized standpoint, anticipate the reactions of others, inhibit undesirable impulses, and thus guide his conduct. The socialized person is a society in miniature; he sets the same standards of conduct for himself as he sets for others, and he judges himself in the same terms. He can define situations properly and meet his obligations, even in the absence of other people, because, as already noted, his perspective always takes into account the expectations of others. Thus, it is the ability to define situations from the same standpoint as others that makes personal controls possible. When Mead spoke of assuming the role of the generalized other, he was not referring to people but to perspectives shared with others in a transaction. (1955:564)†

*Excerpt from *The Social Construction of Reality,* copyright © 1966 by Peter L. Berger and Thomas Luckmann. Reprinted by permission of Doubleday & Company, Inc., New York, and Penguin Press, Harmondsworth, Middlesex, England.

†Reprinted from "Reference Groups as Perspectives," by Tamotsu Shibutani in *The American Journal of Sociology,* by permission of The University of Chicago Press. Copyright © 1955 by The University of Chicago. All rights reserved.

The views of Shibutani are important in understanding the nature of society for the individual: Society provides the perspective from which the individual views the world. Mead's generalized other constitutes another important ingredient of society, a second emphasis in symbolic interactionism. It is the internalized moral order, the controls that the individual develops from interacting with significant others. Both are important for definition, self-direction, self-control.

The development of a generalized other in the individual, according to Mead, accompanies the development of a self, and maturity of self demands a recognition by the individual that one's own needs, one's own goals, one's own ideas must be worked out to some extent only by considering the rules of the wider community. The generalized other seems to represent a moral self to Mead:

> The structure, then, on which the self is built is this response which is common to all, for one has to be a member of a community to be a self. Such responses are abstract attitudes, but they constitute just what we term a man's character. They give him what we term his principles, the acknowledged attitudes of all members of the community toward what are the values of that community. He is putting himself in the place of the generalized other, which represents the organized responses of all the members of the group. It is that which guides conduct controlled by principles, and a person who has such an organized group of responses is a man whom we say has character, in the moral sense. (1934:162–63)

It is the generalized other that the individual uses to direct, control, and judge the self; it is the generalized other that the individual uses as his or her moral guide. As the individual develops his or her individual qualities—self and mind—a social being is also being developed. Self and society become part of the individual simultaneously.

The generalized other is the internalized moral system. It may be different in some ways for each individual, since each individual to some extent internalizes different rules, and the same rules take on different importance for each individual. Furthermore, each individual has different significant others—family, friends, heroes—so each individual will develop a slightly different generalized other. However, Mead saw that continuous interaction depends on individuals who *share* a generalized other, who share a set of rules to some minimal extent.

Importance for Society of a Generalized Other and Shared Perspective

Here it is important to point out that these *products* of interaction, which become central to the individual, are also absolutely vital for society. It is because people come to share a perspective and a generalized other in interaction that a continuing complex society is possible. Mead emphasizes this point:

> The complex co-operative processes and activities and institutional functionings of organized human society are also possible only in so far as every individual involved in them or belonging to that society can take the general attitudes of all other such individuals with reference to these processes and

activities and institutional functionings, and to the organized social whole of experiential reactions and interactions thereby constituted—and can direct his own behavior accordingly. (1934:155)

A shared perspective is necessary for understanding each other in order to accomplish difficult tasks. Warriner says that "men can act with other men because they have come to share notions as to what they will do. And they can come to share such notions (expectations) only through the communication involved in interaction" (1970:98). A shared perspective is necessary (at least to some extent) to define society as worthy of continuation and in order to establish the place of self in the interaction. A set of symbols shared (which is what is meant by perspective) is important for communication, which in turn, is essential for cooperation among individuals.

> Group life is organized around communication. Communication consists not merely in the transmission of ideas from the head of one person to that of another, it signifies shared meanings. "Shared" means more than that terms are used in ways sufficiently alike so that persons understood each other; it also means that terms arise out of and in turn permit community action. . . . We might speak of a group that consisted of only two members provided they were to act conjointly, with consensus, because they shared important symbols. Popular idiom does not usually refer to groups of two persons, but the principle involved is the same whether the groups have three members, ten, one hundred, or more. The members are able to participate in various coordinated activities because they share a common terminology. Groups form around points of agreement, and then new classifications arise on the basis of further shared experience. (Strauss, 1959:148–49)

A generalized other, shared with others, is necessary for self-control and self-direction, allowing the action to go in an agreed-upon direction established in interaction rather than according to the whims of each individual.

> The self-conscious human individual, then, takes or assumes the organized social attitudes of the given social group or community (or of some one section thereof) to which he belongs, toward the social problems of various kinds which confront that group or community at any given time, and which arise in connection with the correspondingly different social projects or organized cooperative enterprises in which that group or community as such is engaged; and as an individual participant in these social projects or co-operative enterprises, he governs his own conduct accordingly. (Mead, 1934: 156)

The basis of society is, therefore, some consensus, a shared understanding about the world, which one must act toward.

> We see, then, that people respond to one another on the basis of imaginative activity. In order to engage in concerted behavior, however, each participating individual must be able to attach the same meaning to the same gesture. Un-

less interacting individuals interpret gestures similarly, unless they fill out the imagined portion in the same way, there can be no cooperative action. This is another way of saying what has by now become a truism in sociology and social psychology: Human society rests upon a basis of *consensus,* i.e., the sharing of meanings in the form of common understandings and expectations. (Meltzer, 1972:13–14)

It is not meant here that these "products" of interaction are things that remain the same. On the contrary: Interaction is an active process, and meaning arises from it, and as a result, meaning too is constantly changing. Group life is a complex process indeed! Shibutani masterfully describes the nature of consensus, communication, and social change:

> The product of communication is not merely the modification of the listener's attitude or behavior through the stimulation, but the establishment of some measure of consensus. Consensus is the sharing of perspectives among those cooperating in joint action; it is an on-going process, a sharing that is built up, sustained, and further developed through a continuing interchange of gestures. The communicative process is rarely a single instance of stimulation and response, such as the reaction to a scream of terror, but a sequence of exchanges within a larger context. Consensus is rarely complete even for purposes of a relatively simple enterprise. It is partial; there are almost invariably areas of uncertainty, and it is about these that most of the interchanges take place. With each gesture the uncertainties are successively minimized or eliminated, enabling each person to contribute his share and to enjoy greater confidence in the responses of others. In most situations, then, communication is a continuing process. Men who are acting together try to develop and maintain mutual orientations to facilitate the coordination of their respective efforts, and the interplay must continue until the task is accomplished. The concept of *communication* refers to that interchange of gestures through which consensus is developed, sustained, or broken. (1961:140–41)

If we combine Shibutani and Mead, the image of society that develops is this: Interaction leads to the development of a generalized other, a set of rules, a guide, which the individual internalizes and which becomes the basis for self-control, self-direction, and self-judgment. It also leads to a shared perspective, an agreement about how to approach reality, a way of defining reality, a consensus about how to define each other, self, and the world out there. The individual may be said to be part of several societies, each one with its own perspective and generalized other, sometimes very different from each other, but often with considerable overlap. Each individual should also be seen as having some consistency between his or her generalized others and perspectives. That might be described as an overarching view of reality and a single generalized other, but it is also important to see the generalized other and perspectives as somewhat situationally related. To some extent, each society has its own perspective and generalized other, and they change over time as individuals interact and as the situation that must be dealt with changes. Shibutani makes this an important point in his work. It makes sense to see the individual in modern "mass society" as part of many societies, not just one. It is difficult to imagine America with an overarching perspective or generalized other. In some situations "America" may be highly relevant as a perspective (e.g., the traveler to other countries), but it is more accurate to see a nation like America as having a multitude of social worlds, each with its own perspective/generalized other, often consistent with many other social worlds, often a variation, sometimes very different, occasionally downright hostile or revolutionary. Shibutani clearly and beautifully describes mass society as separate social worlds:

> Modern mass societies, indeed, are made up of a bewildering variety of social worlds. Each is an organized outlook, built up by people in their interaction with one another; hence, each communication channel gives rise to a separate world. Probably the greatest sense of identification and solidarity is to be found in the various communal structures—the underworld, ethnic minorities, the social elite. Such communities are frequently spatially segregated which isolates them further from the outer world, while the "grapevine" and foreign-language presses provide internal contacts. Another common type of social world consists of the associational structures—the world of medicine, of organized labor, of the theater, of cafe society. These are held together not only by various voluntary associations within each locality but also by periodicals like *Variety,* specialized journals, and feature sections in newspapers. Finally, there are the loosely connected universes of special interest—the world of sports, of the stamp collector, of the daytime serial—serviced by mass media programs and magazines like *Field and Stream.* Each of these worlds is a unity of order, a universe of regularized mutual response. Each is an area in which there is some structure which permits reasonable anticipation of the behavior of others, hence, an area in which one may act with a sense of security and confidence. Each social world, then, is a culture area, the boundaries of which are set neither by territory nor by formal group membership but by the limits of effective communication. (1955:566)

In summary, then, all organized life, what we are here calling "societies" or "groups," are defined as individuals who symbolically interact and cooperate in problem solving. Symbolic interaction and cooperation are made possible by three

FIGURE 11-2

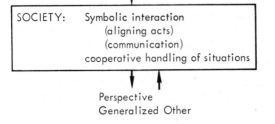

human qualities: role-taking ability, self, and mind. And as a result of interaction, a shared reality emerges called a generalized other and perspective, which serves to promote further symbolic interaction and cooperative problem solving. Figure 11-2 summarizes the nature of society as described in this chapter.

HISTORY AFFECTS SOCIETY

We are born into groups, organizations, societies that have been around for a long time. We enter into interaction that has gone on between other individuals for a long time. America was here before we were born and will probably be here after we are dead. We interact with other Americans, with our family, the Joneses, and with the workers at General Motors. It is correct to see each of these as collectives of *individuals in interaction;* each is a society, sharing, cooperating, solving problems, communicating. It is also important, however, to recognize that each has a *history.* Each interaction situation is not a brand new society but is influenced by interaction that has gone on before. People have interacted in America for a long time and through that interaction, a generalized other and perspective have developed, ever changing but also to some extent retaining some consistency over generations. The perspective and generalized other, continuously shared and continuously being redefined, lead those who interact to define each other, self, and the world outside in somewhat the same way as those who interacted earlier. Included in the perspective is some idea as to how individuals are supposed to act in their positions (roles) as well as formal rules and informal expectations (norms, institutions) to be followed by all.

> There are such matters as social roles, status positions, rank orders, bureaucratic organizations, relations between institutions, differential authority arrangements, social codes, norms, values, and the like. And they are very important. But their importance does not lie in an alleged determination of action nor in an alleged existence as parts of a self-operating societal system. Instead, they are important only as they enter into the process of interpretation and definition out of which joint actions are formed. The manner and extent to which they enter may vary greatly from situation to situation, depending on what people take into account and how they assess what they take account of. (Blumer, 1969:75)

Perspectives and rules are historically developed. The individual learns them in interaction, comes to share them, and may redefine them, but they often influence how the individual acts in a situation.

> A man must be viewed as embedded in a temporal matrix not simply of his own making, but which is peculiarly and subtly related to something of his own making—his conception of the past as it impinges on himself. (Strauss, 1959:164)

LARGER COLLECTIVES AFFECT SMALLER COLLECTIVES

Each interaction, furthermore, takes place within a larger collective; each society is part of a larger one and may be influenced by the larger one. In Blumer's words, each action or transaction takes place within a larger society. Some might call this a "macro-order." My family interaction is embedded in a small, midwestern community, and that in turn is embedded in American society. The sociology department, a group of individuals in interaction, is part of a university, which in turn is part of larger interaction levels. There is interaction between leaders and citizens in the worldwide community, and this interaction begins the development of a worldwide society, which affects each nation. The entire nation does not very often solve problems together, but leaders are elected in order to make decisions for the collective, and various political, military, economic, and educational leaders, because of their wealth, positions, or other power resources, make decisions that affect the whole collective. The point is that interaction at any level has consequences for other levels, maybe slight, maybe great. American culture affects individual family culture; the perspective that arises as people interact at a university will affect classroom interaction, dating interaction, and faculty interaction. Of course the effect varies; many of us reject the perspective and generalized other of the larger collective, many of us redefine them for ourselves, but many of us accept their limits religiously. Many may not accept the perspective and the generalized other of the collective, but the decisions made in the larger society may affect our interaction anyway—for instance, a decision made by leaders to go to war or to increase the interest rate. The individual's definition of his or her situation in relation to the larger collective, however, is vitally important. One may or may not use the larger society to define self, situation, or the world. One may find its decisions totally unacceptable and withdraw from it inwardly, escape it, or work to change or destroy it.

SMALLER COLLECTIVES AFFECT LARGER COLLECTIVES

It is also true that an organized group, such as the American Medical Association, may combine the resources of its members and act to affect the direction of the larger American society by lobbying to influence legislators, by sponsoring television programs and advertisements to influence the public, and by publishing mountains of evidence to support its interests. What is being described here is an *acting unit,* a number of interacting individuals cooperating and directing their leadership to fight for their interests by interacting with political leaders and the public at large, in order to direct the larger society in the direction it desires. And in many cases, a group like the AMA will succeed, as do a number of smaller collectives in American society. America should be conceived of as a number of individuals interacting, some representing themselves, others representing organizations or groups, often trying to influence other organizations or the society at large.

PEOPLE MAKE SOCIETY—SOCIETY MAKES PEOPLE

The interdependence of humans and human society is great. It is through interaction (society) that perspective, symbols, and social objects are created. It is through interaction (society) that self, mind, role-taking skills, and generalized other are developed. On the other side, human symbolic interaction (society) is carried on because humans are equipped with symbols, self, mind, perspectives, role-taking skills, and generalized other. In truth, society provides us with what we are as individuals, and in turn, it is what we are as individuals that makes human society possible.

It is important to conclude this discussion of society with one last idea. Whereas most theories of society almost dare us to show how it is possible for freedom and creativity to exist, the symbolic interactionist shows that freedom and creativity arise *from* society, not in spite of it. In truth, society does "make us" as we interact with others. But with what society provides—symbols, self, mind, role-taking ability—we turn around and make society.

REFERENCES

BERGER, PETER L. and THOMAS LUCKMANN
    1967 *The Social Construction of Reality,* New York: Doubleday. Copyright © 1966 by Peter L. Berger and Thomas Luckmann. Reprinted by permission of Doubleday & Co., Inc., New York, and Penguin Press, Harmondsworth, Middlesex, England.

BLUMER, HERBERT
    1953 "Psychological Import of the Human Group." In eds. Muzafer Sherif and M. O. Wilson, *Group Relations at the Crossroads,* pp. 185-202. New York: Harper & Row.
    1962 "Society as Symbolic Interaction." In ed. Arnold Rose, *Human Behavior and Social Processes,* pp. 179-92. Boston: Houghton Mifflin. Copyright © 1962 by Houghton Mifflin Company. Used with permission.
    1966 "Sociological Implications of the Thought of George Herbert Mead." *American Journal of Sociology* 71:535-44. By permission of The University of Chicago Press. Copyright © 1966 by The University of Chicago. All rights reserved.
    1969 *Symbolic Interactionism: Perspective and Method.* Englewood Cliffs, N.J.: Prentice-Hall. Copyright © 1969. Reprinted by permission of Prentice-Hall, Inc.

MEAD, GEORGE HERBERT
    1934 *Mind, Self and Society.* Chicago: University of Chicago Press. Reprinted by permission of The University of Chicago Press. Copyright © 1934 by The University of Chicago. All rights reserved.
    1936 *Movements of Thought in the 19th Century.* Ed. Merritt H. Moore. Chicago: University of Chicago Press. Reprinted by permission of The University of Chicago Press. Copyright © 1936 by The University of Chicago. All rights reserved.

1938 *The Philosophy of the Act.* Ed. Merritt H. Moore. Chicago: University of Chicago Press.

MELTZER, BERNARD N.
1972 *The Social Psychology of George Herbert Mead.* Kalamazoo: Center for Sociological Research, Western Michigan University. By permission of Bernard N. Meltzer.

SHIBUTANI, TAMOTSU
1955 "Reference Groups as Perspectives." *American Journal of Sociology* 60:562–69. By permission of The University of Chicago Press. Copyright © 1955 by The University of Chicago. All rights reserved.

1961 *Society and Personality: An Interactionist Approach to Social Psychology.* Englewood Cliffs, N.J.: Prentice-Hall. Copyright © 1961. Reprinted by permission of Prentice-Hall, Inc.

STRAUSS, ANSELM
1959 *Mirrors and Masks.* New York: Free Press.

WARRINER, CHARLES K.
1970 *The Emergence of Society.* Homewood, Ill.: Dorsey Press. By permission of the Dorsey Press.

12
SYMBOLIC
INTERACTIONISM:
A FINAL ASSESSMENT

Take any situation: a dinner party, an athletic event, a club meeting, a meeting of the United Nations, a battle, a family feud, a revolution, a conflict between ethnic groups—look at any of these in depth and one has to be amazed at the complexity of human social life. Every one of these—in fact, all situations—can be approached and analyzed from a number of perspectives, each telling us something more, each unlocking new and enlightening aspects of human beings. The lesson has to be humility: No perspective, no matter how useful, can tell us all there is about any situation. A Marxist perspective sensitizes us to inequality, conflict, power, and economics. A sociological perspective will point us to social structure, roles, social stratification, and institutions. A psychoanalyst reveals to us the subconscious at work in situations, drives, defense mechanisms, personality. Social psychologists tell us how individuals are influenced by each other in situations and how attitudes are formed and changed in situations. It is easy to criticize each of these perspectives. We can say that each one is *incomplete,* each ignores some important aspects of the situation, and each probably overemphasizes certain things.

This criticism is true, of course, of the symbolic interactionist perspective. When the focus is on interaction, both personality predispositions and social structure fail to be examined in great depth. Unconscious and emotional reactions are deemphasized. The symbolic interactionist emphasizes that humans are dynamic, they are rational problem solvers, and that society is a process of individuals in interaction—cooperating, role taking, aligning acts, and communicating. The human engages in overt and covert action in the *present;* recalling past, planning for future, and the action that takes place between individuals is an important influence on the direction of individuals and collectives. The choice of concentrating on interaction is a bias—in the same way that all perspectives must concentrate on some things at the expense of others—but this concentration is central to the understanding of what humans do. The symbolic interactionist focuses on concepts few scientists have seriously considered, and thus the perspective has always been a criticism of mainstream social science. Expecting symbolic interactionism to explain everything is erroneous, but it is correct to say, in my opinion, that symbolic interactionism is an exciting and useful perspective for understanding human social life. It has made important contributions to social science, sociology, social psychology, to those who "work with people," and to students interested in understanding themselves and society.

SYMBOLIC INTERACTIONISM AND HUMAN FREEDOM: A REVIEW

Symbolic interactionism is an attempt to break away from traditional social science and to view the human as maker, doer, actor, and as self-directing. It is an attempt to locate what Kant and other philosophers were looking for: a free spirit, a "soul," individual freedom in humans. It is an attempt to locate the freedom that many say scientific sociologists cannot really find. It is, of course, naive to believe that humans are completely free, but this perspective of symbolic interactionism does focus on human qualities—socially created qualities—that break us out of the determining prison of traditional social science. For a moment, perhaps it might be beneficial to summarize how symbolic interactionism conceptualizes the "free" person:

1. Many might argue that it is the "*I*" in the self that is the free person. Indeed the "I" is important, but it is not what this book or what the perspective sees as the real source of human freedom. The "I" tells us that socialization is never complete, that part of us goes untouched by society, that we continuously surprise ourselves in what we do, that we are creative, impulsive, spontaneous. The "I" means that we do engage in action not thought out: This is exciting in the sense that action can be taken, thinking about it can occur afterward, and new ideas about the world can arise, new directions can be taken. I say "no" to my master without thinking, and afterward I realize the possibility of refusing to conform, and "no" becomes a thinking act.

2. It is the *me*, the socialized self, that is the source of human freedom. By giving the human a self, society gives the individual someone to talk to privately, someone to *direct*, someone to think things out with, someone to use to analyze situations. Mind activity is activity that analyzes situations and directs the self performing a certain way in a situation. This is an active ongoing process, causing action to go one way, then another, causing the individual to reanalyze situations, to recall past and construct future as action unfolds. Rather than habit or instinct taking us through social situations, it is definition and planning carried out with the self that is central.

3. *Symbols* are also a source of human freedom. With words as tools, the human is able to construct new ideas, new syntheses, new strategies. Give the human words and the ability to remember and combine them, and there is no way to stop new creative thoughts and acts. In a sense, every sentence is an individual creation, every student essay exam and term paper, every speech, and every telephone conversation is a new creative effort by symbol users, synthesizing and analyzing in unique ways. Humans are not *sometimes* creative but creative in all situations.

4. Humans are constantly changing, constantly "becoming." We are dynamic, our interactions influence what we do and are. We are not damned (or blessed) with our past as a determining agent; we are not imprisoned by the ideas or traits we have developed long ago. It is always in the present that we actively define what is important. Interaction with others and with self constantly shifts our direction, our action, our definition of the world and self.

Freedom, of course, is limited. We act freely, but only within a situation that has parameters. It is the purpose of the social sciences, including symbolic interactionism, to understand these parameters along with the active self-determining nature of the individuals. Briefly, some of the paramaters to consider are the following:

1. The situation will provide some important constraints on what we can do. We are confronted by situations that we must define, but these situations have an existence in themselves. They have a history independent of us: a war is a reality; others may reject us or love us; a class structure in society may place us within its limits; poverty may limit much of our action and concerns; and others may have more resources and, therefore, more power advantage over us—they may at times coerce us, manipulate us, or persuade us. Central here is the fact that actors constantly define situations for others, and people can and are manipulated by this. It is difficult to ignore the situation that confronts us; it is an important parameter.

2. Action is not always directed by symbolic interaction with the self. Alternatives are emotions and habit. Both of these lead us to respond to stimuli without thinking, without problem solving, without considering past and future, without role-taking. There are elements of both emotion and habit in what we do, and to the extent that we rely on these in our action, we are not "free" in the sense that is described above. Some individuals may be highly influenced by habitual or emotional response, unable to deal effectively with new situations or to new variables in situations, unable to interact with others, unable to role-take, unable to cooperate in dealing with complex situations, and/or unable to communicate effectively. Their freedom is limited.

3. A society, a social world, may be so important to us that its perspective not only becomes a *guide* to situations, but actually shapes our action, making our definition a habitual response. This may depend on the extent and nature of our exclusive interaction with certain other individuals and our identification with them. A religious cult, an isolated family life, or the world of a prison may be a closed world where interaction between a few may be continuous and intense and where there may be a constant sharing of a single perspective and a single generalized other. Freedom, creativity, and adjusting acts to ongoing interaction here will be made more difficult; freedom will be small.

4. Human freedom is always limited by language, by our symbols. We can only be free within our symbolic system. That is why learning a number of perspectives, extending our vocabulary, and exposing ourselves to a number of social situations is essential to liberal education. Increasing the symbols available to us for analyzing situations, for thinking, for seeing things in different ways, for directing our self in new directions is essential.

These limits, or parameters, should not cause us to lose sight of the freedom that is human. Perhaps it is better to call it "our active nature": Humans do not respond to situations but are actively involved in both definition and self-direction in these situations.

SYMBOLIC INTERACTIONISM AND SCIENCE

George Herbert Mead argued forcefully for the understanding of human beings through the study of what they *do,* through their action. Action, according to Mead and to the symbolic interactionist perspective, is always overt *and* covert action, what we do in relation to the other and in relation to our self. This may be difficult to study scientifically, since self-action is difficult to measure and difficult to predict. This perspective also seems to go against most of our notions of science since it suggests that there is an important element of human freedom in what we do.

There has always been disagreement over the meaning and purpose of science. All seem to agree that science is a method of discovery, one that relies on empirically gathered evidence, and one that emphasizes a systematic and objective approach to the accumulation and analysis of evidence. Most social scientists have regarded science as a means of testing hypotheses related to causes of human behavior. This has usually involved defining two or more variables and testing a causal relationship between them. Social scientists, in their attempt to be scientific, have adopted from some natural scientists a model of science for studying human behavior. As a result, the symbolic nature of the human being has been neglected; covert-minded activity has been considered "outside of science"; action in the present has been overlooked as a cause; and, in the end, "the definition of the situation" by the actor has not been considered an important element in the situation.

Symbolic interactionists are critical of traditional social science, its use of scientific methodology for the study of human beings, and its definition of "important causal variables." The way we study humans, as in anything else in nature—for instance, bugs, stars, rocks, or rats—must be determined first and foremost *by the nature of the empirical world under study.* We must develop empirical techniques that take into account the central qualities of human behavior. Science must understand how humans *define situations,* how they *act in the present* by applying past experiences and future plans, how they *solve problems* confronting them. This means that scientists must recognize that past events alone do not *cause* present action without an active person defining the situation and directing the self in the present. The purpose of symbolic interactionism as a scientific perspective is to understand the cause of human action, but "cause" is transformed to mean human definition, self-direction, and choice in situations. We must better understand how humans think, solve problems, role take, apply their past, and look to the future in situations. Science for understanding human action must recognize that part of human action is choice, is creative, is free, and thus, paradoxically, the role of science becomes one of understanding how, and to what extent, freedom plays a role in what we do.

The symbolic interactionist regards a careful *description* of human interaction as a central goal of social science. Careful observation of social action, description of the important "elements" involved, and a careful description and redefinition of these elements should be achieved. That does not necessarily mean understanding which variable causes which variable, although the important elements at work in social situations may someday be causally linked. In a sense, a "formal sociology" is one of the goals of the symbolic interactionist, the purpose of which is to isolate and carefully describe such central concepts as conflict, role taking, cooperation, problem solving, rehearsal of action, situations, definition of the situation, identity, self-direction, symbol, social objects, embarrassment, appearance, poise, and the like. It is important to see every one of the concepts at work in a number of situations, comparing and contrasting instances of them, clarifying them, describing how they play a role in a number of situations, and how they seem to be absent from others. I might observe human action and recognize some important process taking place. Then I describe it: "This is what embarrassment is, this is what happens when people are embarrassed, this is what people think, what they do, this is what happens to the ongoing interaction." Then I analyze a number of situations where embarrassment exists and also analyze where it is absent. Edward Gross and Gregory Stone's article on embarrassment (1964) is a model of this kind of analysis.

Another important principle that symbolic interactionists use in scientific research is the gathering of data through the observance of *real life situations.* Much social science research is done in laboratories or on questionnaires; scientists should carefully describe people in real settings—how they interact with others and with themselves in situations that must be worked through. This kind of description is not to be impressionistic and journalistic, but as careful, critical, systematic, and objective as possible. Interaction in a controlled lab situation might be used to supplement real-life situations. Videotapes of both real situations and lab situations provide an excellent way of analyzing "side by side" several instances of interaction. Opportunities to discuss ongoing interaction with other scientists is also made easier through such an approach. But it is always the definition of and the action taken in real situations that must be the central laboratory for understanding human behavior.

Norman Denzin has done significant empirical work within the perspective of symbolic interactionism. In 1971 Denzin attempted to spell out principles that should govern the methodology of this perspective:

1. Denzin calls his methodology "naturalistic behaviorism." It is a commitment to studying the behavior of actors in their own worlds through entering those

worlds and understanding them from the actor's perspective. It is imperative to understand overt action and definitions actors give their actions, even if this means simply asking them for "retrospective accounts of past actions."

2. Introspection is a basic part of the methodology. The researcher must examine his or her own self and his or her views of experience. The researcher's own life becomes an important source of data, and he or she must be open to all sources of data for understanding interaction.

3. The researcher must develop a technique for describing "in a rich and detailed fashion the experiences, thoughts, and languages of those he studies." This must show the time sequence involved and also how actors influence each other's acts as they go along.

4. The researcher must balance his or her theoretical concepts with the actual situation being described. There is a need to generalize, yet there is also a need to respect the empirical world itself, to see it as one unique, real-world experience.

5. The scientist must build up confidence among those he or she studies, must get close to them, and must rely heavily on them for understanding the situation.

6. Any social situation might be analyzed from a number of angles, but researchers should be sure to focus their attention around a carefully selected set of concepts, each sensitizing them to a different aspect of the situation, but together offering important insights. For example, scientists should look at "language," "self," "social objects," "social setting," and "joint actions." Whatever concepts are chosen, however, will determine the particular strategy of investigation.

7. It is important to determine ways to describe the study in such a manner that others are able to replicate it, to check it out, to add to it, and/or to criticize it. The scientists "must repeatedly address the question of replication and whether or not his findings can be built upon by others." For example, the method of sampling situations must be carefully described.

Denzin gives a more detailed account of the technical aspects of scientific investigation, but these seven principles summarize his major points. Both this description and Denzin's own work stand as examples of a symbolic interactionist approach to scientific investigation.

Symbolic interactionism stands as an important criticism of using traditional scientific methods in social science. The study of attitudes, values, animals in laboratories, and people in experimental situations gives some insight into human behavior, but it is not enough. The symbolic interactionist calls for a different direction, as summarized by Blumer:

It [symbolic interactionism] believes that this determination of problems, concepts, research techniques, and theoretical schemes should be done by the *direct* examination of the actual empirical social world rather than by working with a simulation of that world, or with a preset model of that world, or with a picture of that world derived from a few scattered observations of it, or with a picture of that world fashioned in advance to meet the dictates of some imported theoretical scheme or of some scheme of "scientific" procedure, or with a picture of the world built up from partial and untested accounts of that world. For symbolic interactionism the nature of the empirical social world is to be discovered, to be dug out by a direct, careful, and probing examination of that world. (1969:48)

Note the formation in recent years of the Society for the Study of Symbolic Interaction, and the publication of a journal by that organization. The articles in this journal, as well as in several others such as *Sociological Quarterly,* contain excellent examples of the empirical work done by symbolic interactionists. The empirical studies are tremendously diverse, but each focuses on interaction, definition, meaning, and/or social worlds. Each conforms to a great extent to the scientific principles outlined here. Most are based on interviews with people about their worlds, their action, and their perspectives; some draw from everyday examples of interaction or are based on participant-observation. Symbolic interactionism is more than a statement of empirical principles and more than a criticism of social science: it is also a perspective that has struggled to develop its own methodology and has increased our understanding of human interaction through its many empirical findings.

SYMBOLIC INTERACTIONISM: SOME REPRESENTATIVE STUDIES

The studies that have been inspired by this approach are too numerous to include here in any systematic way. However, five interesting examples might help give some idea of what can be done.

Lonnie H. Athens (1980) investigated violent offenders to find out why some people choose violence in their life situations. Sociologists and psychologists have traditionally examined the social and personality factors that cause rape, murder, aggravated assault, and other crimes of violence. As a symbolic interactionist, however, Athens was interested in the *thinking* involved, in how actors define situations that call for violent action. Each person is thought to be an "*actor* who organizes his actions to fit the situations that confront him" (1980:13). Athens interviewed fifty-eight offenders who described in detail what happened in situations where they committed violent acts and what they were thinking, if anything. The data "show that violent actors *self consciously construct* violent plans of action before they commit violent criminal acts . . ." (1980:19). They take the role of their victims, always interpreting actions as symbolic acts, and they take the role of a violent generalized other that approves of this type of action in this situation. Continuous definition is important:

> Once actors have formed violent plans of action, whether or not they carry them out depends upon what happens during the process of interpretation, that is, it depends upon whether they stay in a fixed line of indication or form a restraining or overriding judgment. (1980:38)

View of self, type of generalized other, and length of violent careers are all factors that contribute to the definition of the situation as one of violence. And actions by the other are interpreted and in turn influence maintaining a violent definition or altering the definition.

In *Sexual Stigma* (1975) Kenneth Plummer examines sex and sexual deviance from a symbolic interactionist perspective. What is a sexual act and what is not?

> *Nothing is sexual but naming makes it so. Sexuality is a social construction learnt in interaction with others.* This is not, of course, to deny the existence of genitals, copulation or orgasms as biological and universal 'facts'; it is simply to assert the sociological commonplace that these things do not have 'sexual meanings' in their own right; these have to be bestowed upon them through social encounters. The 'mind' has to define something as 'sexual' before it is sexual in its consequences. (1975:30)

Plummer asks us: Is it a sexual act when a child plays with his or her genitals, when a couple are naked together, when a man and woman copulate out of duty, or when a girl takes her clothes off in public? We often define them as such, but they are not necessarily so.

This is, of course, also true of sexual behavior labeled as "deviant." We are not biologically programmed to engage in a certain type of sexual act. We are characterized by a great plasticity. We learn how to be sexual, and so "why individuals are led to certain kinds of 'sexual experiences' and not others . . . [requires an understanding of] interaction with significant others, and . . . the abstract meanings lodged in the 'objective reality.'" Like all other human action, sexuality must be understood as consisting of a stream of action involving decisions influenced by interaction with others and with self. (1975:56-57) And this process is lifelong, causing the actor to go first in one direction, then another. And the full importance of interaction can be grasped only if we realize that our world is highly complex, made up of a great diversity of sexual directions, often contradictory, and always changing. Thus, homosexuality, defined in a certain society as deviant, is deviant only because of the prevailing definition, and the reasons for an individual's choosing that path rather than another are contained in a process of definition and interaction. Like all identities, this identity emerges through a continuous definition by others and the actor, and the stream of action involves a series of changes we might call a sexual "career."

Samuel Heilman (1976) described life in an orthodox synagogue from a symbolic interactionist perspective. How people interact in such a place is carefully described, always with the purpose of understanding the world from their perspective. Actors do things in relation to each other, they communicate, they interpret, they change actions according to what other people do. Meanings arise in such interaction, and while the outsider might interpret a situation one way, the actors themselves see the situation according to a common perspective, developed over a long period of time. The example of the *"schnorrer"* is described in this context. What is a *schnorrer* to the people involved in the synagogue, and how do they act toward him? How does he communicate that he is not a beggar but needs financial help? How does he express the fact that he is like everyone in the synagogue except he has had misfortune? How is he successful in getting financial help without demeaning himself? The interaction is critical:

> With the end of the prayers, the schnorrer steps forward toward the *bimah* (the pulpit in the center of the room). He holds in his hand two letters of reference, which he calls to our attention. They are his credentials. But this money-collector will go beyond the letters; he will tell his story.
>
> He speaks in Yiddish (perhaps because he has seen a copy of the *Jewish Daily Forward* in Velvel's pocket, perhaps because he wants to emphasize his Jewishness, or perhaps because he speaks no English). He explains aloud to all those assembled that he has worked hard all his life, as they have, but he has now come upon hard times, especially because he suffers from "arthritis" (the only English word he uses). In his hand he holds a cane. He has a family to support, as we all do, and if we could give him some financial help, he says, he would be most appreciative.
>
> The man's forthrightness has frozen the participants in their places. No one has sneaked out the door or even tried to leave. No one can claim ignorance of this stranger's needs. He has shined a spotlight on all of us by putting one on himself, knowing that, if he can tap one or two people for money, the rest will feel impelled to give in domino-like fashion. A few of the men begin to take out their wallets, looking at the others' actions. All the donations are bills, and all are handed to Rabbi Housmann. Some members ask Housmann for change—something that could not be done without embarrassment were the money being given directly to the schnorrer.
>
> While Housmann is collecting the money, those who have already given wait and talk. The ritualized giving is evidently not yet complete. Some members complain aloud about the need to give, one man saying, "I don't understand. In these times of social security benefits and all. . . ." But the grumbles are hardly as abusive as those made to beggars, and everyone who grumbles still donates. In response to some complaints about the need for giving, Velvel says, "It's a *mitzvah* (positive and mandatory ritual commandment) to give him (that is, the schnorrer) some money." Giving is a religious responsibility, as important for the donor as for the recipient. The others agree and add, as one man puts it, "God forbid that we should ever need it," a comment never heard in the presence of any other kind of mendicant.
>
> The schnorrer receives the money from Housmann and thanks the people aloud. Then, as the people shuffle out, the schnorrer approaches some directly, shaking their hands and offering words of blessing. Finally, he approaches Harwood and asks for a ride to another synagogue nearby, the next stop on his journey. He gets his ride. (1976:117–118)

Always Heilman points out, there is an attempt to establish a commonness between himself and the potential donors: dress represents a middle-class status, for example. There is an attempt to shake hands, to converse, and to do what a "guest" rather than a simple beggar might do. The schnorrer always tries to build bonds and feelings of acceptance before he "gives his pitch," since he knows that his only chance of success is to ask only *after* establishing his Jewishness and telling his sad story. No matter how often the schnorrer returns, he does not become a friend and a guest to those in the synagogue, but remains an outsider, "stigmatized by his plea for money." (1976:119)

Heilman's account presents to us a picture of life in one part of our world through firsthand and sensitive observation. No scientist could hope to capture the many complex aspects of interaction, communication, interpretation, and presentation of self through other types of methodology.

Mary K. Zimmerman (1981) examined the abortion clinic after abortion became legal in this society. Her study is a follow-up of the work done by Donald Ball in the 1960s when abortion was illegal. Both Zimmerman and Ball's studies focused on how those who run abortion clinics attempt to *define the situation* for clients. Ball found that before they became legal, clinics were made to appear as sterile and medical-like as possible, in order to assure acceptance by the patient. The fact that abortion was illegitimate demanded that abortion clinics give the appearance of legitimate medical facilities, not unlike a doctor's office or a hospital. Zimmerman, in her study of two clinics in the 1970s (which included observations and interviews with staff and patients) noted that the clinic still found it essential to define the situation for clients, but the type of definition had shifted:

> Specifically, the shift from illegal to legal abortion has been accompanied by a shift in "rhetoric of legitimation" from one emphasizing medical professionalism to one that deemphasizes it, stressing instead "personalized," "individualized," nontraditional care. (1981:51)

The attention turned to relaxing the patient, supporting and assuring the patient, encouraging discussion of doubts and fears.

Throughout the history of abortion clinics, staff have attempted to take the role of the patient, to try to understand what she wanted, and to present the clinic in that form. Through understanding the patient's perspective, clinics, like all businesses and agencies that deal with the public, decide how consumers view their services, and they attempt to build on that, so that there is a consistency in how the clinic presents itself and how the consumer needs to see it.

From abortion clinics we move to Little League Baseball, another social world that can best be understood through firsthand observation. Gary Alan Fine (1981: 269) examined teams in four communities for three years. His interest was in seeing how preadolescents develop social skills, skills in presenting themselves to others. Such skills are not learned through a "rote learning of behaviors or of an encyclopedia of practical knowledge." Preadolescents learn social skills through interaction with others, dealing with common situations, learning to fit one's own acts with those of others, learning to take each other's roles, interpreting each other's acts, and so on. Fine reports the following from his field notes:

> Hardy sees Tommy get on the bus and announces loudly, "Tommy sucks." Rod adds: "Tommy's a wuss." In unison Jerry and Rod tell Tommy as he approaches, "You suck." Rod particularly is angry at Tommy. "Harmon can't play because of you. What a fag!" Tommy doesn't respond to the abuse from

his older tormentors, but looks dejected and perhaps near tears (which is what Rod and Hardy later tell Harmon). The insults build in stridency and anger as Hardy calls Tommy a "woman." Jerry knocks off his hat, and Rod says, "Give him the faggot award." Finally Jerry takes the baseball cap of Tommy's friend and seatmate and tosses it out the window of the moving bus. (1981: 269)

What is the point? Why is this a significant encounter? What appears as cruelty and insults to outsiders is part of a social world where preadolescents learn about each other's expectations, where they learn how to present themselves to others, what limits exist to insults, how to react to insults. In fact, if acts go "too far," as was the case in throwing the hat out the window, one learns how to apologize. Organized baseball teams provide an opportunity for interaction among friends, which teaches the necessary skills for successful interaction. And, because there is a relationship among friends developed over a period of time, people have a history of interaction, and any isolated episode is not likely to be very threatening to self-perception. We feel comfortable around friends; we are more likely to be open; we learn many of the essentials of interaction.

The final example is a study by John Carling of "Bachelorhood and Late Marriage" (1977). What happens to the man who seems to be a confirmed bachelor, when he suddenly gives that up and decides on marriage? The study concentrates on "interaction": how interaction influences bachelorhood to begin with; then how it alters that status. Forty men were studied. Half were over thirty-five and never married, half married after the age of thirty-five. Here the research technique used was in-depth interviews, the collecting of life histories from the men.

Almost all of the men reported that "in adolescence they had a great deal of difficulty in peer-group interactions." (1977:47) They entered adulthood without much dating experience, *and* they entered without much pressure from significant others (both parents and friends) to date. If they had friends, the friends usually did not date either. "None of them had parents who asked 'Why aren't you dating like others your age'?" About one-third were very involved in interaction with family, which prevented them from seeking relationships outside the home. There is no one quality that influenced bachelorhood; there is a cluster: "Rather, bachelorhood arises in the context of a web of situations and definitions that make marriage unlikely at various points in the life histories of individuals" (1977:51).

Those who decide on marriage after thirty-five are best described as going through a process of "conversion." They are seekers: The old social world within which they lived their lives was "crumbling," and they were lonely. Friends were marrying, and parents died. A turning point occurred for the late-married that did not really occur for those who did not marry. "Most of the late-marrieds had short courtships; they were at turning points that made them ripe for marriage and they wasted little time in becoming involved with the woman who happened to be available at the time" (1977:50).

These empirical studies are good examples of the perspective of symbolic interactionism. All attempt to capture interaction, definition, and decision making over a period of time. The actor changes, situations are dynamic, action goes first one way, then another. The human is understood as a highly complex problem solver, defining and redefining directions in which to go in situations.

SYMBOLIC INTERACTIONISM: SOME EVERYDAY EXAMPLES OF APPLICATION

A student in a class on symbolic interaction asked me: "This is all fine and dandy, but what in the world does this perspective have to do with anything? What is its relevance?" I could not believe that this perspective, so powerful for me, could not be applied by the student. "It's relevant to everything human," I began. "All situations can be described using this perspective—this classroom interaction, for example, race relations, war, a football game, a family, a party. . . ." and I went on and on, patting myself on the back as I proudly announced all the applications. "But I'm going to work with delinquents," was the reply. "How can I use this to help them, to change them, to make them better?" Then I knew that relevance to this student meant changing people—how do we as teachers teach better, how can we alter behavior for the better, change attitudes, make a better world? For me relevance has always meant just plain understanding—how well does Marx understand society, or Freud understand it, or George Herbert Mead? In fact, the point of the symbolic interactionists seems to be that human beings are not easily manipulated, altered, predictable. I realized that the perspective may aid my understanding of *human complexity,* but not necessarily suggest how to successfully change or manipulate others.

Another student who was in business management told me: "The thing that symbolic interactionism taught me was that it is very difficult to manage people any way one chooses; people are active and thinking, and they determine their own directions in interaction with others and with themselves. This is important when I go out into the business world and deal with people." Symbolic interactionism may not yet be relevant to those who want to systematically alter people in a given direction, but it is a very relevant perspective for understanding human social situations. As it does this more and more accurately, prediction and the ability to change people may result (if that is what one chooses to do with knowledge).

The point of the business management student cannot be taken lightly: It is interaction that affects the direction of the individual, and the nature of interaction—overt and covert—is difficult for one to control or direct except in a small number of situations. We can teach our children values, but these values will be effective in directing the child only if they influence the child's interaction and only if they continue to be important in the perspectives he or she shares with others. It seems that the teacher or parent must be prepared to see these values transformed or put aside during interaction with others who become the new significant others or reference groups. The convicted criminal can be put away in a prison community, can learn new values, can take on a different perspective, can have a different "personality," but when released these things will be effective only if *interaction* is influenced, and only if interaction does not lead the individual to define the world in the same way he or she defined it before imprisonment. To change the person is to change his or her interaction, social worlds, reference groups, and perspectives, and thus alter the person's definition of self and situations. Given the nature of modern society this goal seems difficult for one person to set for another.

Symbolic interactionism is a perspective that can be applied to all social situations and can help illuminate them. This goes for two people on a date, for a college classroom, for any game like chess or football, for bringing up children, and for social problems such as crime and inequality. All of these involve interaction as well as interaction within individuals with selves, minds, symbols, perspectives, analyzing, problem solving, cooperating, sharing, communicating, and aligning acts. I have tried to apply this perspective to my world, and I find it full of insights. If it is going to be useful, one must take the concepts and use them to analyze situations. I would like to give briefly some examples of how I have applied this perspective to things that concern me.

Symbolic Interactionism in Sex, Marriage, and Family Relationships

Asking someone for a date was always a major event in my life. As I asked someone for a date I communicated something (I am interested in you *or* I need company so please join me *or* I'm scared *or* I'm cool *or* I like having a good time *or* . . .). The other person interpreted my request: he's nice, he's interested in me, I wonder what he really wants, he's really nervous, and so on. We role take, we communicate, and often if we do not understand, we ask for clarification of meaning. We meet, we interpret each other according to dress, looks, acts, speech, the objects we surround ourselves with, and so on. We do this in order to assure the continuation of interaction, or in order to get away from the other as fast as possible, or in order to influence the other. Each time we act, there is analysis of meaning, a greater sharing of meaning, an emerging perspective, more and more knowledge of how to align acts toward each other. Kissing and lovemaking are symbolic acts too: They stand for past experience, future intent, and current feelings and thoughts. Over time a society may emerge between us, we become significant others when we are around each other and, increasingly, in situations where we are apart. Conflict with parents may occur, perhaps because a new emerging perspective is replacing an older one, a new significant other is replacing an older family reference group. Interaction with parents may occur less often, and a failure to take each other's role or to understand each other's meaning takes over. Where symbolic interaction with self was once necessary for aligning acts between ourselves and our parents, automatic emotional response to each other now predominates, and the accompanying failure to align acts cooperatively ensues. Habitual reactions, not acts attempting to take account of the other, become commonplace. We may marry the one we date and love even though parents may object. Marriage may lead to a redefinition of the situation for all. Interaction patterns will change, the reference groups will increasingly become the new family for husband, wife, and any children. The conflict with parents may cease, and cooperative interaction may occur as the older parents increasingly see their child's family as a reference group. On the other hand, the husband and wife may drift further apart, actually diminishing interaction, and those outside the family may become significant others and reference groups. Problems of communication, failure to role take and align action accurately may lead to a breakdown of the family and society.

We can also see each family event as symbolic interaction: preparing a thanksgiving meal, deciding on whether to have children, deciding where to live, and dividing up tasks around the home. All of these events are decided through husband and wife interacting, role taking, sharing, and so on.

Interactionism in the Classroom

Symbolic interactionism, when applied to my own life as a teacher is awfully humbling. I started my career hoping to influence students, to get them to look at the world sociologically, humanistically, or through the symbolic interactionist perspective. I hoped to teach something that would remain with students, to make a difference in some important way. I was a teacher, in part, to try to create a better world. I woke up one day when a student stated: "You know, this is all very interesting, this is even relevant to my life, but this classroom is the only place I ever discuss these things or hear anything about them. Outside this classroom there just is not any interest or knowledge about them. I won't remember any of this when the class is all over." I realized then why things are so easily forgotten after a final exam. A perspective is remembered if it is applied and found to be useful in a number of situations. But this is unlikely to happen unless other people around us also use it regularly and share it in interaction. A perspective is remembered if one has a reference group that shares it, if it is associated with our significant others. The different perspectives gained in the classroom cannot be expected to be remembered and applied—they are forgotten unless they continue to be shared through interaction. College itself can be an important perspective that we remember—it can become a reference group providing a perspective for our present situation—but whatever was gained will be changed considerably as we interact *now* with new people. Unhappily, for those of us who think we can actually teach something lasting, what will probably happen to our students is this: They might learn the perspective we are trying to teach, barely remember it after the exam, or they may interact with others who share it or take another class that shares it, (or may never take another class like it or interact with others who share it). They will probably graduate with little except a dim memory that will, in turn, be transformed as they interact with others in the work world who may share a perspective that contradicts or even ridicules the perspectives learned in college. Realistically, the classroom experience is part of a long stream of action for each person. A teacher may influence the direction that stream of action takes. He or she may influence the student's desire to interact with others who share an academic, sociological, psychological, or biological perspective, or, at least, may influence the student's desire to continue to interact with those who are open to discussing these perspectives intelligently.

Symbolic Interactionism and Social Issues

The problems that exist between blacks and whites in American society or between Arabs and Israelis in the Middle East, or between Americans and Russians can, in part, be understood from a symbolic interactionist perspective. Conflict can indeed result from the fact that one group gains at the expense of the other, which a Marxist perspective may emphasize. But conflict may also result from a breakdown in communication, a misinterpretation of symbols, inaccurate role taking, poor communication with the other, misinterpretation of situations, or failure to align acts appropriately and/or cooperatively. Individuals and collectives may find conflict rather than cooperation characterizing their interaction, but, in most cases, interaction will involve both cooperation and conflict. Their behavior may be subtly influenced in one way, and then another. Misinterpretation and failure to understand intentions may lead to questioning and redefining tasks; failure to take each other's roles properly may lead to judging each other unfairly, expressing anger, and then uniting to work out intelligently what really is on each other's mind. We will find that when interaction is systematically cut off between groups, a perspective cannot be easily shared, the acts of each cannot be understood by the other, and situations cannot be cooperatively understood and worked out. Cooperative problem solving then becomes impossible, aligning acts fails to materialize, and emotion and habitual response replaces symbolic interaction between the groups. This is one of the results of segregation in society.

The symbolic interactionist perspective describes everyday situations that we all encounter, as well as complex problems such as war. The perspective has been applied successfully to understanding deviance in society. It can be applied to anything that involves human action and interaction. It has illuminated the problem of mental health and mental illness, which has always been a central interest to me. The problem of mental illness can be looked at in a different perspective when it is defined as a "chronic failure to interact successfully with others." Symbolic interactionists will emphasize four possible problems that might account for this failure in interaction: problems with symbols (understanding others and/or being understood), problems with role taking (either a lack of ability or an unwillingness to role take with others in interaction), problems with applying inappropriate reference groups—significant others—or perspectives to situations, and problems with habitual and/or emotional responses to situations that call for symbolic interaction with self. When any or all of these become chronic, then the individual will have difficulties in social situations. There will be problems in communication, a failure to analyze and define the situation and one's place in it, a failure to assess others accurately and align acts, a failure to define the situation accurately for self, and a failure to decide on a line of action that will allow one to work out the problems in the situation cooperatively. Everyone has these difficulties, but when they are continuous, then group life becomes impossible, and the individual increasingly confronts conflict, isolation, frustration, self-control problems, self-rejection, powerlessness in situations, and stress associated with having to work out problems. This framework for understanding personal problems works for me; it helps me understand other people and myself. The description may be naive and admittedly it is highly speculative, but it is one direction in which the symbolic interactionist perspective leads me: It suggests the ways a symbolic interactionist might approach a problem such as mental illness.

The list of situations that can be looked at from the perspective of symbolic interactionism can go on indefinitely. It is a rich perspective, and it can be used to comprehend all individual and group action. That has been its strength for me and for many others.

THE IMPORTANCE OF THE SYMBOLIC INTERACTIONIST PERSPECTIVE

The symbolic interactionist perspective is important for all *social science*. It is a criticism of social science, calling forth an alteration of direction and a set of new assumptions about human action. It is revolutionary. By emphasizing the active nature of humans, it questions the scientific potential for fully understanding and predicting human behavior. It asks that we focus on a definition of the situation, which is an active process, impossible to predict exactly, but to some extent understandable through careful and systematic investigation. It questions the attempts to understand human behavior by studying attitudes or values the human chooses on a questionnaire. It sees experiments done with non-symbolizing animals as limited approaches to the understanding of the human being, and it questions the validity of applying certain accepted scientific methods uncritically to the understanding of human action. Symbolic interactionism sees the human as too complex an organism to be studied by such methods. Action is seen as caused not by something from a distant past, but by symbolic interaction between and within individuals. It emphasizes that actions have a long continuous history, the cause of any isolated act is not easily located, and that each action shifts direction from time to time. In the end, symbolic interactionism calls for social science to see humans from a different perspective, and to adjust its scientific focus and techniques accordingly.

Symbolic interactionism has a number of important implications for *sociology* specifically. It is critical of traditional sociology in the same ways it is critical of all social science. But it is also extremely enriching and adds immeasurably to the important insights of this field. For example, it adds to our understanding of the sociology of knowledge, it describes the social nature of reality, how our group life or our society creates our definition of reality, internal and external. It tells us of the power available to those who control symbols, perspectives, and definitions. The perspective can be applied to understanding further the "collective consciousness" in Durkheim, the "class consciousness" and "false consciousness" in Marx, the religious perspectives in Weber, and the "forms of interaction" in Simmel, to name only the most obvious ties with sociological theory. Symbolic interactionism has been applied to the theoretical and empirical study of deviance, emphasizing the importance of definition, self-definition, interaction, and power. It has been applied to socialization, collective behavior, and various social problems. Its definition of society is useful since it emphasizes both society's dynamic nature and the kinds of action between individuals necessary for its continuation. It seems to me that symbolic interactionism, more than any other perspective in sociology, clearly describes the intricate interrelationships between the individual and society: Society makes the individual through creation of the self, mind, symbols, generalized other, perspectives, and symbolic role taking. Conversely, it is the human individual that makes human society through active interpretation, self-direction, role taking, aligning his or her own acts with others, and communicating. By regarding the human as so thoroughly social and symbolic, and by describing the complex ways this is so, symbolic interactionism makes a major contribution to the sociological perspective.

Symbolic interactionism also has much to offer the *disciplines outside of social science,* such as the humanities, communications, and philosophy. The nature of reality, the meaning of the self, the emergence and importance of society, the nature of symbols, the importance of human communication, and the future of humanity are all topics symbolic interactionists share with these other disciplines. George Herbert Mead seems to relate increasingly to more and more people outside of sociology, and other symbolic interactionists recognize this. Indeed, the Society for the Study of Symbolic Interaction is a multidiscipline organization, appealing to many more than sociologists.

Symbolic interactionism also relates to psychiatrists, ministers, social workers, clinical psychologists, teachers, and *other professionals whose purpose is to improve the lot of other individuals.* It shows the great importance of interaction as a source for change, since the development of new reference groups provides important anchors for changing the individual's perspective and, thus, his or her definition of the world. It emphasizes *action,* with others and with self. The individual's interpretation of others as well as his or her precise communication with others is critical for cooperation—thus it focuses our attention on the central importance of communication, role taking, and problem-solving skills. It suggests that self-communication, including self-judgment, self-analysis, and definition of other people in situations may involve consistent inaccuracies that may be examined and worked out in a therapy group. Instead of focusing on one's past, this perspective suggests focusing on the *present,* especially how the individual defines the situations he or she encounters, including how the past and future are defined in the present. Furthermore, the perspective's message is that those people who are being helped are *active,* they are self-directing and creative, and they cannot easily be directed by us. Those of us who try to help others are only single people; our interaction with them is limited since many other individuals enter interaction with those we are helping. Thus, we must be prepared to see our work neutralized, made less important; because of that, the interaction is difficult for us to control. Perhaps we can hope to influence the direction people take, to encourage them to go one way rather than another, to interact with certain others, to use certain reference groups in their repertoire, to communicate and understand better, to role take and problem solve more accurately, but we cannot hope to change a person dramatically through our interaction with him or her.

The symbolic interactionist perspective, finally, is important to those of us who are *students* interested in understanding human life and the nature of action, society, truth, and freedom. That is the appeal the perspective has had for me, and that has been the underlying theme of this book. This perspective contributes to a liberal arts education: It deals intelligently and systematically with some of the most important questions concerning human life.

REFERENCES

ATHENS, LONNIE H.
> 1980 *Violent Criminal Acts and Actors: A Symbolic Interactionist Study.* Boston: Routledge and Kegan Paul.

BLUMER, HERBERT
> 1969 *Symbolic Interactionism: Perspective and Method.* Englewood Cliffs, N.J.: Prentice-Hall. Copyright © 1969. Reprinted by permission of Prentice-Hall, Inc.

DARLING, JON
> 1977 "Bachelorhood and Late Marriage: An Interactionist Interpretation." *Symbolic Interaction*, 1:44–55.

DENZIN, NORMAN K.
> 1971 "The Logic of Naturalistic Inquiry." *Social Forces* 50:166–182.

FINE, GARY ALAN
> 1981 "Friends, Impression Management, and Preadolescent Behavior." In eds. Gregory Stone and Harvey Farberman, *Social Psychology through Symbolic Interaction.* 2nd ed., pp. 257–72. Lexington, Mass.: Ginn.

GROSS, EDWARD and GREGORY P. STONE
> 1964 "Embarrassment and the Analysis of Role Requirements." *American Journal of Sociology* 70:1–15.

HEILMAN, SAMUEL C.
> 1976 *Synagogue Life: A Study in Symbolic Interaction.* Chicago: University of Chicago Press.

PLUMMER, KENNETH
> 1975 *Sexual Stigma: An Interactionist Account.* London: Routledge and Kegan Paul.

ZIMMERMAN, MARY K.
> 1981 "The Abortion Clinic: Another Look at the Management of Stigma." In eds. Gregory Stone and Harvey Farberman, *Social Psychology through Symbolic Interaction.* 2nd ed., pp. 43–52. Lexington, Mass.: Ginn.

INDEX

A

Action, 113–31
  and definition, 123
  and goals, 115–17
  habitual, 124–25
  influence of the past and future on,
    125–27
  and interaction, 22
  and mind, 89
  overt and covert, 123–24
  and the past, 23
  and the present, 22–23
  and self, 72–82
  social, 129–31, 113
  and society, 158–59
  stream of, 113, 114–15
Acts, 113–23
  cause of, 117–20
  four stages of, 120–23
  social (*see* Social acts)
  as social objects, 115
"Altercasting," 144–45
Ames, Van Meter, 85, 89, 92, 94–95
Aronson, Elliot, 18, 19

Asch, Solomon, 21
Athens, Lonnie, 181–82
Attitudes:
  Mead's view, 90–91, 125
  and perspectives, 23–24
  in social psychology, 18
Autobiography of Malcolm X, 4–6
Averchenko, A., 1–2

B

Ball, Donald, 139–40, 184
Becker, Ernest, 149–50
Becker, Howard, 36
Behaviorism, 27, 30, 31
Berger, Peter, 13, 14, 15–16, 66–67,
    77–78
  and Thomas Luckmann, 140–41,
    165–66
Blumer, Herbert, 26, 27, 30
  and action, 116–17, 122–23
  and definition, 116
  influence of, 26

Weinstein, E.A., and P. Deutschberger, 144–45
Wells, L., and Gerald Marwell, 80
White, Leslie, 49

Z

Zborowski, Mark, 36–37
Zimmerman, Mary, 184